Network Planning and Management: Your Personal Consultant

Network Planning and Management: Your Personal Consultant

Steve Rigney

Ziff-Davis Press
Emeryville, California

Editor	Valerie Haynes Perry
Technical Reviewer	Steve Bosak
Project Coordinator	Barbara Dahl
Proofreaders	Carol Burbo and Nicole Clausing
Cover Illustration and Design	Regan Honda
Book Design	Regan Honda
Word Processing	Howard Blechman
Page Layout	M.D. Barrera
Indexer	Carol Burbo

Ziff-Davis Press books are produced on a Macintosh computer system with the following applications: FrameMaker®, Microsoft® Word, QuarkXPress®, Adobe Illustrator®, Adobe Photoshop®, Adobe Streamline™, MacLink®Plus, Aldus® FreeHand™, Collage Plus™.

If you have comments or questions or would like to receive a free catalog, call or write:
Ziff-Davis Press
5903 Christie Avenue
Emeryville, CA 94608
1-800-688-0448

ISBN 1-56276-309-1

Manufactured in the United States of America
10 9 8 7 6 5 4 3 2 1

This book is dedicated to my family: Shandra, Stephen, Mom, Dad, Frank, and Marlene. I also wish to thank my coworkers, Keith and Scott, and all of my clients.

TABLE OF CONTENTS

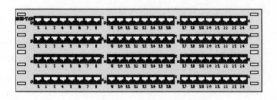

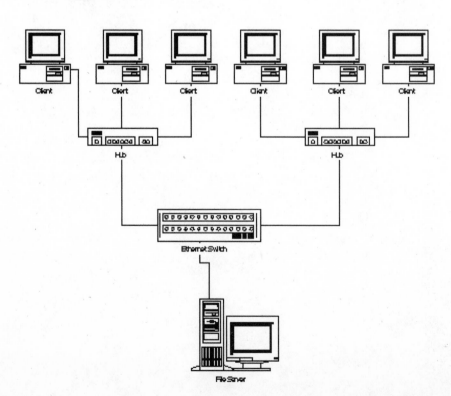

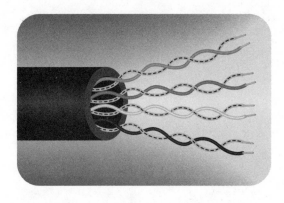

FOREWORD

If you want to fly from New York to San Francisco, you'd rather have a pilot who makes the trip every day instead of one who doesn't know the way, right? If you want to know how to do something, you ask someone who's done it, right? Well, if you want to know how to select, install, and maintain your network, ask Steve Rigney, because he does it every day. Inside this book you'll find the most practical information and insight you can get on the dos and don'ts of networking and communications.

Nothing shows Steve's hands-on approach better than his network Field Notes. He uses these true stories as illustrations, guides, and cautionary tales. Because his company has hundreds of clients, Steve has been through every practical kind of installation and problem from making links to IBM AS/400 minicomputers to helping clients understand why they can't compress already compressed drives.

Writing with clarity, wit, and insight, Steve sets his book apart from the "pirate software" manuals that tell you how to run unlicensed programs and from the "theoretical" tutorials with little practical value. This is a book for savvy managers with tight budgets, for newly minted network administrators, and for old heads looking for new tricks.

On the bottom line, this book is a great compilation of practical and useful advice. It can make you a hero in your own company. Buy a couple of copies because people will steal it from you.

—Frank Derfler

ACKNOWLEDGMENTS

I would like to thank all of the professional people at Ziff-Davis Press who helped me with this book. I especially want to thank Cindy Hudson for giving me the chance to write this book and Valerie Perry for all of her editorial help and guidance.

I would also like to thank Frank Derfler for writing the foreword to the book and for all of his help, patience, and support over the past few years. Steve Bosak, the technical editor, also did a great job keeping my facts straight.

INTRODUCTION

In every office that uses PCs, there is one person who is regarded as the computer guru. That enlightened individual may the accountant, secretary, or janitor, but that person knows more about PCs than anyone else in the company and he or she is constantly being sought out by coworkers for advice and help. This book is tailored to the needs of the computer guru. If your boss comes to you and asks you to design and install a PC-based network, *Network Planning and Management: Your Personal Consultant* will provide you with all of the information you need to successfully design, implement, and maintain a network.

The book is structured around a document that I write for my clients called an SAR (survey and recommendation). When a client wants to install a network, I gather all of the pertinent information and write it down in an easy to understand document that I give to the client. This SAR explains every step involved in choosing the hardware and software, designing and installing the cable, and installing and configuring the network applications. You can think of this book as a very long and very detailed SAR.

Each chapter includes a section called "Field Notes," which documents true stories of networking problems I have encountered over the years. The Field Notes are designed to stress the importance of a tip or procedure. If you fail to follow directions and plan for the future, you might find yourself starring in the lead role of one of my Field Notes.

What's in the Book?

The first chapter focuses on initial planning and setting your goals. In this chapter I help you determine your needs for installing a network. I discuss practical concerns such as creating a budget, drawing a diagram, and planning for your future needs. In Chapter 2, "Research," I take the planning stage further and provide you with tips on researching the products you will use on your network. I discuss several ways to gather information from reading magazines and calling online services.

Chapter 3 deals with WAN links and remote access. I provide you with a breakdown of the different types of network connections and the pros and cons of each. Chapter 4 is a time to slow down and make sure that you have everything in place and ready before the installation day arrives. I devoted Chapter 5 to upgrading because every installation is basically an upgrade.

In Chapter 6, "Installation," I look at the different steps involved in installing different NOSes, including Novell NetWare and Artisoft LANtastic. After you install your network you have to keep it running, so I discuss maintenance and upkeep in Chapter 7. Chapters 8 and 9 deal with LAN and WAN management, respectively. I look at specifc network management products and discuss the most comon management standards including SNMP (Simple Network Management Protocol). Because PCs break fairly often, I delegated the topic of troubleshooting to Chapter 10. I provide you with specific information to solve specific problems.

I have also included two appendices. Appendix A provides a list of software and hardware vendors that I mention in the book plus a few other products that you might find useful. Appendix B includes a list of books, magazines, and online services that you can use to gather research information or learn about new products.

This book is a culmination of years of hands-on network consulting. I could not cover every situation or product, but I do provide you with enough information to install, maintain, and troubleshoot the most popular and common networks. I hope you have as much fun reading this book as I had writing it.

CHAPTER

Initial Planning

I'm

a network consultant—that's how I make my living. I've staked out a position that says I don't sell hardware or software. I sell skill, knowledge, experience, and advice. Throughout this book I'll offer you those same things, but I'll also add some insight and specific recommendations. However, you can't take advantage of this advice if you don't know what you need or want. You have to do a needs assessment to ensure satisfaction with the final result. So let's explore some ways to plan your network needs.

Setting Your Goals

It may sound like a funny question coming from a network consultant, but the first thing I always ask a client is: "Do you really need a network?" The answer serves two purposes. First, it can save a client a lot of money and second, it makes the client think about the goals they want to accomplish by installing a network. Too many organizations decide to install or upgrade an existing network just because it sounds like a good idea and the competition has one. A network is an investment of your time and money and, like any other investment, you need to have a reason for making it.

Networks are for sharing. Computer networks are designed to allow you to share information such as files, applications, and electronic messages; and resources such as disk drives, printers, modems, and faxes. Unfortunately, many people believe that a network will solve all of their needs and increase productivity tenfold. But a poorly designed network or the wrong kind of network can hurt your productivity and your bank book.

An important question you need to ask yourself is: "What do I want the end result to be?" The end result can be as complex as implementing an e-mail system for a nationwide network or as simple as sharing a laser printer or plotter. You may find that a simple printer sharing device may be all that you need and in turn save yourself a lot of money and frustration. You may also determine that the network you need is too expensive for your budget.

In my experience, most companies decide to implement a PC-based network in order to use a "vertical" or business-specific software program. If a program is available that will increase your business and productivity, but requires a network, chances are you will install that network. In fact "the software dictates the hardware;" I use this phrase throughout the book. The true benefit of computer networking is the ability to run software applications that will make your life easier and more productive even though many companies install networks just to share printers and files.

The details of upgrading and installing networks are covered in Chapters 5 and 6, respectively.

Planning for the Future

One of the most frustrating chores a network consultant must do is explain to the client why he or she has to install a new hard disk drive or wiring hub only six months after they installed their new network. Too many people say, "Oh, I only need DOS, all of our apps are DOS-based." That doesn't mean the app vendors won't write a Windows version of that app tomorrow that you may want to use instead of DOS. In fact, it's almost impossible to use the plan of your existing system to design your new one because you can't predict the future. On the hardware side, just because you only have five users now doesn't mean you won't need enough network cable and disk space for ten users within a year.

For the reasons just mentioned, it is always smart to design a system that provides at least double the resources you currently need. The best examples of this are the size of your hard disk and the amount of RAM in your PC. If you currently have 200 megabytes (MB) of data on your existing system, buy a new system with at least 500 to 1,000MB of disk space. Most new applications use a graphical interface and require a lot more disk space than your old WordPerfect 5.1 documents. It is also a lot easier and usually less expensive to purchase a larger hard disk than you will ever need than it is to add more disk space down the road.

A good rule of thumb to remember is what I call the "three-to-five-year rule." You want to design a network that will cover your needs for three to five years. While technology surpasses itself approximately every 18 months, the new computer you buy today will probably still run the majority of software that is available three to five years from now. It may run slow, but it will probably still run. For example, most new PCs are based on either the Intel 80486 or the Pentium processor. These new PCs are capable of running 32-bit and 64-bit operating systems, respectively, but most of them still come bundled with Microsoft's or IBM's 16-bit DOS.

Field Note: Take the Long View

A local land survey and design firm decided it was time to install a PC-based network to share CAD drawings and its new expensive HP plotter. I met with the owners and asked them how many surveyors and/or CAD designers they planned to employ over the next year or two. They said they currently only had nine employees and there was no way they would ever exceed that number. I asked them several more times and they stuck by their original estimate.

In the survey and recommendation (SAR) I presented to them, I suggested both a 10- and 20-user license of the network operating system and a 10- and 20-port wiring hub. To be honest, I had to explain to the owners that the 10-user license of the software and 10-port wiring hub would work, but I also urged them to consider planning for the future.

The owners decided on short-term savings and purchased the 10-user license of the software and subsequently only installed enough network cable for 10 users. Within the last six months they have hired 10 new surveyors and added at least 10 more PCs to their network. As a result, they spent approximately $2000 more to upgrade their existing system than they would have if they had taken my advice from the start.

Determining Specific Business Tasks

Since I contend that the software dictates the hardware, software should be your first priority. You probably have recognized a need for networking in order to share some resources, but what are the particular jobs and functions that must be carried out? Which business applications or specialized programs do you want to use? You can often find the information you need about specialized programs in special business-related publications and at focused trade shows. For example, if you are a dentist looking for a billing system, a plumber looking for an inventory system, or a librarian looking for a check-out system, the best place to search for software is in the magazines and trade shows that serve your profession.

Once you find the business software you need and determine its requirements, then it's time to select the appropriate network products that you can weave into your system. Start by making a big wish list and later determine what's practical and affordable. Sit down with a piece of paper and a stack of mail-order catalogs and computer magazines, and write down product names and prices. You are not looking for exact brand names or products, but you need to get an idea of prices and availability.

It is also a good idea to write down choices for every product. There is always a product that will get the job done and another you would just love to have. Seeing it on paper will ensure that you don't forget any major pieces or parts.

The next chapter offers details on how to continue your research once you are ready to seek out the products and solutions that will meet your networking needs.

Timing Your Installation

I live and work in a small resort town on the Gulf of Mexico. Our local economy is tied directly to the number of tourists that come to visit us each summer. This means summer is the slowest season for my network consulting business—because nobody wants to make a major change or install a new system when they are busy and making money. Winter is when the managers and owners can sit back and discuss the problems they faced during their last busy season and take the time to think of possible solutions.

Every business has its own "season" whether it's tax time for accountants or the holidays for retailers. The idea behind a network is to increase your productivity, not to disrupt your business. If you are planning a major network installation or upgrade, it should be scheduled during your slowest time. You will also need to set aside some time for training your employees and debugging the new system.

Preparing a General Budget

You need to decide how much money you *want* to spend as opposed to how much money you *can* spend. Throughout this book, I will provide you with current pricing information on products that I mention. While prices do change rapidly, it is usually possible to use these prices to determine a ballpark figure for your budget.

After you complete your wish list, you may decide your budget isn't big enough to complete the entire job. Then you may want to consider breaking the project up into stages. It is usually better to break the project into sections than it is to scrap the whole idea. It is also advisable to spend a little extra money up front to design a system that will meet your needs for years to come.

When is a project too expensive? One way to answer that question is to decide how long it will take your new system to pay you back in terms of increased productivity and business revenue. While that's a pretty hard formula to figure out, it may or may not help you justify a big up-front cost.

In some cases, it is pretty easy to determine how much time and money a new system will save you. For example, if a new network accounting package can do the payroll for your entire company in a third of the time it took your outside accountant, you have a real dollar amount you can put into a spreadsheet. Subtract the price of the accounting program and the hardware required to run it from the amount you are paying an accountant every month, and you'll see how long the program will take to pay for itself.

The following checklist details the components that are necessary for a PC-based network. Your list may contain more items, but without the following, you don't have a network capable of performing file and printer sharing.

Check List for Your General Network Budget

✓ Network file server, either dedicated or nondedicated

✓ PCs for network clients

✓ Network operating system

✓ Network adapters

✓ Network cable

✓ Network applications

✓ Network installation

✓ Network training

✓ Network or stand-alone printer

Drawing an Up-to-Date Diagram

If you are just planning to install a peer-to-peer network between two PCs across the room, you probably don't need a detailed diagram. However, if you are installing a larger network that will cover multiple offices or buildings, it is extremely helpful if you have a diagram of every office that will be affected during this installation or future upgrades.

You have several choices when it comes to designing a diagram of your network. You can use a paper and pencil to draw a floor plan of your office and sketch in where you plan to place your PCs and other peripherals such as printers and fax machines. You may also be able to get a blueprint of your office from the builder or one of the electrical contractors. The blueprint is the better option, but it may be overkill if you are designing a small LAN.

If you have to draw a diagram by hand, make sure you prepare two—one without the network, another detailing where the PCs and printers will reside. You will also want to note the location of power outlets. If you will use an existing blueprint you will need to sketch in where you plan to put the network components. Until you see the configuration on paper, your installation plans may not mean much. You'll find that studying your drawing will prevent you from making mistakes such as placing a printer in front of a frequently used filing cabinet. Your diagram should also include the actual scale of your network hardware, to make sure it will fit where you want it.

If you are installing a network that will span multiple offices or floors, you will need a diagram of any existing cable runs in your building. This diagram will help you determine the best place to install new cable. You may find that you will be able to use some of your existing cable, or at least the conduits, for your network connections. However, before you plan on using any existing cable, always contact a professional cable installer to scan and certify your existing cable for the type of network you are using. A thorough wiring diagram will detail all of the florescent lights, elevators shafts, and other points of possible electronic interference that you want to avoid.

If you can't get a floor plan or blueprint of your office, but you want to create a professional looking diagram, there are several software drawing programs that you can choose from. Shapeware's Visio 3.0 (see Figure 1.1) costs $199 and allows you to create a very detailed network diagram. It includes an adequate collection of clip-art images of hardware such as PCs, modems, printers, and cable. There are also high-end drawing programs including Microsystem Engineering Company's SysDraw 7.1 (see Figure 1.2), which costs $999. The more expensive programs include thousands of images of actual network products. For example, you could use SysDraw to diagram a network consisting of only a Compaq SystemPro file server, a Cabletron MiniMMAC wiring hub, and a Hewlett-Packard LaserJet 4M Plus printer.

While both of these products are Windows-based and offer an easy-to-use graphical interface, they do require some investment of your time and money. I only recommend using a software package if you are installing and managing a medium to large network or multiple small LANs.

The method you choose to create a network diagram should be based on the size of your network and how often you anticipate that it will change. A good working diagram will prove invaluable to you and to any consultant that needs to troubleshoot a network problem down the road. It is amazing how many network problems are solved by tracking down a faulty cable connection in the broom closet, which was undocumented. Good, accurate documentation also prevents you from wasting time searching for the faulty equipment.

After Planning

After you decide to install a network or upgrade your existing one, and determine that you may be able to afford it, the fun begins. The following chapters provide greater detail on planning, installing, and managing your network.

Figure 1.1
You can choose from hundreds of images in Visio to diagram your existing or future network.

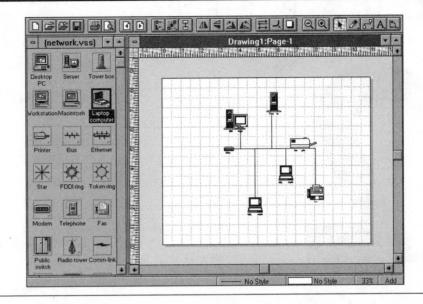

Figure 1.2
SysDraw includes thousands of images of actual network products. In this diagram, a Compaq SystemPro server is connected to an HP LaserJet 4SI, using a Cabletron hub.

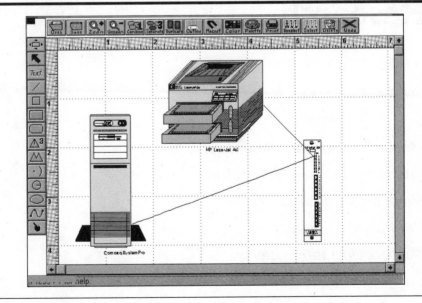

CHAPTER

2

Research

Congratulations, you have just finished the most difficult step in designing and implementing your network. The initial planning/needs assessment stage is hard because it forces you to look into the future and make decisions or solve problems before they happen.

While the initial planning of your network is probably the most difficult, researching products and solutions requires the most time. A good analogy for researching a network is grocery shopping. In this chapter, I will help you check your cupboard to see what items you need, choose a grocery store, decide between similar products, pick the right check-out line, and decide who should carry your bags to the car.

Magazines and Other Resources

I consider myself an expert at research. Not only am I good at it, I actually enjoy it. In addition to being one of the most important steps in designing your network, research is also a learning experience. I have never researched a topic without learning something about a totally different but useful topic. The most important trick to becoming a good researcher is to use the tools and resources that are available to you.

Its pretty obvious that there is a great deal of information available to anyone who chooses to use it. You cannot just go to one source to get the entire picture. Good research takes a lot of time and you can't just jump at the first solution or product that looks good.

Unfortunately, you don't always have a lot of time to call vendors and scan through piles of information on online services. Always set aside as much time as possible for research. If you do a good job checking on products, it will save you time when it comes to installing them and making them work together.

Magazines

The first place you should begin your research is at your local newspaper and magazine kiosk. Computer magazines are published weekly, biweekly, and monthly. You can easily find a magazine that provides detailed information on everything from computer games for kids to high-end satellite receivers. The major computer trade magazines are divided into two types, the weekly magazines that mainly focus on current news, and the biweekly and monthly magazines that provide more in-depth product reviews and technical overviews.

Some magazines including *LAN Times*, *Network Computing*, *Communications Week*, and *Network World* focus solely on network products and information. Other popular magazines including *PC Magazine*, *Computer Shopper*, *Info World*, *PC Week*, and *Byte* only allocate a section of the total magazines' pages to network discussions.

When you are doing your research, the best magazine articles to read are product comparisons. I have written hundreds of product reviews over the past few years and I know how much effort is put into them. A stand-alone review of a product can provide you with a helpful list of features, but a head-to-head comparison will help you make the best buying decision.

It's also smart to read reviews of the same product in different magazines. While Magazine A may love a product and give it a good review, Magazine B may not. Usually all of the magazines find the major pros and cons of a product but they differ on how they report the product's features and on what is important to the reader. It's difficult to make practical comments about a product by reading the press releases—as many reviewers do. Look for hands-on reviews.

Online Services and the Internet

Online services such as CompuServe, Prodigy, and America Online are another great source of information. In addition to having access to vendor forums and technical support, you can also chat or exchange e-mail with other people that are working on or have finished research on a network project.

CompuServe

Of all of the popular online services, CompuServe is probably your best choice for research. Most major network vendors including Microsoft, Novell, Artisoft, and IBM provide a free a forum you can use to download product information and exchange e-mail with technical support people. CompuServe is fairly inexpensive at approximately $5 to $10 an hour for basic services depending on the speed of your connection.

You can connect to the CompuServe online service using almost any DOS or Windows-based communication program. CompuServe also offers a Windows-based utility called WinCIM. As you can see in Figure 2.1, WinCIM allows you to configure a menu of your favorite places and navigate CompuServe with a click of your mouse. WinCIM comes bundled with many modems or you can download it from CompuServe for approximately $15.

Microsoft Network

Another exciting new online service is called the Microsoft Network. The Microsoft Network promises to be a strong competitor to CompuServe and other online services. One of the strongest selling features of the Microsoft Network is the fact that the software you use to access the service is bundled with every copy of Microsoft's Windows 95. If you want to connect to the Microsoft Network, all you do is select the desktop icon and fill out a form. There is no cost for the software, only for the time you are connected.

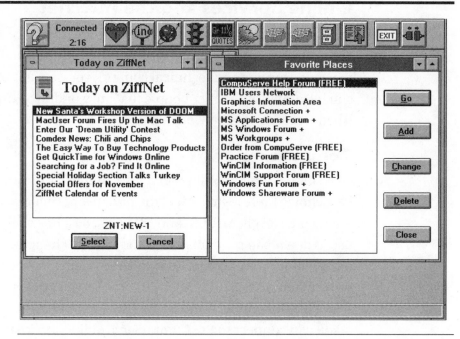

Figure 2.1
WinCIM allows you to customize menus of your favorite places to visit on CompuServe.

The Microsoft Network is designed as an open system and individual service providers can determine what types of services they want to provide and how much to charge for them. The Microsoft Network also works closely with your existing Windows applications. For example, you can select the online icon from within Excel and request help with a particular formula or receive tips on creating charts. No other online service is as tightly integrated with your desktop operating system.

The Internet

Everyone has probably heard enough hype about the Internet to either love it or hope it disappears. Whether you like the Internet or not, you can't deny that it provides a gateway to a wealth of information that you can't get anywhere else. The Internet was the first WAN (wide area network) and therefore it is still a favorite place for people to get together to exchange ideas on networking.

One of the biggest complaints about the Internet concerns the amount of effort it takes to navigate through the thousands of network nodes to find the information you are looking for. Fortunately, many Internet sites have set up a World Wide Web (WWW) server. You can use a graphical communications program such as NCSA's Mosaic, shown in Figure 2.2, to connect to a WWW server and find information without knowing where it is located. WWW servers provide hypertext links that connect thousands of servers together based on a simple subject or text string. For example, if you select a hypertext word such as "network" you may be transported to a WWW server located in a different country. If you select another hypertext word, you may go back to where you started. The Web is a lifesaver for users who do not know how to navigate the Internet.

There are several books that simplify the process of connecting to the Internet. *The Traveler's Guide to the Information Highway* by Dylan Tweney and *How to Use the Internet* by Mark Butler (both published by Ziff-Davis Press in 1994) are good resources. *The Whole Internet; User's Guide & Catalog* by Ed Krol (second edition, published by O'Reilly & Associates, Inc. in April 1994) is an additional reference that will help you find Internet service providers as well as numerous tips and examples for navigating the Internet and finding what you are looking for.

Dial-up access is another drawback to using the Internet as a research tool. Unless you work for the government or a large university, you probably don't have a free high-speed Internet connection. While you can use a standard PC, modem, and communications software to access most online services, the Internet is usually a different story. Because the Internet is basically a giant network, many connections require a network protocol. This means you have to install network drivers on your PC. While this is not an impossible task, it is a lot of work for a dial-up connection. Local Internet dial-in connections are also not as widely available as other services including Prodigy, CompuServe, and America Online.

Figure 2.2
NCSA's Mosaic is a shareware program you can use to access World Wide Web servers on the Internet.

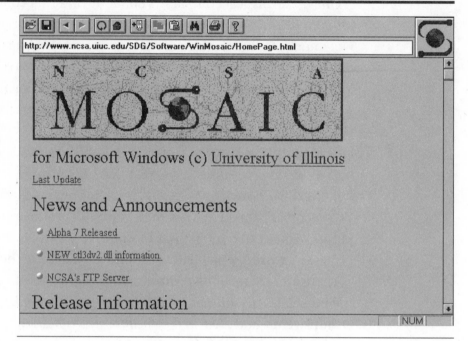

Fax-Back Services

If you have ever called a company for technical support or information on a product, you will appreciate fax-back services. Most large companies are implementing a dedicated fax machine that does nothing but send technical and product information to people that call and request it. The concept is simple, you dial a number and request information, punch in your fax number and hang up. A few minutes (or sometimes hours) later you receive a fax with everything you wanted to know about that product.

Not only do fax-back services save you time and money, they also furnish you with a tangible piece of information you can file away for later access. Some companies offer a canned menu you can choose from to receive your information, while others require you to talk to a live person and get a fax document number. Either way, fax-back services are a lot better than listening to piped-in music while you're on hold for three hours.

CD-ROMs

If you are installing a large network or multiple small ones, you will want to become familiar with some of the CD-ROMs that are available. Unlike magazines and online services, CD-ROMs can provide you with approximately 650MB of information that you can look through without paying a connection fee. There are three CD-ROMs that I use every day; Computer Library's Computer Select, Novell Network Support Encyclopedia (NSEPRO), and Microsoft's TechNet.

Computer Select, shown in Figure 2.3, is a collection of computer magazine articles and other information that is published every month. Each CD contains six months worth of articles from magazines including *PC Magazine*, *PC Week*, *Mac Week*, and *Computer Shopper*. The CD includes a viewer for DOS and Windows and the search engine allows you to search on individual topics or text strings. For example, I could do a search on CD-ROMs and within seconds have 1,000 articles to read through.

Novell's NSEPRO (see Figure 2.4) contains technical support information, software updates, and all of the NetWare user manuals. NSEPRO can save you a lot of time and money if you frequently need to solve NetWare configuration problems or update network drivers. You can also use NSEPRO to learn about Novell's education and certification programs.

Like the NSEPRO CD, Microsoft TechNet, shown in Figure 2.5, also offers technical support information and software updates for Windows-based networks and other Microsoft products. I frequently use the TechNet CD to find missing software such as printer drivers for brand new printers. Most of these CDs cost approximately $300 to $500 for a yearly subscription, but the time they can save you in research is worth the price. (Fortunately, these CDs are available for free via online services, including CompuServe and the Internet.)

Chapter 2: Research

Figure 2.3
Computer Select allows you to search for a certain topic based on information such as publication, author, and date.

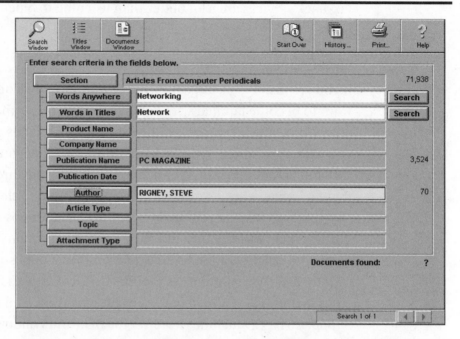

Figure 2.4
You can use the NSEPRO CD to learn about Novell products and search for help on a particular NetWare problem.

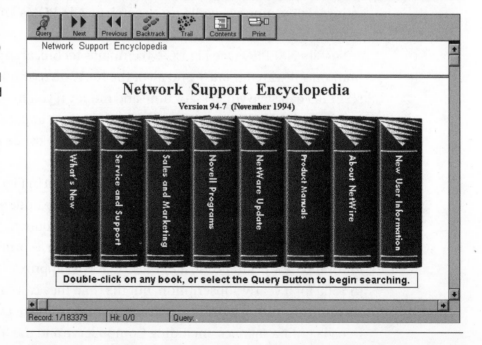

Figure 2.5
The Microsoft TechNet CD includes new drivers for your Microsoft applications and a large database of technical information.

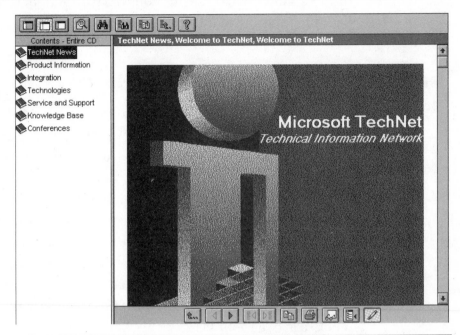

Use the Experts

There are hundreds of salespeople whose job it is to help you understand network products and how they work. Most major network vendors offer toll-free phone numbers that you can call to talk to a salesperson about specific products. Many companies will also send you detailed evaluation material about its products. While you have to be objective and take this information with a grain of salt, it is a good place to start. It is also interesting to request information from several vendors to see how each company claims its products compare to those of competitors.

Some consultants, including myself, are usually happy to spend a few free minutes on the phone explaining the major differences between products. A consultant or reseller who really wants your business will bend over backwards to help you understand the technology. If a person seems annoyed with your questions, you have probably called the wrong place.

Inventory What You Already Have

Every installation is basically an upgrade of your existing system. Don't think that you have to throw everything away and start afresh when you install a network. If you have an up-to-date inventory of your equipment, you may be able to upgrade your existing hardware instead of replacing it with new equipment. A basic inventory will include information such as processor type and speed, hard-disk size, amount of memory, and the type of video. There are many utilities you can use to create an inventory of your existing PCs. Microsoft even bundles a utility called Microsoft Diagnostics (MSD) with MS DOS 6.x and Windows 3.1. MSD is ideal for performing a quick scan of all your PCs.

If you already have a network, there are several hardware and software inventory programs such as Saber's LANWorkstation that will help you keep track of all of your existing components. Products such as LAN Workstation also allow you to create detailed reports on the types of software and hardware on your network. For example, you can use a LAN Workstation to create a report of all the 486 PCs on your network that have 8MB of memory and a 200MB hard disk.

After you perform your survey, you may find that a simple memory or hard-disk upgrade will allow you to use your existing PCs with your new software or network. There are many simple rules you can use for deciding if you can use an existing PC with your new software. The following "Rules of Thumb" chart details some of the bare-bones minimums you need to have for most major network and desktop operating systems.

"Rules of Thumb" Bare-Bones Minimums

Software	Required RAM	Required Disk Space	CPU
Novell NetWare 3.1X or higher	16MB per gigabyte	500 or more MB	486 DX 33MHz
Microsoft Windows 3.1 or higher	4MB, prefer 8MB	120MB	486 SX 25MHz
Microsoft Windows 95	8MB, prefer 12MB	200MB, prefer 500MB	486 DX 33MHz
Microsoft Windows NT server	16MB	500MB, prefer 1 gigabyte	486 DX 33MHz
Microsoft Windows NT workstation	8MB, prefer 12MB	300MB, prefer 500MB	486 DX 33MHz
IBM OS/2 2.1 or higher	8MB, prefer 16MB	300MB	486 DX 33MHz
Artisoft LANtastic server 6.X or higher	8MB	200MB	486 DX 33MHz
Performance Technology POWERLan server 3.x or higher	8MB	200MB	486 DX 33MHz

These are not the minimum requirements recommended by the vendors. They are the minimum requirements I recommend based on several years of experience installing and maintaining these programs.

XTs and ATs May Still Be Useful

Not every user on your network is going to need a fast PC, and some may not even need to run a graphical operating system such as Windows 95. You'd be surprised by how many people still have IBM XT and AT systems that they use daily. I have seen some networks that have as many as 20 or 30 ATs. When I ask the owners about upgrading, they say "Why? They still work." Old 8088 and 80286 based PCs with at least one megabyte of RAM will work great as DOS-based word processors running older versions of WordPerfect or Professional Write.

ATs also make great print servers for most network operating systems, including Artisoft LANtastic and Novell NetWare. All you need is a 80286 based system with a small hard drive and at least a megabyte of memory. Even if you don't plan on using these old systems, save them just in case.

Using Existing Cable

Your existing cable may work with the network you are installing. If you are installing a network in a large building with an existing cable system you will want to have the cable checked to see if you can use it with your network. Many new buildings may have an adequate supply of EIA/TIA certified Category 3, 4, or 5 Unshielded Twisted Pair (UTP). Even if the cable is currently only used for your digital phone system, there may be enough extra pairs that you can use for your network.

This is only a viable option if you are installing a network topology, such as 10BaseT or Token-Ring that can run over UTP cable. If you are planning to use coaxial or 10Base2 cable, you probably don't have an existing supply of usable cable.

The best way to check your cable is to call a professional cable installer. Most cable installers use devices called cable analyzers that can certify your cable for the type of network you are installing. Many cable analyzers, such as Microtest's PentaScanner, can even print a detailed certification report. If you have a copy of the certification report, you will be in a better position to argue with the cable contractor if a problem arises.

See Chapter 4, "Prepare for the Network," for details on cabling.

Shopping for Installers

Your network is only as good as the people who installed it. You may pay a little extra up front to have an experienced professional install your network, but it will almost always save you money in troubleshooting bills down the road. I have learned the hard way to stick with experienced contractors for every stage of an installation.

Let Your Fingers Do the Walking

The best place to begin looking for experienced network installers is in the Yellow Pages. Most Yellow Pages are divided into sections that you can use to track down the exact type of service you are looking for. For example, there should be a section for network consultants and another section for computer resellers.

If you live in a large city, you will probably also want to find a network consultant who is close by. When you have a problem, you don't want to have to wait several hours for help to arrive. Many businesses also advertise in the local newspaper and that is another good place to look.

Word of Mouth Is a Powerful Tool

After you have scoured the phone book and the newspaper, ask other businesses in your area which company they used. If you know a person who is proud of their company's computer network, ask them who helped them with the installation. Unless they are your direct competitors, other businesses are usually happy to help you out.

Approximately 80 percent of my new clients were referred to my company by existing clients, and the other 20 percent stumbled across my name in the phone book or local newspaper. Word of mouth is probably the best tool you can rely on in your search for a network consultant. A consultant who does a good job and does not charge an arm and a leg will probably get a call back from you and hear from your friends as well.

Certification Programs

Almost every network operating system vendor has some type of certification program it offers to its installers and resellers. While a certification does not mean that one vendor is always better than the competition, it does show an effort to learn more about the software and hardware that vendor is selling and/or installing. The following chart lists some of the certifications from three of the largest network software vendors; Artisoft, Microsoft, and Novell.

Company	Certification	Description
Artisoft	Artisoft Premier Partner	Premier Partners must have $50,000 in sales every year, and pass three exams, or take two training courses and/or a combination of both.
Artisoft	Artisoft Advantage Partner	Advantage Partners must have $10,000 in sales every year, pass three exams, or take two training courses, and/or a combination of both.
Artisoft	Artisoft 5 Star Consulting Program	Artisoft 5 Star Consultants must pass three exams, or take two training courses and/or a combination of both.
Microsoft	Certified Systems Engineers	CSEs are required to pass four operating system exams and two elective exams, such as Microsoft Mail or SQL Server.
Microsoft	Certified Product Specialists	CPSs are required to pass at least one operating system exam and the elective exam on the product they specialize in.
Novell	Certified NetWare Administrator (CNA)	CNAs are required to pass an exam for one version of the NetWare operating system. You can become a CNA for multiple NOS versions.
Novell	Certified NetWare Engineer (CNE)	CNEs must obtain 19 credits from exams ranging from different operating systems to electives such as remote access.
Novell	Enterprise Certified NetWare Engineer (ECNE)	ECNEs must possess a CNE certificate and complete an additional 19 credits of exams including the NetWare operating system and other electives.
Novell	Certified NetWare Instructor (CNI)	CNIs must submit an application and pass an exam based on the course they wish to teach.

In addition to software vendors, hardware vendors such as Compaq and IBM also offer certification programs for resellers and installers. Most major network vendors provide their own certification of third-party products. For example, you can buy a network file server that has been certified by Novell. It is always smart to use certified installers and purchase equipment that has been certified to work with your network operating system.

Working with Multiple Companies

I don't sell hardware or software and I don't pull cable. Therefore, when I submit a network installation SAR (survey and recommendation) to a client, it includes recommendations for other companies that provide hardware, software, and network cable. I have worked on networks that included up to six different companies that provided different services and products.

It is very unlikely that you will find a network consultant who also installs cable. It requires a lot of time to keep up with new technologies and the tools and knowledge required for the two services are totally different. I would steer clear of any small consulting firm that claims they can provide all of the hardware and software for your network and install the cable. The major problem has to do with the tools required. A network consultant's toolbox is usually filled with a stack of diskettes and maybe a network sniffer or analyzer. A network cable installer will probably arrive in a truck or van with ladders on the top and will likely be wearing a tool belt.

It may seem like it could become confusing working with multiple companies on a single project. The trick is in the coordination. A good network consultant will meet with all of the companies involved and coordinate between them. In fact, you may not even have to talk with the individual companies, and the only interaction you will have with them is paying their bill when the job is completed.

A good consultant will provide you with everything you need to know for your network installation or upgrade. When I submit a SAR to a client, that client will have all the information they need to perform their project. You cannot take anything for granted when you are planning a network installation.

Requesting Proposals

Most resellers and consultants will not charge you to create a proposal. You can also call most hardware and software vendors and request a proposal via fax. It does not take a long time to call individual companies and stand by the fax machine to wait for the proposals to arrive. By requesting multiple proposals you will have a ballpark price on how much the installation is going to cost you.

Even if you already do business with a company, request proposals from its competitors. You never know if a new and better company has opened up in your area. You may still decide to use your existing consultant, but additional proposals will give you a good idea if your company is treating your fairly.

Evaluating Bids

After you have received all of your proposals, sit down with a calculator and compare costs. You will want to read the proposals carefully to see what parts and services are included with the price and what is going to cost you extra. Ask your business colleagues which company or vendor they used and how much they paid for the service.

I am a big believer in purchasing hardware and software from mail order companies whenever possible. It is always good to use a reseller, especially if they are going to perform the installation. However, if you are planning to perform the labor yourself or use a network consultant, compare the prices between your local reseller and a national mail order company.

Most large PC vendors such as Compaq and IBM allow you to purchase their systems direct via a toll-free phone number. While you can't always purchase some of the high-end systems direct, you can get most PCs from the manufacturer cheaper than you can from a reseller. The manufacturer's warranty and on-site service policies are usually just as good as a reseller's, and you don't have to worry about large computer vendors taking a vacation.

If you have done your research properly, you should have a table top full of information on different hardware and software. After you have gathered all of your information it is time to start making decisions.

Network Operating Systems

There are two basic types of network operating systems, peer-to-peer and server-centric. Peer networks do not require a dedicated server and allow you to designate any client PC as a network file or print server. Peer LANs, such as LANtastic, Windows for Workgroups, and POWERLan, shown in Figures 2.6, 2.7, and 2.8 respectively, are ideal for two to ten PCs that need to share applications, printers, and exchange e-mail. As you add more users and more powerful applications, your peer network will become sluggish and eventually you will need to designate a client PC to act as a dedicated server. Because most peer network operating systems run on top of DOS, you will eventually overpower your peer server's multitasking capabilities. Fortunately, most popular peer networks offer an upgrade path to more powerful server-centric networks.

Server-centric networks require a dedicated file server, but can handle more users and network intensive applications such as SQL database programs. Most popular server-centric networks, such as Novell NetWare, Windows NT Server, and Banyan Vines, offer true 32-bit multitasking operating systems that run on powerful dedicated

Figure 2.6
In addition to basic file and printer sharing, Artisoft LANtastic 6.0 includes the Exchange Network Scheduler. You can use the Network Scheduler to schedule group or personal meetings.

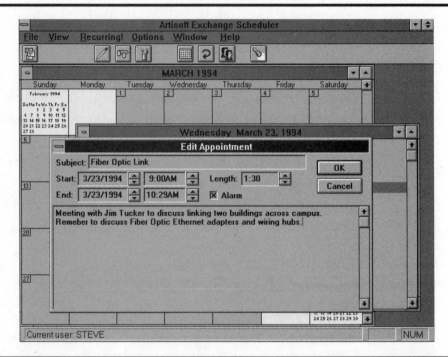

Figure 2.7
Windows for Workgroups includes a graphical interface for connecting to other PC's network disk drives and printers.

Figure 2.8
POWERLan provides one of the easiest to use interfaces of any peer or dedicated server network. If you want to connect to another person's PC, you simply drag the cable to the network resource.

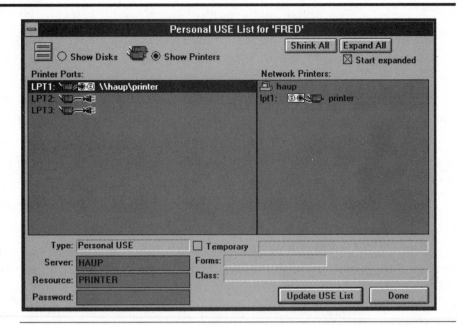

servers. The choice between server-centric and peer networks should be based not only on the number of client PCs and the geographic size of your LAN, but also on the types of applications you are using.

Probably the most important factor that determines the type of network you will use is your application software. Most application vendors certify their software with specific network operating systems. If you do not follow the vendor's recommendation when you install your network, you may face problems in the future. In my experience, if you call a vendor with a problem and you are not using the recommended network, the vendor will claim that the problem was caused by the network, and not by their product.

Remote Access

As the price of portable computers drops and people begin working from home or on the road, remote access is becoming an important component on most networks. The ability to call in to your network from home or the road and check your e-mail or transfer data can be a real time saver.

Remote node and remote control are still the two major ways to access a host network from a remote location. *Remote node* allows you to connect to your host network over a dial-up line and access the network's resources just like a local network client. When you are connected as a remote node, you have access to all of your local resources and your network drives and printers. If you access a file or program on the host network, the entire file or application is downloaded to your PC's memory to run.

In my opinion, remote node is not the right solution for most people. You've got to have some pretty specific client/server applications in mind before you plunk down money for a remote node solution. These connections try to jam a lot of traffic down a relatively slow pipe. A remote node connection or BBS provides a safe and easy way for people to get into the LAN to drop off and retrieve files. These connections require some administration, but that work is less than the work involved with setting up even a couple of remote users. With a remote control or BBS connection, the remote PC only has to run a single communications program, with a remote node connection, you have to completely reconfigure the remote PC's startup files.

Conversely, *remote control* connections allow you to run almost any application located on the host network, but you give up access to your local disk drives and programs. With a remote control connection, you only send keystrokes and screens across the dial-up connection. Remote control is designed for users who need to run server-based applications such as accounting software. Performance is usually not an issue for remote control connections unless you frequently transfer large files.

In the next chapter, I will provide more detail on specific remote access products and the pros and cons of each. Fortunately, remote access is something you can easily add to your network at a later date and it does not require drastic changes to your existing LAN.

Servers and Clients

You also need to decide what kind of file server and client PCs you will need. As I mentioned earlier, you may be able to use some of your existing hardware. If you are planning on using your existing hardware you may only need to purchase hardware upgrades such as more memory or disk space.

The most important computer on your network is the file server. When your file server goes down, you go down. Most peer networks have more than one PC configured as a file or print server. For example, you may have one PC for a file server and another PC configured as your printer and CD-ROM server. The PC that you use as your file server will need more processing power than the PC processing your print jobs and CD-ROM requests. Furthermore, if you are also using your file servers as client PCs, you will need a computer that is capable of completing the network requests and simultaneously running Windows or DOS-based applications.

You can probably use your existing PCs for a peer network if you plan your network and segment your applications across a few high performance PCs or a PC that you dedicate as a network server. The basic requirements for either a non-dedicated or dedicated peer server should include: a 486 DX 33MHz CPU, eight or more megabytes of RAM, and an eight-to-ten millisecond IDE or SCSI hard-disk drive—the size of the hard disk is based on your storage requirements. You will find that the amount of RAM for cache, and the speed of your hard disk, will increase your network performance more than a minimal increase in CPU speed. For example, a 486 DX 33 MHz PC with 16MB of RAM and a fast SCSI hard drive will usually provide better performance for most tasks than a faster 486 DX2 66 MHz with only 8MB of RAM and a slow IDE hard disk drive. This is particularly true for file servers. It is not always beneficial to spend a lot of money on a single peer network server; sometimes it is better to distribute the load over two or three lower priced 486 based PCs.

Designing a dedicated PC for a server-centric network requires more planning and offers more choices and challenges. Server-centric packages such as Novell only provide a single server license, so you can only have one file server on your LAN without purchasing a new server license. Most server-centric networks, such as Windows NT Server, Novell NetWare, and Banyan Vines, include detailed instructions on the type of hardware you need for your file server. A good rule to follow is to take the minimum requirements for the network file server and exceed everything by a third. For example, if the file server needs 8MB of RAM, install 10 to 12MB. The minimum requirements are for the network operating system only and do not always take your applications into consideration.

Server-centric networks are true 32-bit operating systems, so plan on at least a 486 or faster CPU. 486 SX PCs don't include a math co-processor, so be sure the CPU is a DX based chip or has an equivalent math coprocessor. If you plan to run CPU intensive applications such as graphics or SQL databases on your server, you should consider a Pentium processor. For normal word processing and spreadsheets, a 486 PC is adequate.

Memory or RAM is one of the most important factors for increasing performance on your dedicated server. The more RAM you have, the more cache your system can create. Memory cache eliminates the need for lengthy disk searches that can slow down your entire network. While memory is expensive (approximately $40 to $50 per megabyte), you need to start with at least 8 to 16 megabytes of RAM in your server and leave yourself room to add more in the future. As you add network peripherals, such as CD-ROMs or tape backup drives, to your server you will need to increase the amount of RAM.

You should also only use 70 nanosecond (ns) or faster memory chips in your system. If you mix 100 ns chips with 60 ns chips, the system will default to the slower chip speed.

The Hard Drive

The hard drive is the most important component in your system. Without a hard disk, you have no data to share and without data, your network is useless.

SCSI and ASPI Controllers   Start with a fast, 8 to 10 millisecond, SCSI (Small Computer Systems Interface) hard disk and a ASPI (Advanced SCSI Programming Interface) complaint SCSI controller. A SCSI controller will allow you to daisy-chain in one PC a total of eight SCSI devices, such as CD-ROMs, tape backups, optical juke-boxes, and hard disks. ASPI provides a common language between the controller and the OS. The type of applications you use will determine your hard disk storage requirements. For example, if you need to store large graphic files, start with a one gigabyte hard drive. A good general size for a hard drive is 500MB.

RAID Subsystems   Larger mission-critical organizations need to consider using RAID (Redundant Array of Inexpensive Disks) disk subsystems. There are several layers of RAID support, ranging from total disk mirroring and fault tolerance to standard disk duplexing. A RAID system will protect you from any down time associated with data corruption or a hard disk failure. Most RAID systems also offer hot swappable disk drives, so you can replace a faulty hard drive without interrupting the server.

Bus Architectures   The internal slots on the motherboard of your PC are referred to as the PC's bus. Of the three main bus architectures, EISA, ISA, and MCA, the EISA standard offers the most flexibility for your file server. The EISA bus can use both 8- and 16-bit ISA cards in addition to 32-bit EISA adapters. There are EISA cards available for network adapters, SCSI controllers, and video controllers. Another benefit of EISA is the ability to automatically detect and configure your adapters. If you have ever had to change an interrupt or memory address, you can appreciate EISA's automatic configuration. There is also a new technology called local bus that may become the wave of the future, but for flexibility and performance stick with EISA.

Most new Pentium-based PCs also include a slot called the PCI (Peripheral Component Interface) bus. Unlike EISA, PCI adapters provide a 64-bit data path and contain internal processors. Similar to EISA adapters, PCI cards are software configurable and you don't have to worry about jumper settings or dip switches. There are several PCI adapters available for network adapters, hard-disk controllers, and video cards.

Wireless

The most popular solution to the problem of connecting your portable PCs and desktops to the network is to pull network cable and use an internal network adapter, external parallel port adapter, internal PCMCIA adapter, or a docking station. Unfortunately, there are several situations where installing network cable is impossible or impractical. For example, older buildings or warehouse environments don't always allow you to install cable in all of the places you need to have a computer. It is also expensive to install network cable through concrete walls or floors for only a few nodes.

Portable PCs are being used everywhere in the work environment. People carry them into conferences to take notes, into meetings to check spreadsheets, and into presentations to show the slides. While PDAs (personal digital assistants) didn't achieve the popularity initially predicted for them, there is no doubt that hand-held productivity tools will eventually become common sights around the corporate campus. But it's difficult and typically impractical to wire every conference room and meeting space with enough network connections for every attendee. A wireless LAN allows people to network together around a conference table and to access the work-group or corporate network services to retrieve information and to make links to extended networks.

Choosing Vendors and Installers

Now that you have a good idea of the products and services you need, it is time to call the individual companies and plan meetings. If you are ordering components from a mail order house, you will want to go ahead and place your orders. There is usually not a delay on common products such as printers and CD-ROMs, but it may take a while for your PCs to show up. After you have decided on the companies you will use, you want to call them and check on product availability and possible dates for the installation.

Here's a checklist that may prove useful as you go through this process:

- **Meet with Everyone Involved**   If you will use separate compa-nies for each phase of the installation, such as cable, hardware and software products, and installation, you need to sit down with everyone at one time. This will give the individuals a chance to meet each other and discuss their respective roles. If the per-son that installs your network cable does not meet with the per-son that will install your PCs, it will be a nightmare for them to find all of the wall jacks and trace cables.

    I have never installed a network without walking through the en-tire building with the cable installer. The cable installer may also need to call me if they find a problem or have a question. A good network consultant will coordinate with all of the people involved.

- **Go Back to the Budget Process to Reevaluate and Check Validity**   Chances are, the research phase uncovered a lot of questions and products that you did not budget for in your ini-tial planning stage. As people learn more about networking and see all of the neat things they can do, they seem to forget about the costs. Make sure that your research covers your existing needs not your wish list.

Because the budget process takes so long, and computer prices change daily, recheck your prices. You may find that the quote you got on a PC a month earlier has dropped in price. Also check that the original installation costs have not changed. Most consultants will include a quote expiration date.

Reread all of your proposals and make sure there are no hidden costs. For example, does the network installation cover setting up security and printers? Is training separate? If your network is installed properly, it will appear seamless to the end users, but you need to allow for some type of training on general maintenance and navigation.

Conclusion

As I stated at the beginning of this chapter, research requires the most time of any step in designing and installing a network. Research can be fun and it is definitely a learning process. The payoffs of doing research are definitely worth the investment. A good network installation requires a certain amount of time and effort. It is less expensive and stressful to spend your time planning and researching versus troubleshooting and upgrading. The next chapter will look closely at various optional network components, such as remote access, and LAN-to-LAN links.

Field Note: Experience Is the Best Teacher

Several years ago, when 10Base2 coaxial cable was still the most popular medium for Ethernet LANs, I decided to switch one of my clients over to a 10BaseT UTP topology.

We were constantly replacing coaxial connectors and every time there was a problem, the entire network went down. Most 10Base2 networks use a topology called linear bus. A *linear bus* network uses a single piece of cable that snakes around to every node on the network. If there is a single break or bad connection in the line, the entire network goes down. A 10BaseT network uses a star topology. A *star topology* requires a central wiring hub, but each node is connected to the network via its own cable segment. If a cable breaks on a 10BaseT network, only the node that is connected to that cable is affected.

Because of the reliability and fault tolerance of 10BaseT, we decided it was the best solution to our 10Base2 cable problems. While I was familiar with 10BaseT networks, I had never used the topology before, and the cable looked like fat telephone cable with bigger connectors. Because it looked like telephone cable, I decided to call a telephone contractor to perform the installation.

I should have become nervous when I had to explain the cable pin-outs and connectors to the contractor, but I still thought it should be a simple task for someone that had experience installing telephone systems. Boy, was I wrong; we spent the next two weeks after the installation tracking down bad connectors and faulty cable runs. We eventually had to call in an experienced network cable installer to reinstall the entire network. Needless to say, I didn't send the client a bill for my time, but fortunately I learned a priceless lesson.

CHAPTER

3

Preparing for WAN Links and Remote Access

Almost as soon as you establish your "local" area network, you'll face the need to expand the connectivity beyond the thousand feet or so of cable that define the term "local." People in your organization will want to access files and services on the network from home and other distant locations. This will be the beginning of your transition from a LAN (local area network) to a WAN (wide area network).

Overall, the major difference between LAN and WAN operation is the LAN uses short, fast connections while the WAN uses long and slower connections. The fast LAN links (the LAN cables) are a luxurious transmission scheme. They allow you to organize central files in elaborate arrangements in order to move a lot of information between clients and servers. The long, slow WAN connections are typically telephone lines although other connection options, such as city and nationwide wireless links, are becoming available. These connections create a discipline that forces you to organize your network files more carefully.

WAN Categories

It helps to divide your thinking about wide area networking into two areas: PC-to-LAN and LAN-to-LAN. You'll use the same technologies and terms in both areas, but the sociology (a factor often as important as the technology) will be very different. The chart below compares several dimensions of LAN and WAN segments.

	LAN	LAN-to-LAN	PC-to-LAN
Medium	Local cables	Telephone lines	Telephone lines
Speed	4 Mbps–100 Mbps	56 Kbps–1.5 Mbps	9.6 Kbps–128 Kbps
Distance	Approximately 1,000 feet	Beyond 1,000 feet	Any distance

	LAN	LAN-to-LAN	PC-to-LAN
Connection Devices	Network adapters	Communication servers and modems	Communications servers and modems
Connected Systems	Clients and servers	Local network to local network	PC to local network
Management Concerns	Reliability and capacity	Invisibility	Security Connection reliability Ease of use

The following sections discuss LAN-to-LAN and PC-to-LAN operations in greater detail.

LAN-to-LAN

When you set up LAN-to-LAN systems, your goal is always to make the operation invisible to everyone using computers on either side of the link. In modern networks, devices called routers serve as the regulating portal on each LAN. Routers examine the contents of each packet of data on the network and determine if the packet is addressed to a node on a distant LAN. If the address is across the gap, the router will strip off the local information such as the Ethernet address and error-control bits from the data packet, compress the rest of the information, and send it across the LAN-to-LAN link. All of this happens without any special action from the user.

Router Setup

Router setup is an arcane art, and router companies typically run one-week courses for the hardware and similar courses for the software. You should plan on taking those courses! The best advice I can give you is to choose your router vendor as carefully as you would choose a spouse because buying a router is the equivalent of entering into a marriage.

The communication between routers typically uses techniques proprietary to each company, so buying a router is an investment in that company's technology. Some of the larger router vendors include

Cisco, and Bay Networks, formerly Wellfleet, and Synoptics. High-end multiprotocol routers range in price from $1,000 to approximately $15,000 depending on the speed of the connection and the accompanying software.

In addition to the high-end routers from Cisco and Bay Networks, there are also several remote node access servers that provide basic dial-up routing. The more expensive routers are usually used for leased lines that are used to connect two LANs together 24 hours a day or at least during business hours. If you only need a LAN-to-LAN link for a few hours every other day, and you can live with slower analog telephone line connections, a low-end dial-up router such as NEC's DR. BonD, or the Shiva LANRover may work for you. Some of these products also work with faster digital lines such as switched 56 or ISDN.

Here are some things to consider when you select a router:

- Each router only works with a specific set of one or more network protocols. Typical network protocols include IPX (the Internetwork Protocol Exchange) and TCP/IP (Transmission Control Protocol/Internet Protocol). IPX was developed by Novell for its NetWare line of software, but Microsoft has also adopted it for Windows networking.

- Routers are primarily software products. Almost all router companies sell both hardware and software, but there is a trend toward putting router software into computers, wiring hubs, and other devices instead of into stand-alone hardware. While software-based routers are less expensive than a total hardware solution, they do require a lot more time to install and configure.

- You may want to consider using NetWare for your routing. Novell includes IPX routing software in every NetWare server and the company sells a separate multiprotocol router that is very successful.

Figure 3.1 shows the configuration of a WAN-to-WAN system using NetWare routers. Note that the routing functions shown inside the NetWare servers could alternatively be performed by separate network-connected boxes containing specialized router hardware.

Figure 3.1

You can use Novell's Multi-Protocol routing software to link two networks together without the added cost of an extra hardware router. The software-based router resides on the server. Note that only network packets with a remote destination address travel across the WAN link.

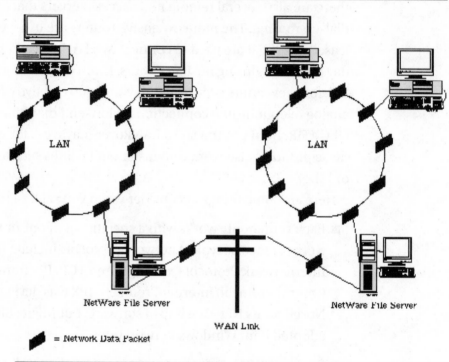

PC-to-LAN

The systems that connect remote PCs to LANs aren't nearly as invisible as LAN-to-LAN links, although some of the same techniques apply. As I said in Chapter 2, remote node and remote control are still the two most common ways people access their LAN from a remote PC. The two remote access methods are very different and you should not purchase a product or design a solution until you consider what types of applications you will be using on the remote PC. Once again, the software dictates the hardware and in this case the remote access method and product you use is considered the hardware.

Along with file servers, print servers, and fax servers, remote access servers are becoming a standard component on most LANs. As more people begin working at home and using portable PCs when they travel, remote access solutions are becoming not only a convenience but a necessity. As a network consultant, I could not live without my remote access server. Whenever I travel a long distance to a client's site, I can always dial into my office and retrieve the file I forgot. The amount of time and mileage it saves me more than pays for the price of the remote access server.

Remote Control

As their name implies, remote control products allow you to remotely control a PC on the LAN from a remote location. When you type a letter on the remote PC, it is just like typing it on the host PC. You can think of remote control products as a long extension for your keyboard and video cables. Figure 3.2 shows an example of a remote control setup between two PCs. Because you are only sending video and keystrokes across the dial-up connection, performance is comparable to what you would see if you were actually in the office typing on the host PC. All of the processing of information is taking place on the host PC, so it does not really matter what type of PC you are using on the remote. In fact you may be able to use an old 8088 or 80286 PC on the remote side and use a faster PC for the host.

There are several excellent remote control products on the market. Some of the more popular products include Symantec's pcAnywhere, Ocean Isle's ReachOut, and Norton-Lambert's Close-Up. All of these products range in price from $100 to $200 and work with both DOS and Windows-based PCs. Overall, these products are similar in both features and performance. Most remote control

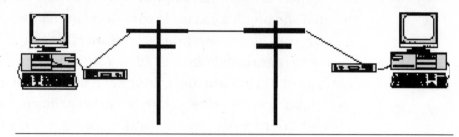

Figure 3.2
During a remote control connection between two PCs, only keystrokes and screens are transferred across the telephone lines.

packages that I have used over the years have proven very easy to install and use.

Windows-Based Programs   My biggest complaint with Windows-based remote control packages, is that they mess up my WIN.INI and SYSTEM.INI files. In order to provide acceptable performance over a dial-up connection, most Windows-based remote control programs include a proprietary keyboard, mouse, communications, and video Windows driver for the remote PC. This allows you to remotely control a Windows-based PC, but use your own video, keyboard, and mouse drivers.

If you have ever tried to remotely control a mouse, you know that the movements are jumpy, if the mouse cursor even works at all. While these proprietary drivers are necessary if you want to get your work done, they can cause compatibility problems with your other Windows programs. Many existing Windows programs require your traditional Windows drivers and if your remote control product replaces them, your programs may not work. It is bad enough that these programs make changes to your INI files, it is worse when they don't annotate the changes they make. For example, if a program is going to replace my communication driver line in my SYSTEM.INI file, it should label the changes or at least make a backup of my original file.

Remote Control on a Network

In addition to remotely controlling a stand-alone PC, many vendors also offer a product you can use to remotely control any PC on the network. Products such as pcAnywhere LAN allow you to use your network cable instead of a modem to take control of another PC on the same network. Network remote control is a great tool for network administrators. Instead of walking across campus or down the hall to fix a problem, the network administrator can simply take control of your PC and perform troubleshooting tasks or make changes to your configuration files.

Another benefit of network remote control programs is that they work well with remote node servers to provide a complete remote access solution. If you combine a network remote control program with a remote node access server, you can use your remote node connection to remotely control any PC on the host LAN. A combination of remote node and remote control is the best of both worlds.

Remote Nodes

Instead of extending your keyboard and video cables, remote node products extend your network cable. Figure 3.3 illustrates a basic remote node server configuration. While remote control programs only send keystrokes and screens over the dial-up connection, remote node programs send the entire network protocol. Because of the overhead involved in sending the network protocols over a telephone line, remote node connections are usually slow and only useful for very specific applications.

While most remote control products are software-based, most remote node products include both hardware and software. This is due to the fact that most remote node solutions are a lot harder to install than their remote control counterparts and require a lot more integration between the software and the hardware. A remote control

Figure 3.3
During a remote node connection, all of the network packets, not just keystrokes and screens, are sent across the telephone lines.

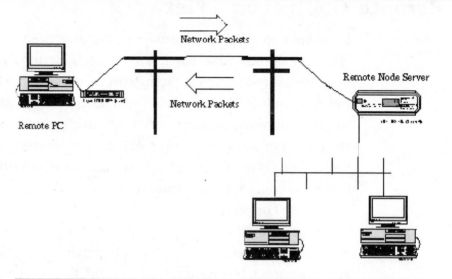

package only requires two PCs, two modems, and a phone line between them. Remote node products require PCs, modems, and phone lines, but they also need a network adapter on the host side and network drivers for both the remote and host PCs. Remote node products are also more expensive and can range in price from $2,000 to $10,000 depending on the number and speed of the dial-in connections.

Some remote node products such as Novell's NetWare Connect and Stampede's Remote Office are software-only products and require a dedicated PC or file server, a multi-port I/O adapter, a network adapter, and several hours of your time to install and configure. While software-based packages offer most of the same features as remote node hardware solutions, I prefer the turnkey solution. Turnkey remote node solutions cost about the same as software-based products, when you figure in the price of a dedicated PC, and they are lot easier to install and troubleshoot.

The two best remote node solutions currently on the market are the Microcom LANexpress 2.0 and the Shiva LANRover 3.0. The

Field Note: The Software Dictates the Hardware

One of my clients has both a NetWare LAN and an IBM AS/400 mini-computer. The AS/400 is connected to the NetWare network using a combination of Novell's NetWare for SAA on the file server and IBM's PC Support on the clients. All of the clients can simultaneously access the file server and AS/400. In addition to the central office, the company also has several satellite locations that need to access both the NetWare LAN and the AS/400.

The first solution I thought of was to use a remote control program such as pcAnywhere LAN. After all, pcAnywhere can run on any network client with a modem and it's cheap. Unfortunately, PC Support requires several device drivers that must be loaded in your local PC's memory in order to access the AS/400. When you use remote control to connect to a host, you no longer have access to your local PC's disk drives or device drivers.

The only way to allow the satellite offices to connect to the AS/400 was to use a remote node solution. A remote node server will allow you to connect to the host network but still have access to your local disk drives and any memory resident drivers loaded in your local PC's memory. The best product available was the Shiva LANRover/E.

The LANRover solved the problem of connecting to the AS/400, but it was too slow to use for running applications located on the NetWare file server. I decided to install pcAnywhere LAN on a dedicated PC and use the remote node connection to remotely control that PC.

By using both remote node and remote control, I was able to design a remote access solution that covered all of my clients needs. I would have rather just used one product, but that is not always possible.

LANexpress server ranges in price from $3,499 for a two port Ethernet unit to $11,899 for a 12-port Token Ring server. The LANRover Plus is also fairly expensive with a retail price tag of $4,299 for the four port model to $8,499 for a server with eight internal modems.

LANexpress and LANRover Plus

The most appealing feature of both the LANexpress and the LANRover Plus is their installation. All you have to do to install the hardware is connect the phone lines to the modems, connect the network cable, and turn on the power. Both products include a Windows-based SNMP (Shiva network management program) that allows you to configure the access server, remote users and dial-in and dial-out security. I have installed both products numerous times, and it has never required more than two hours to get the servers up and running.

The LANexpress expressWATCH management software, shown in Figure 3.4, provides numerous statistics and configuration information. For example, you can use the expressWATCH software to monitor over 250 statistics, including the quality of your dial-up connection, the number of packets sent and received, and any connection errors that occurred. You can also customize expressWATCH to only show errors or information you are interested in. ExpressWATCH allows you to keep a history of all connection information and monitor usage and other information via a graphical chart.

Figure 3.4
You can use the LANexpress express-WATCH software to monitor individual port utilization for all of your connections.

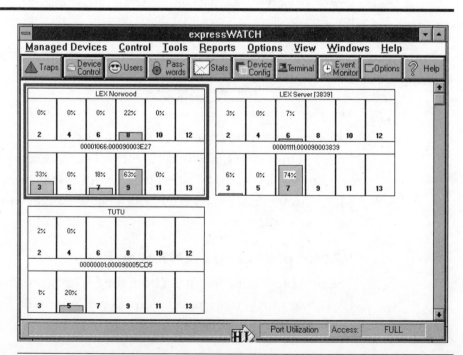

The Shiva network manager (SNM) software shown in Figure 3.5 offers configuration features similar to expressWATCH, but it does not provide the same in-depth statistics. While expressWATCH is a Windows-only application, Shiva provides an SNM package for Macintosh computers. Unfortunately, LANexpress does not offer any support for Macintosh PCs. LANexpress's lack of Macintosh support is a big problem for all of the people that own PowerBook PCs and need to access their host network.

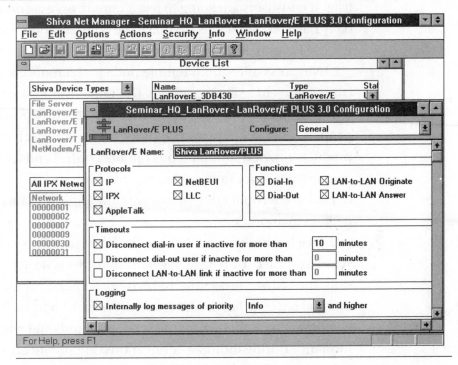

Figure 3.5
The Shiva Net Manager utility allows you to control all of your remote node servers from a central location.

The LANexpress and LANRover Plus servers allow you to connect to the local network using several different protocols including TCP/IP, IPX, and NetBEUI. Only Shiva offers support for the AppleTalk and the Apple Remote Access protocols. Both products include drivers for NDIS and ODI so you can use almost any network operating system on your remote PC.

One unique feature found in LANexpress is the ability to select your network connection type when you boot your PC. For example, when you turn on your PC, you get a pop-up screen that allows you to select a remote network, local network, or no network. This is ideal for people that don't know how to create separate batch files for remote and local network access. Shiva and most other products leave the task of creating individual configuration files to the end-user. If end-users are going to use a remote access connection on a daily basis, vendors need to make the configuration process on the remote PC as painless and transparent as possible.

LANexpress offers both remote node and remote control dial-up connections in a single package. The LANRover Plus only provides remote node access, but you can use a third-party product such as pcAnywhere LAN to provide remote control connections. Both products provide simultaneous remote control and remote node connections. For example, you can use both products to establish a remote node connection in one window and a remote control connection in another.

Unlike the internal modems in the LANRover Plus, which use standard UART (Universal Asynchronous Receiver Transmitter) calls, the LANexpress contains high-speed parallel bus modems. The internal LANexpress modems use the parallel port technology to eliminate the bottleneck of the serial port and offer sustained performance during multiple connections. Microcom also offers external and PCMCIA internal modems that use the parallel port technology. If you have already invested in external modems or need to use high speed synchronous connections such as ISDN or Frame Relay, you should stick with the LANRover Plus, or another product that doesn't include modems.

The LANRover Plus gives you the ability to use any modem or serial connection you choose. The LANexpress server offers better management and statistics, but it is more expensive and you have to use the Microcom internal modems. While the LANRover Plus offers better performance at a better cost per port, it does not bundle a remote control solution.

The LANexpress and LANRover servers are only two of dozens of remote node solutions. I like these products because they are easy to install and maintain. LANexpress and LANRover are designed for multiple dial-in connections and you may only need to provide one or two remote connections at a time. Fortunately, you can find single and dual port remote access servers that offer the same features of the larger multi-port servers but without the high cost.

Setting Up Your Remote PC

If you do decide that remote node is the best remote access solution for your network, there are some things you must remember when you setup your remote PCs. The most important step is to copy frequently used network programs to your local PC. Any program you access on the host network is copied to your computer's memory over a relatively slow connection. For example, if you connect to your host NetWare server and run the login program, you are actually downloading the entire program to your PC. The login program is approximately 112K, so it will require over a minute just to logon to the server using a 9600 bps modem. The same is true for other NetWare utilities such as Syscon, Map, and Pconsole. You should copy all of the network utilities you use to your local disk drive and make sure that you do not try to launch them from the remote server.

You will also want to create separate login scripts for your remote users. It can take as long as five minutes to connect to a remote server, if the host login script is configured to map 14 different network drives and attach you to three different servers. The easiest way to do this is to set up a network group for your remote users. You can create a shortened version of your main login script for everyone in the remote group.

Security

Security is one of the biggest concerns for people planning a remote access server for their LAN. The idea that someone could dial into your network while you are at home asleep is a real nightmare. Fortunately, most remote access products provide powerful security features and if you use these along with your network's built-in security, you are reasonably safe.

You may also want to invest in a third-party auditing utility, such as Saber's LAN Workstation, or use NetWare's built-in auditing features to track usage. An auditing utility will allow you to see who accessed the network and what information they retrieved or added. You can also restrict users from connecting to the network during certain hours and days of the week and control their access to individual files and subdirectories.

The best way to prevent unauthorized access when no one is around, is to turn the remote access server system off when you leave at night. Not every company closes at night, but not every company has remote users that need to access files at 2:00 a.m. either. Never give the telephone number of your remote access server to anyone that doesn't need to have it.

Dial-Up Routing versus Dial-Up Computing

What's the difference between a dial-up router and a remote node access server? They certainly look alike and generally have the same types of connections. In some cases, there is no difference in the equipment except in how you use it, many dial-up routers can perform most of the functions of an access server, but in most cases there is a difference in capability and in the accessory software.

Devices like the Centrum Inc.'s CentrumRemote 3000, Telebit NetBlazer, and Shiva's NetModem come equipped for both roles. While other devices such as the Livingston PortMaster and Networks Northwest Inc.'s BReeze 1000 only perform dial-up router functions.

Dial-up routers are devices designed to link LANs. Their primary role is to call another identical router on a distant LAN. Their firmware has the capability, called dial-on-demand, of recognizing the destination address of a specific frame on the LAN and initiating a connection to the distant address. The dial-up routers on each end must have routing table functions that can decode addresses and gather information from routing information packets. The routing tables eliminate excess traffic over the dial-up line, a very important task for expensive long distance dial-up connections.

Remote node access servers are designed to answer calls from distant calling nodes and to provide network connections to the calling PCs. They don't have to have internal dial-on-demand functions, but access servers must have software for the calling node. This software typically conforms to the ODI or NDIS LAN card driver standard, but instead of a LAN card it addresses a serial port. Because of the economies of scale, remote node access servers such as DCA's RLN, Shiva's LANRover, and the Microcom LANexpress have multiple ports—a feature found in only a few dial-up routers such as the NEC America Dr. BonD. Generally, it's as tricky to compare the costs of these products as it is to compare their features.

Remote access products such as the $1699 NetModem/E from Shiva provide a single dial-in and dial-out connection for remote computing in addition to connecting to another NetModem to create a dial-up router. Dial-up routing products such as the Livingston

PortMaster retail for $2,395 for a single connection but do not support remote node access.

The dividing line between dial-up remote node versus dial-up routing is being blurred by the existence of multifunction products like the NetModem, Dr. BonD and NetBlazer. Dial-up computing is designed to extend the remote network to your local desktop or notebook PC via a modem and a telephone line. Remote node is useful for transferring small files and e-mail across the dial-up connection, but usually too slow to run applications from the remote network. Dial-up routing is designed to link two remote networks. Dial-up routers can provide the bandwidth necessary to transfer files and run applications located on the remote LAN.

Telephone Lines: The Common Links

Both LAN-to-LAN and PC-to-LAN systems use telephone lines to carry the data. Three things happen when you send signals across any kind of long-distance circuit: the signals distort, they degrade in strength, and electrical noise enters the signal path. Repeaters and amplifiers can remove distortion and noise and increase the signal strength, but they're expensive. Because of these factors, long distance circuits are slower than LAN cable connections and they can be costly.

Warning: Long distance circuit costs can sneak up on you. These costs typically include a one-time charge for installation and a recurring monthly charge for service. You can often shop competing vendors and find monthly prices that differ by 10 to 15 percent or more. However, sometimes hidden up-front costs make a big difference in the overall amount you pay.

When you read the words "telephone lines" you probably think about the voice circuits you use every day. You use these same voice circuits when you make phone calls using modems. Modems—the term stands for "modulator/demodulator"—are devices that change the digital data coming out of your computer into analog tones. But when you get serious about making LAN-to-LAN and even PC-to-LAN links, then you'll want to use a digital instead of an analog service.

There are three types of digital data services you can buy: leased lines, circuit switched connections, and packet switched connections. Each of these is listed in the table below.

	Leased Line	**Circuit Switched**	**Packet Switched**
What?	Digital Leased Service	Switched 56, ISDN	Frame Relay, X.25
Why?	Higher Reliability	Lower Cost	Multi-point and Reliability
Who?	Local Carrier or Long Distance Company	Local Carrier or Long Distance Company	CompuServe, MCI, AT&T, WilTel
When?	Connect time is greater than 4 hours per day	Short connection times	All types of service

The following sections provide details on the individual services.

Leased Lines

Leased lines are circuits that you lease from a carrier on a full-time basis from point A to point B. The leased line carrier might be your local telephone company, a long distance or, as they are more formally known, an interexchange carrier, or some independent provider such as a company called Teleport that is active in many U.S. cities.

The basic increment of connection is one 64 Kbps circuit, although because of arcane network considerations this 64 Kbps circuit often actually uses 56 Kbps signaling. You'll typically buy service in increments of 64 Kbps. So, you might go to your local telephone company (the folks who give you dial-tone) and lease connections between a headquarters building and a warehouse in the same city with a signaling speed of 64 or 128 Kbps in order to link a remote warehouse computer into the corporate LAN. A common configuration consists of a dozen 64 Kbps circuits in one bundle known as a T1 circuit. T1 is said to have a signaling speed of 1.544 Mbps and carriers can break it apart into any combination of channels using signaling speeds that are multiples of 64 Kbps.

Leased line circuits are priced by the mile and according to the signaling speed. You pay more to go farther faster. Typically, if you don't use the circuit for any more than three to five hours a day, it is less expensive to use a dial-up or "circuit switched" service.

Digital Circuit Switched Services

When you dial a telephone call, you are using circuit switching. Through the number keys, you send commands to a telephone company central office computer that tells it how to complete a switched connection. Digital switched services work the same way.

Switched 56 and ISDN

A digital switched service called "Switched 56" is often offered by your local telephone company as part of a package of services known as Digital Centrex. Centrex, or central exchange, is a service that precludes the need for you to buy a local private branch exchange (PBX) for your telephone services. Instead of owning and installing your own local equipment, the local telephone company uses their central office equipment to forward, switch, conference, and ring calls within your offices. Digital Centrex adds digital connectivity.

Using Switched 56, you can connect between networks or dial into networks that also have switched 56 service. The calls typically cost about the same as a voice call on a business line. However, the up-front costs are higher.

A newer form of switched digital service that is exploding in popularity is the Integrated Services Digital Network or ISDN. ISDN was originally designed to allow the mixing of digital voice and computer data on the network. The digital voice service is a flop (the phones cost too much, are difficult to connect in extensions, and fail when the power goes off), but the digital services are set to explode.

ISDN provides "bearer" or B channels, each using 64 Kbps signaling. So, if they are "bonded" or aggregated together, the ISDN device can dial calls and have full 128 Kbps connectivity. Because the system uses a separate "data" or D channel for signaling, the calls are completed in tenths of a second. An ISDN router can initiate a call, transfer data between LANs, and disconnect the call in seconds. Since ISDN calls cost generally about twice as much as a standard voice business call, using ISDN can be more economical than using leased line services in many applications.

Packet Switching

Packet switched services combine the economy of dial-up services with the convenience of leased lines. There are many packet-switched service providers—ranging from your local exchange carrier to the interexchange carriers such as AT&T, MCI, Sprint, and WilTel, to special "value-added" carriers such as CompuServe.

These carriers take your data and form it into packets with specific destination and control information. The packets travel (typically over leased lines) to special packet switches. These switches examine the destination and select the best route. However, if the best route is congested or out of order, the switches choose alternate routings from within the vendors extensive network of cross-connected switches.

Packet switching offers reliability and flexibility. It's particularly useful if you have many points of operation—such as point of sale, credit checking, or reservation operations. In the U.S. today you'll typically use frame relay packet switching. This technology uses less error-checking (and therefore has less overhead and is more efficient) than the older X.25 packet switching systems found internationally.

Wireless: The Wave of the Future

If telephone lines are the common links of today, then wireless services are most definitely the links of the future. The major national wireless services and products are currently too slow for LAN-to-LAN links, but they are usually acceptable for PC-to-LAN connections and remote access. Another problem with present-day wireless services is the lack of availability in all areas. I live in a small town and I probably won't have wireless access for another two to three years. However, if you live in a large city and do a lot of your work from the road, or in your car, wireless services are worth looking into.

National Wireless Services

While some people successfully use analog modems to send data and faxes over cellular telephone connections, digital wireless systems provide more reliable service. But today's digital wireless services are a hodgepodge of offerings. The first of their kind, and the most widely available services, ARDIS and RAM Mobile Data, are typically best used for exchanging simple text messages. In addition to the first wireless services, there are several new wireless networks that promise to provide greater flexibility and performance. Metricom's Ricochet and the Cellular Digital Packet Data (CDPD) technology are expected to become the powerful competitors in the wireless networks of the future.

IBM and Motorola fielded the ARDIS system in the late 1980s primarily as a way for IBM service technicians to exchange messages with their local headquarters. Now as a subscription service, ARDIS is available in approximately 400 U.S. cities. True to its roots, its main value is still in the transmission of short status messages.

ARDIS operates in the 800 to 900 MHz frequency range and requires special wireless modems to transfer messages and data. The original ARDIS networks only provided a throughput of 4.8 Kbps and any user with old ARDIS compatible equipment is stuck at that speed. The service has increased the raw data rate to 19.2 Kbps and all of the new ARDIS equipment will allow you to switch between the two data rates. However, even at the higher signaling speed, you might only see a throughput of 1 to 2 Kbps using certain applications and network protocols.

RadioMail Corp's RadioMail is the most popular ARDIS service. You can use RadioMail to send text-based messages to other wireless users and you can even send e-mail over the Internet. RadioMail is fine for short messages, but it does not allow you to send large binary attachments with your e-mail. ARDIS subscriptions are usually based on usage and you can expect to pay around $100 a month for the services.

The RAM wireless network, which began service in 1992, is similar to ARDIS in performance and price and is available in approximately 100 U.S. cities. ARDIS and RAM are currently the only nationwide wireless services in full operation. RAM also operates in the 800 to 900 MHz frequency range, but it only provides a raw data rate of 8 Kbps. Like ARDIS, RAM is designed for message traffic. You can use the RAM network to connect to services such as RadioMail. You can also use applications such as Airsoft's AirAccess to perform file transfers and other tasks across the RAM network. RAM does not have the same coverage as ARDIS, but it is available in most major U.S. cities.

The CDPD Standard

Building on the concept of digital wireless computing, a group of companies developed CDPD (cellular digital packet data), which is an open standard for packet data communications that takes advantage of the technology of the existing cellular telephone system. CDPD provides a raw data rate of 19.2 Kbps and is designed to work with wireless modems available from companies such as Sierra Wireless and CMI. Another advantage of CDPD is the ability to switch between analog voice and data using the same wireless device.

CDPD uses a channel hopping technology to move between the existing cellular telephone radio channels. Because the CDPD hardware is an add-in to the standard cellular technologies, CDPD provides the same coverage and range as your cellular phone. CDPD is currently only available in several cities and the monthly cost ranges between $15 and $120, based on usage and services.

Metricom's Ricochet services uses a technology called Micro Cellular Data Network (MCDN) that operates at a signaling speed of 77 Kbps. Unlike the other services, Ricochet is a spread spectrum, frequency hopping network, similar to wireless LAN products including Xircom's Netwave and Proxim's RangeLAN/2. Metricom provides $495 wireless modems that use the Hayes AT command set and provide network connections using the PPP network protocol. Metricom offers a flat rate of $29.95 a month and provides unlimited usage of the Ricochet network.

The Ricochet network uses special wireless modems that communicate with small transceivers placed on poles throughout a geographical location. The Ricochet modems can roam from transceiver to transceiver, but you will loose your connection if you are traveling faster than 6 mph in a moving vehicle. An area can always add more transceivers to increase the bandwidth as more people join the service, but don't plan on using the service in a moving vehicle. Ricochet is currently only available in a few cities in California.

Both Ricochet and CDPD are designed for a variety of applications including network e-mail, file transfers, and remote control and remote node network connections. ARDIS and RAM are best suited for basic messaging, and they provide better coverage. Your choice of a wireless service should be based on the applications you want to run, performance, price, and for now, availability in your area.

Wireless LAN-to-LAN

If you need to connect multiple network nodes or LANs together in a small campus area or between a distance of less than a mile, it is not always feasible to pay for a leased line connection. There are several infrared and wireless radio products that will allow you to send data at speeds close to 2 Mbps over distances up to a mile or more.

Infrared devices offer better performance, but the transmitters and receivers must be within sight of each other and heavy fog and other environmental conditions can interfere with your connections. You can also plan on spending around $10,000 to install an infrared link between two buildings. As with land-lines, infrared connections are priced based on the speed of the connection and the distance.

Wireless radio LAN links are usually less expensive than infrared, and they do not have to have a line of site connection or worry about environmental conditions such as heavy rain or fog. Wireless radios have another problem, interference. Depending on the frequency they use, wireless radios can receive interference from a host of outside sources including radio stations, radar, and even microwave towers.

Until wireless links become less expensive and more readily available, you should stick with cable, namely fiber-optic. You can use approximately one mile of fiber-optic cable to link your LANs or nodes together and fiber is only a one time cost. Fiber-optic cable is immune to any type of interference and you may be able to use it for other services including telephones and multimedia.

Bottom-Line Advice

If you need to link LANs or to provide callers with high speed access to a LAN, you need a friend in the telephone business. If you are outside the U.S., you typically don't have a choice of carriers. Although England and few other countries now allow competition for commercial digital service. In the U.S., you should start with your local telephone company. I'd like to say that they all understand digital connections, but that's far from true. Either way, your next call should be to the local offices of a carrier like AT&T, MCI, Sprint, or WilTel. These companies have many alternative services for you. They can often install and lease you everything from the router to the leased line.

In addition to shopping for the best price, you should also shop for responsive service. If the would-be provider doesn't understand your data needs, they'll never know how to fix a disrupted service.

ISDN services are important for both LAN-to-LAN and remote LAN access. Many people in your organization will be able to get ISDN connections at home and the prices of ISDN interconnection devices are dipping. Give ISDN careful consideration for any digital connectivity needs.

Other Alternatives

The world of internetwork communications is changing fast. Cable television companies are moving quickly toward offering interactive digital connections and wireless connections offer mobility unmatched by any other connection option. Even the electrical power companies in some parts of the country might view digital services as just another utility connection that they can run over their existing poles and conduits.

The alternatives open to you will depend on your location. Some cities will be slow to update their old telephone communications infrastructure, while new wireless services will be popular. New telephone systems will probably have an advantage in suburban areas where distances challenge wireless coverage. You'll have to take each case and location individually and evaluate all of your options for cost and support.

LAN-to-LAN and PC-to-LAN connections will be increasingly important to all organizations. These technologies will help to frame how your company does its business over the last half of the 90s and into the next century.

C H A P T E R

Preparing for the Network

There is a lot more work involved in preparing for your network installation than just making check marks on your component list and calling the installers to confirm the dates. Installing a network is a lot different than installing a new word processor or replacing a failed hard-disk drive. A network installation will disrupt business as usual and you want the job to go as smoothly and quickly as possible.

To make procedures easier and faster, in this chapter I will provide you with some steps you can complete before the dreaded installation day. In Chapter 6, I will go into greater detail on connecting your network client and servers and configuring the network software. While you can't do everything, I think you'll be surprised at how many minor things you have to worry about before you can even start connecting your users to the network. Installing a network is really a two-step process. First, all the components must be in their place and checked out; then you can hook everything together and see if it communicates.

In addition to checking all of your network components, you also need to check your office space. Remember that you'll need several AC outlets at each client location and extra phone jacks in places where you want to use a modem. You can even go as far as stocking up on paper before installing your new laser printer.

Readying the Site Most people wouldn't install an expensive carpet in a house before the drywall was installed and painted. Likewise, you wouldn't install your network client PCs before the power outlets, network cables, and connectors had been installed. Most preinstallation tasks are just common sense, but some of the steps are so obvious it is easy to overlook them.

Starting with the Cable

Depending on the type of cable you are using, make sure that it is installed in every location, any wiring hubs you need are working, and that you have enough drop cables for all your network nodes. In addition to verifying that you have cable everywhere you need it, also make sure that the cable meets the specifications for the type of network you are installing. It is frustrating when you arrive at a client's office to begin a network install and discover that the cable was not installed properly or that it's the wrong type for your network.

You can't use any type of copper cable for your network and you can't just install it in your building without understanding the rules. In order to check your network cable installation, you need a basic understanding of the different types of network cable and how they compare in terms of features. The chart below and the following sections will give you a brief understanding of the difference in network architectures and cabling topologies.

Feature	Unshielded Twisted Pair (UTP)	Shielded Twisted Pair (STP)	Coaxial	Fiber-Optic (FO)
Network Architectures	Ethernet, Token-Ring, ARCnet	Ethernet, Token-Ring	Ethernet, ARCnet	Ethernet, Token-Ring, ARCnet
Throughput	Approx. 100 Mbps	Approx. 100 Mbps	Approx. 350 Mbps	Approx. 1 trillion bps
Physical Topology	Star or Bus	Star	Bus or Star	Bus or Star
Benefits	Inexpensive, flexible	Resistant to interference	High performance, resistant to interference	High performance, immune to interference, long distance
Drawbacks	Susceptible to interference	Expensive, hard to install	Expensive, susceptible to faults in Bus topology	Very expensive, difficult to install
Suggested Use	Small to medium LANs	LANs and inter-LAN backbone	Small LANs and inter-LAN backbone	Inter-LAN and WAN backbone

Coax, STP, and UTP

The three main types of network cable for Ethernet, ARCnet, and Token-Ring are coaxial, shielded twisted pair (STP), and unshielded twisted pair (UTP), with fiber-optic slowly gaining acceptance. Each type of cable is shown below.

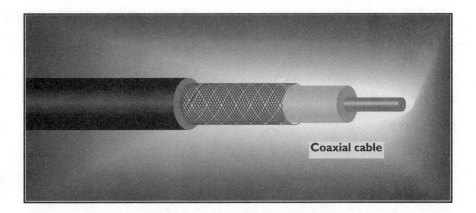

Coaxial cable

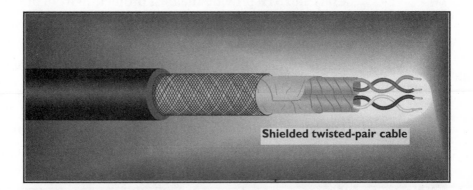

Shielded twisted-pair cable

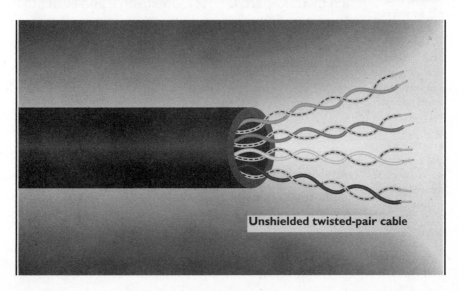

Unshielded twisted-pair cable

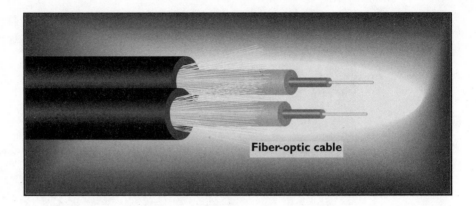

Fiber-optic cable

Checking the Wiring Peripherals If you installed your network cable using a star topology, you not only have to check the cable installation, but you also have to check other components, including the wiring hubs and patch panels. It is always smart to have your cable system in place and organized before you begin connecting your network nodes. The amount of time involved to set up your wiring closet will depend on the size of your network and the number of cable runs you installed.

Coax and STP provide the best protection from outside interference and offer greater distance, but they are expensive and harder to pull through walls. UTP is more susceptible to interference, but it offers flexibility and is less expensive. UTP is also shaping up to be the medium of choice for most new network architects including 100 Mbps Ethernet.

Distance is another factor to consider when choosing your network cable and topology. The thin Ethernet cable scheme does not offer fault tolerance, but it is inexpensive and can connect PCs up to 185 meters apart. UTP is more flexible and easier to install, but is limited to a distance of 300 feet between the network device and the wiring hub.

Because of its high cost, fiber-optic cable is normally reserved for very high-speed and high-capacity data communication needs. However, in some situations it can prove less expensive than copper cable and a lot more dependable. Fiber-optic cable does not transmit any magnetic or electrical signals, so it is not susceptible to any outside interference. Likewise, it will not cause any outside interference. You can also use fiber-optic cable to cover more than 10 times the distance of normal copper-based network cable. I will discuss more uses of fiber-optics in the following chapter.

I have found the best way to design a medium to large LAN is to use a combination of different types of cable. For example, if the network covers multiple floors in a building, I try to use coaxial or fiber-optic as my backplane to connect the different floors and UTP to connect the PCs on the individual floors. Coaxial can cover a longer distance and it is less sensitive to electric interference from devices such as power cables and elevators. UTP is a flexible and inexpensive solution for my individual nodes. As long as you use the same MAC network protocol, you should not encounter any problem mixing your cable types.

Understanding the Architectures

A network architecture is a set of protocols or rules that describe how a product should perform network activities such as transferring data. The type of network cable you choose is tied directly to the network architecture you are using. Products that adhere to the same network architectures can communicate and work with each other. The three major network architectures used to share the network cable are ARCnet, Ethernet, and Token-Ring. The network architecture not only dictates what type of network adapter you should buy and the cable you use, it also defines other things, such as how many PCs you can connect together and how far apart they can be. Over the years network architectures have also begun to encompass other specifications such as network management.

The I Triple E Standards

Most network architectures in use today are defined by individual subcommittees of the Institute of Electrical and Electronics Engineers (IEEE), pronounced "I Triple E." The IEEE provides a set of standards that specify the network architectures including cabling, physical topology, electrical topology, and media access control

(MAC). Basically, the IEEE standards define how the network nodes share access to the network cable and what type of signals they send across it. The main committee in charge of the standards is called the 802 committee. Smaller subcommittees that define the different architectures are also part of the larger 802 committee and they are distinguished by a decimal point and corresponding number. For example, the subcommittee in charge of 10 Mbps Ethernet is called 802.3 and the group in charge of developing standards for Token-Ring is referred to as the IEEE 802.5 subcommittee. Likewise, the architecture standards are also called by the name of the committee that defined them. Architectures such as ARCnet that do not completely fit into any of the standards are referred to as 802. (dot) something.

Media Access Control (MAC)
The access protocol, or MAC, is the most important distinguishing factor for comparing the three different network architectures. A good analogy of the access protocol is a traffic cop. The traffic cop, I'll call him Mac, sits at every node and controls access to the network cable or highway. Mac has a set of rules that tell him when to let a node travel on the highway. The rules are designed to prevent a collision, but they also explain what to do in the event of an accident. While the different network architectures can usually use the same type of network cable, each network architecture uses a different access protocol.

ARCnet

ARCnet has been around for awhile and has a fairly large installed base. The drawbacks of ARCnet include a relatively slow throughput of 2.5 Mbps and a lack of third-party vendor support for replacement hardware. Over the years, ARCnet has lost its popularity and you will usually not see it used for new installations. ARCnet typically runs over RG-62 coaxial cable and uses a star-topology with multiple wiring centers or hubs.

In an effort to revive the life of ARCnet, Datapoint Corp., the inventors of ARCnet, developed a new product called ARCNETPLUS. ARCNETPLUS provides a maximum throughput of 20 Mbps and you can gradually introduce it into your existing network without replacing all of your cards and hubs at the same time. Unfortunately for Datapoint, ARCNETPLUS did not help stop the decline of ARCnet networks.

I only have one client who still uses ARCnet, but the cost of upgrading 200 PCs has kept that client from making the move to a more popular and scalable architecture. I would not recommend ARCnet for any new network installations. If you currently use it, consider upgrading to either Ethernet or Token-Ring. Even if you did want to continue using ARCnet or install a new network using the ARCnet architecture, you would have a very hard time finding products and support.

Ethernet

Ethernet is the most popular network architecture. Most current Ethernet networks operate at a signaling speed of 10 Mbps. However, the IEEE has recently defined a standard for running Ethernet at speeds up to 100 Mbps. One reason for Ethernet's popularity is the fact that it is usually the least expensive of all three architectures. You can usually find a good 10 Mbps Ethernet adapter for less than $100 compared to $200 to $300 for Token-Ring adapters. You can install Ethernet using coaxial or unshielded twisted-pair (UTP) cable in either a star or daisy chain topology. Ethernet is becoming the architecture of choice for both peer and server-centric networks.

To further the appeal of Ethernet as a network architecture, several vendors have developed a specification for 100 Mbps Ethernet. There are two major specifications for 100 Mbps Ethernet, 100VG-AnyLAN and 100BaseT. 100VG-AnyLAN was developed by Hewlett Packard and provides a transmission speed of 100 Mbps for both Ethernet and Token-Ring. The 100VG-AnyLAN architecture is defined by the IEEE 802.12.

The 100BaseT specification was developed by several companies including 3Com, Synoptics, and Intel. 100BaseT is also called 100Base-X and Fast Ethernet. The IEEE 802.3 subcommittee is currently responsible for 100BaseT. While 100VG-AnyLAN changes the Ethernet network architecture media access protocol, 100BaseT uses the existing Ethernet MAC specification. Both architectures require you to use new hubs and network adapters which are more expensive than existing 10 Mbps Ethernet products. I will discuss 100 Mbps

Ethernet and other new products in greater detail in Chapter 5, "Upgrading."

Token-Ring

Token-Ring is the most robust but expensive architecture of the three. Token-Ring operates at a rate of 4 or 16 Mbps and uses a star topology to ensure that your network is safe from cable failure. Token-Ring cable and network adapters are expensive and some peer networks don't include network drivers for Token-Ring cards. Most existing Token-Ring networks run over shielded twisted-pair (STP) cable installed in a star topology. Newer Token-Ring networks are switching to the more flexible and less expensive UTP cable.

If you have invested a lot of time and money in an existing Token-Ring network, you will probably want to stick with Token-Ring. However, if you are planning a new network or a large overhaul of your existing system, Ethernet is a lot less expensive and the performance differences are negligible.

Understanding the Topologies

The physical topology of a network describes the type of cable you use and the way you connect it to your client PCs and file servers. The two major network topologies are daisy-chain or linear-bus, versus star or hub. The daisy-chain or bus topology shown in Figure 4.1, is typically associated with thin Ethernet (10Base2) in which the network cable goes from PC to PC in a linear fashion and both ends of the cable are terminated. If a single connection breaks along the chain, the entire network goes down. While the physical-bus topology is normally the cheapest to install, it provides the least protection from faulty connections.

In an Ethernet star topology, such as the 10BaseT network shown in Figure 4.2, the network cable runs from each PC to a central

Figure 4.1
A simple network-bus topology. All of the network nodes are connected using a single cable. If the cable breaks or a connector fails, the entire network will go down.

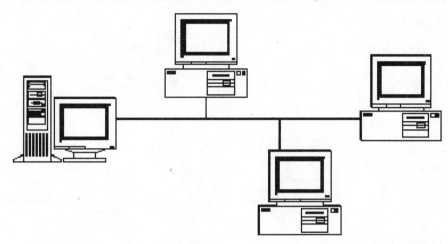

wiring center or hub. If a single cable goes bad, the hub partitions off that bad segment and the network continues working. The star topology offers good fault tolerance, but it does require the added expense of a hub.

A unique $229 product from Farallon called the Etherwave adapter allows you to daisy-chain your 10BaseT client PCs. The Etherwave solution is ideal if you only want to add one or two new nodes, but you don't have any available ports on your wiring hub and all of your cable runs are in use. It is a lot less expensive to install an Etherwave adapter than it is to buy a new hub and install more cable. While the bus topology is acceptable for small, one to two room, network installations, a star topology offers greater flexibility and protection for larger networks.

Installing Patch Panels

Patch panels, like the one shown in Figure 4.3, may look confusing, but they are a great tool for eliminating the rat's nest in your wiring closet. Patch panels serve two basic functions. First, they allow you

Figure 4.2
A star topology uses a central wiring hub and separate cable runs to connect all of the PCs and peripherals on the network. If a single hub port or cable fails, the rest of the network is not affected.

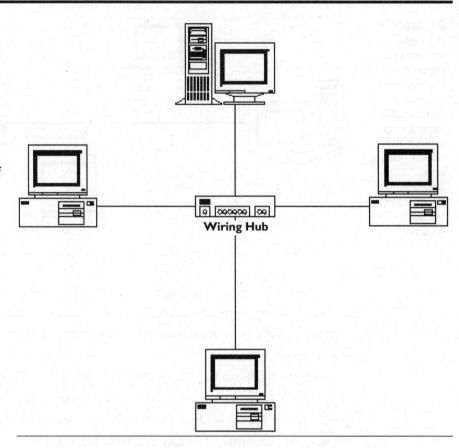

Wiring Hub

to neatly organize your UTP cables. Second, they allow you to make changes to your cable segments and add new devices without moving PCs around or installing new cable.

The patch panel is installed between your network cable and other devices such as wiring hubs. This allows you to switch entire workgroups to a different hub or combine two LAN segments if one of your wiring hubs or file servers goes down. While you could do all of this with a standard wiring hub, it would take a lot longer and soon you would be pulling your hair out trying to remember which cable goes where.

Figure 4.3
All of the ports on a patch panel are numbered so you can keep them in order. Most patch panels are stackable, so that you can add ports as you need to.

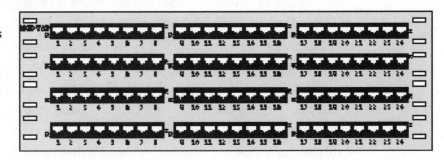

I like patch panels because they allow me to label and keep track of all of my network cables. If you took my advice and planned for the future, you probably have multiple cable runs that are not in use. As opposed to connecting them to a wiring hub or purchasing a larger wiring hub, you can terminate them into the patch panel and connect them to the network as needed. If you have ever gone into a wiring closet that has hundreds of loose cables hanging from a hole in the ceiling, you can probably appreciate patch panels. Patch panels are also ideal for tracking down a faulty cable or hub port.

Designing Your Wiring Closet

I use the term "wiring closet" to signify everything from a large glassed-in computer room with removable floor tiles to a walk-in closet in the corner of your one-room office. When you install a network, there is usually one area that you designate as your wiring closet. The wiring closet is where you usually place your UPS (Uniterruptable Power Supply), wiring hub, file server, and even the phone system. While you may not venture into your wiring closet very often, that doesn't mean that you should stack the components in a pile or put them on the floor.

The best way to arrange your wiring closet is to use either shelves or racks. Shelves are fairly inexpensive and you can design them any way you want. Racks are nicer, but are usually limited to 19 inches in width unless you have them custom built. Not only does using shelves or racks add to the look of your wiring closet, it also helps you make the best use of a limited space and keeps your components off the floor. Plan on enough space for all of your UPSs, wiring hubs, and any PCs or printers that need to be out of the way, but accessible.

Because electronic equipment is extremely sensitive to dangers from dust and heat, also make sure you have proper ventilation for all the devices in your wiring closet. You don't want to walk into a wiring room on a hot summer day and pass out from the heat swells coming off your UPS.

A problem I found with the design of many wiring closets is the lack of adequate power outlets. Sure, you can always use extension cords and multiple outlet strips, but that is dangerous and it contributes to the rat's nest you are trying to avoid in the first place. If I walk into a client's office prepared to begin a network installation and I see that the wiring closet is not set up or is a mess of cables and equipment, I mentally add an hour or two to my bill.

Configuring Your File Server

Whenever I plan a new network installation, I always try to take the file server back to my office before the actual date of the install. This allows me check out all of the hardware and do a test run to make sure the PC will work as a network file server. If I do find any software or hardware problems, it gives me time to fix them before the scheduled installation date.

If your file server is going to have problems, experience shows that they will usually show up during the first week or two of operation.

This is another reason I like to configure it before the actual installation and run it through some tests. The file server is the most important PC on the network, and if it doesn't work you don't want to find out the morning of the planned install.

The ability to configure the file server before the major installation will not only help you diagnose and prevent any hardware and software compatibility issues, it will also save you a lot of time. Most major network operating systems, including NetWare and Windows NT Server, can require as long as three hours just to install the software. That's three hours you will need when you start connecting your clients to the network and configuring your applications.

Using Existing Products

As I mentioned in Chapter 2, you may be able to use your existing products, including PCs, printers, and backup devices, with your new network. Before you plan on using these components, you want to make sure that they will work with your network hardware and software. It is always wise to check your hardware before you start the installation.

If you wait until the installation date and discover that the existing PCs you wanted to use do not work with your network operating system, you are going to have some users that won't have access to the new system until you purchase replacement PCs. This can have disastrous effects on your budget in several ways. First, you will have to find the money to purchase the new PCs. Second, you will have to pay the network consultant to make a separate trip to install them.

Memory Requirements

One of the biggest problems you will find if you try to network your existing 286 and older PCs is the lack of enough available Random Access Memory (RAM). While these PCs may work fine with your

Field Note: Avoiding Incompatible Hardware

Recently, I was asked to recommend a complete network system for a new client. The owners had done their homework and "thought" they new exactly what they wanted, but they decided to contact my company for a second opinion. I met with the client and went back to my office to prepare the SAR. In the SAR, I recommended a brand-name PC for use as the file server and even went so far as to recommend the type of hard-disk controller they should purchase.

After they read over my SAR, they called me back in to discuss it. They had been browsing the pages of a computer magazine and found a mail-order company that could provide a no-name PC for a lot less money. I asked them if they told the salesperson at the mail-order company that the PC was going to be configured as a Novell NetWare 3.12 file server. They said "of course" and guaranteed me that everything would be great and, of course, they would save money.

Fortunately, the file server arrived before some of the other network components and I had a chance to pick it up and take it back to my lab. I immediately popped the cover to see what was inside this "inexpensive" file server. The first thing I noticed was the presence of a no-name SCSI controller instead of the one I recommended. I quickly looked for a book and some disks so I could find the NetWare drivers.

I was starting to get nervous, and when I saw the internal modem in a PC that was supposed to be configured as a NetWare file server, I knew I was in trouble. NetWare does not support internal 2400 baud modems! I removed the modem and tried to install NetWare anyway.

I could not find the driver disk for the no-name SCSI controller, so I called the mail-order company to ask for help. The salesperson at the mail-order company knew the name of the card vendor, but not the phone number. I decided to find the company's phone number myself. After all, I'm a professional network consultant and writer; if a company existed I could find it. Wrong. Not only could I not find the phone number, I could not even find anyone who had heard of the company.

I noticed that the SCSI hard-disk controller had a major manufacturer's chip set on it, so I called that manufacturer for help. The technical support person I spoke with had no knowledge of the card I had, but told me that if it had their chips set, it might work with their driver. Unfortunately, the driver didn't work.

I eventually returned the card and begged the mail-order company to send me a NetWare compatible card. The company sent the new card, but then we encountered other problems and finally had to declare the PC unfit for use as a NetWare file server. The client agreed to return the system and buy the one I recommended in the first place. Unfortunately, all of these problems delayed the network installation by two weeks and made a lot of people angry.

existing stand-alone applications, such as word processors and accounting programs, they may not have enough RAM after you load the network drivers. A good rule to remember is that if your older PCs don't have at least one megabyte of RAM, don't plan on using them on the network. By the time you load DOS, the network drivers, and any other memory resident program, PCs with only 640K of RAM will barely be able to boot, much less run your applications. If you are going to use a Windows-based network, such as Windows NT, each client will need to be at least a 486 PC with 8MB of RAM and a 180- to 200MB hard disk. You could probably use an older 386 PC, but the performance would usually be too slow.

If you are going to install a new application along with your network, check with the software vendors to get the minimum requirements for your client PCs. Different NOSs have different memory requirements, but plan on losing about 70K of your PC's memory to the network drivers.

Backup Systems

If you already have one or two stand-alone PCs, you may already have a tape backup system. If you want to use your existing backup devices, make sure they are capable of backing up data from network drives. Those devices should also be able to hold all of your network data (and preferably all of your applications, too). While you really don't have to back up the network software (if you have the original disks), it is a lot easier to restore from a tape than it is to reinstall all of the software and set it up the way you want it.

In a perfect world, you would install a network backup system that works closely with your network operating system and also allows you to back up both your file server and your client PCs. A good network-based backup system should also allow you to back up and restore security information, such as user names, passwords, and file access rights.

Establishing Network Security

Unless you work in an environment where your data is not very confidential or you completely trust your co-workers, you are going to want some level of security. Even if you only need to set up user names and passwords, it can save you time if you think about them now. It only takes a few minutes to sit down with a pen and paper and create names and passwords. You may even want to let the users pick their own passwords because they are the ones who will have to remember them.

If you are planning to implement file and directory level security, it will take longer than just picking user names and passwords. Unless you plan to set up the file level security yourself, you will need to provide the network consultant with all of the information before the installation.

Using a Professional

I never tell a client they can use any existing PCs, software or backup devices until I personally check out each one. Chances are everything will work fine, but it's better to be sure. If I don't check, I could look unprofessional and the client might have to purchase something they did not have in their budget.

Call your network consultant. He or she should be more than happy to do a quick check of all your existing hardware and software. If you are installing a new software package with your network, you should also call the software vendors and ask them about using existing components.

Making Sure You Have All the Pieces

Everything I mentioned earlier is important, but nothing is more important than checking your inventory and confirming the installation dates with your installers. It is great if you can test every component before you try to use it, but if you don't even have the component, you can't do anything. Below is a check list of all the major pieces and parts of a network installation. If you are missing any of these items, you may not be ready to install the network.

Check list for preparing for your network installation

- File server PC

- Network client PCs

- Network operating system

- Cable installed in the walls

- Drop cables for each network node

- Patch panels and wiring hubs in place

- Adequate AC power outlets for all your components

- Adequate telephone lines for your modems and FAX

- UPSs and surge protectors for your PCs and wiring hubs

- Network adapters

- Printer and printer cables

- Shelves and racks for equipment

- Adequate desk space for PCs

- Other accessories and cables (modems, CD-ROMs, and so on)

If you followed the checklist and did even half of the tasks I discussed in this chapter, you are in good shape for your network installation. Whether you are installing a network, cooking dinner, or planning a trip, the secret is all in the preparation.

In Chapter 6, I will discuss the actual installation process. When you install a network, it can go smoothly or it can become one of the most frustrating experiences you ever have to go through. While you can never predict any problems you may encounter during the installation, you can take some preventative measures. If you perform the preinstallation tasks in this chapter, I think it will make your life much easier on game day.

CHAPTER

5

Upgrading Your Network

People usually decide to upgrade their network for two main reasons. First, their business is booming and they need to add more PCs so the new employees can handle the workload. Second, they failed to plan for the future when they designed the network. In this case, business may not necessarily have increased, but the network lacks enough resources to handle the day-to-day tasks. In either case, you need to plan your upgrade just as carefully as you should have planned the initial network installation. If you don't, you may need to upgrade six months down the road for the latter reason.

A network upgrade is not limited to adding new parts to an existing piece of equipment. An upgrade can include anything from adding more disk space to your file server to installing a remote access server for dial-up connections. In this chapter I will cover the key areas of upgrading a PC-based network. I will look at both software and hardware upgrades and the reasons for doing or not doing both. I will also discuss some specific upgrade tasks you can perform to increase network productivity and performance. No matter what your reasons, you need to be thorough and research all of your options before you invest in a hardware or software upgrade.

Why You Should Upgrade

The main reason you are upgrading is because your network can't handle the workload. I have some clients who have been using the same network hardware and software for several years. It is old and slow but it does the work they need and it hasn't broken yet, so they don't care to upgrade. I also have clients that seem to call me once a week with a new computer or software program they want to install. Some people treat their computer network as a tool for doing a particular job, similar to a hammer. It doesn't matter if the hammer is old and rusty, as long as it still drives nails, there is no need to replace it. These are the people that usually don't have an adequate backup, but yell the loudest when their data is lost. Other people like to live on what I call the "bleeding edge," and tend to buy new hardware and software just to play with it and see how it works. These are the people that never understand why their system is always slow if it even works at all. Neither philosophy is right. You always need to perform some maintenance upgrades on your network, but you should not buy new products without a reason.

Keep in mind that software and hardware vendors love to send you information on their latest wares. The sales brochure usually includes a special introductory price, but not much information on the product's new features. If you are upgrading just for the sake of having the latest and greatest hardware and software, you need to think again. It is always nice to have the newest hardware and software, but if your system is working properly, you should consider saving your money for when you really need to upgrade or have a problem.

You can't blame the vendors; it's their job to convince you to upgrade every time they introduce a new product. That's how they make money. The best way to determine if you should upgrade is to use common sense. For example, if a new version of your word processor is available that offers features that will increase your productivity, you should consider upgrading. Another reason for upgrading is to receive vendor support. Most small software vendors will not provide technical support unless you are using a new version of their product. Even larger companies, such as Novell, do not support early releases of their software, such as Netware 2.1.

Assessing the Benefits

Most people think that a hardware or software upgrade will make their life a lot easier. In most cases the new product will increase productivity and in some cases performance, but at what cost? Before you purchase a software or hardware update, ask yourself, "What benefits is this product going to give me, and in addition to the cost of the upgrade, how much time and money will it take to install and configure it?" Whenever you add a new component to your system, you have to make sure that it will work with your existing products and that you can afford the cost of the installation.

It is not unusual for clients to call me about an upgrade or new product they want to install, and then complain when I explain what is involved in the upgrade. In some cases they decide to go ahead with the installation, but complain when the installation bill exceeds the cost of the product. Other times they may decide that the cost of upgrading is not worth the time and money involved.

Software and Hardware Bugs

Unfortunately, some new releases of hardware and software can contain problems and bugs that cause more trouble than the new features are worth. Many experienced users will not even buy a software package if it is new or if it is a major revision of an existing product. Many people believe that any software that has a ".0" at the end of the version number is going to have problems. While this is not always the case, a few good examples of problems with new software releases include Microsoft's Windows 3.0, DOS 6.0, and Novell's NetWare 4.0. These software releases had different problems ranging from data corruption to incompatibilities with certain hardware. If possible, it's always better to wait until a major software package has been on the market for a few months before you purchase it. Let other people, like myself and other writers and consultants, find the problems first.

You usually don't hear a lot about hardware bugs, but they do exist. The major problem with new hardware is incompatibilities

I never like to install a network or do any kind of major job without discussing it with the client and writing an SAR (survey and recommendation). Unfortunately, I occasionally get suckered into a job without knowing what I'm walking into. About a year ago, I installed a LANtastic network for a local insurance agency. The client recently called and told me he had purchased three new PCs and a new version of LANtastic. He asked if I could run over and make the changes. I should have told him that it would take some time depending on the type of PCs and network adapters he had purchased in addition to the time it would take to reconfigure the network for the new version of LANtastic. Instead I said, "Sure, see you in a minute."

When I got there I was happy to see that he had purchased name brand PCs and that he had the proper number of upgrade licenses for LANtastic. To save time, I decided to install the new PCs with the existing version of LANtastic to make sure they worked.

A mere three hours later, I had the three PCs communicating nicely with the old version of LANtastic; now it was time for the upgrade. I installed the LANtastic upgrade on the existing PCs without a hitch. However, when I tried to upgrade the new PCs, I found out that the new version of LANtastic did not have a driver for the new adapters. I was not worried because I knew I could use the generic NDIS drivers, it would just require more time.

I eventually upgraded all of the PCs and decided to test out the new network. When I tried to run some of the DOS applications, I received an out of memory error on the new PCs. After troubleshooting, I determined that the NDIS drivers required more RAM than the standard LANtastic drivers. I decided to start optimizing memory wherever I could to fix the problem. My client did not seem to understand why the new network could not do the same things as the old network.

After a full day and a half of sweat and hair pulling, I eventually got the network back up the way it used to be. The client and I discussed the time it took, and he determined that his idea to upgrade entailed a lot more work and frustration than he had planned on. He paid my bill, but hopefully he will ask an expert's advice before he decides to upgrade in the future.

with your existing software and hardware. While it is fairly easy to avoid incompatibilities by checking with the vendor before you purchase a hardware product, there are some other bugs that may not be so obvious. The best and most current example of a hardware bug is the Intel Pentium chip. The Intel Pentium had a problem in the FPU (floating point unit) circuit that could cause incorrect re-sults in some floating point math calculations. Most users will never see the problem, but it still makes you nervous when one of the world's largest vendors is shipping a product with bugs.

Checking Out the Products

If you want to check out an upgrade or new product before you purchase it, and none of your colleagues have a copy, you should look through a few computer publications. If the vendor has a CompuServe forum or Internet site, you should also go online and read the messages. Read all of the messages carefully to make sure that the problems users are experiencing relate to your system. Just because a single user is having a problem with a product doesn't mean that there's a problem with the upgrade. There could be other hardware or software problems on their system. I don't usually take a complaint of a product seriously unless multiple users experience it. For all I know the complainant may work for a competing vendor.

Another way to check on a new product, before you buy it, is to call the vendor's technical support number. When a vendor releases a new product, the company is usually flooded with people calling with questions and problems. It make take you awhile to actually talk to a warm body, but if you never get through to technician or if they don't call you back for a day or two, you should think twice about purchasing their product.

Planning Your Upgrade

The main reason you are upgrading is because your network can't handle the workload. You don't want to install a quick fix solution that will force you to upgrade again in the near future.

There are several network components that you will need to add or upgrade as your network grows. The most common include the file server, cable, clients, network operating system (NOS), and remote access servers. Every time you add or change a network component you are essentially performing an upgrade. A network upgrade is not only intended to increase productivity and performance, it can also fix what's broken.

Upgrading Your File Server

Because the file server is the most important hardware component on your network, it is also the one that you tend to upgrade more often. As Figure 5.1 shows, a server upgrade usually entails adding memory, disk space, and remote access capabilities.

Each of these factors are discussed in the following sections.

Figure 5.1
Path to Server Upgrade. The most common file server upgrades include adding memory, disk space, and remote access.

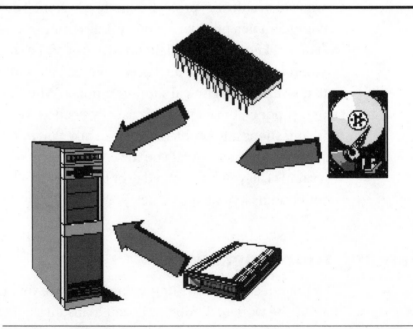

Adding Memory to Your File Server

My biggest problem with computer memory is that it is the only hardware component that has not decreased in price over the last two or three years. I recently built a 486 DX2 66 MHz PC to use as a test machine in my lab. I paid more for the 16MB of RAM I installed than I did for the motherboard and hard disk combined. All complaints aside, memory is as important as your CPU and hard disk in terms of file server performance and capacity.

It doesn't matter how fast your computer's CPU is, it can only handle one job or request at a time, unless you have multiple CPUs. In order to handle multiple jobs, the computer stores all of the subsequent requests in memory until the CPU has time to handle them. While most requests can be stored on your hard disk, it is a lot slower than memory. Memory operates at a speed of 60 to 70 ns (nanoseconds) compared to 8 to 10 ms (milliseconds) for even the fastest hard-disk drives. The more memory you have, the faster your jobs will be completed.

Disk Caching

The most common way your file server uses memory to increase performance is a process called disk caching. Most network operating systems will store the most recent or frequently requested blocks of data in memory. This allows the NOS to retrieve the requested data from the faster memory versus the slower hard disk. Disk caching does not get your request to the server any faster, only the response. The more memory your file server has, the more requests it can store in memory and the less time it has to read and write to the hard disk.

Novell NetWare converts some of your file server's memory into areas called cache buffers. Cache buffers are areas of memory where network requests are stored until the CPU is available. You can use the NetWare Monitor utility to monitor the amount of cache buffers

you have on your file server. You always want to have at least 60 percent cache buffers available on your file server. As you can see in
Figure 5.2, my server has 64 percent free cache buffers. If I added
more disk space, software, or users, I would have to increase the
memory in my file server. If you get below 50 to 60 percent cache
buffers, you will not only lose performance but you may also experience server crashes.

Figure 5.2
The NetWare
Monitor utility
provides a
host of useful
information,
including the
remaining
percentage of
cache buffers.

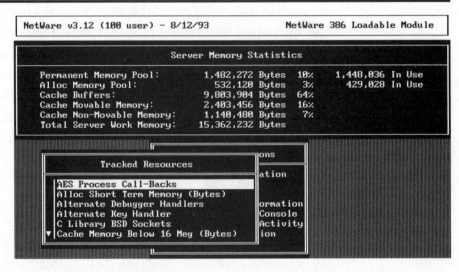

Disk caching is not only reserved for server-centric network operating systems such as Windows NT and Novell NetWare. Both peer-
to-peer network and desktop operating systems include some type
of disk cache. If you want to see how important disk caching is to a
stand-alone PC, remove the Smart Drive or other cache program
from your DOS PC and try running Windows. Without the added
cache, in most cases, you will experience a 30 to 40 percent decrease
in performance, not only when you start Windows, but also while it
is running.

Add-on Utilities and NLMs

Disk caching is not the only memory hog on your file server. Optional add-on network utilities, such as backup, virus protection, and network management utilities also require a lot of system resources. There are hundreds of optional add-on network utilities that you can load on your file server to perform specific tasks. While these programs usually provide a helpful function, they eat up a lot of your memory.

The most common type of file server add-on is a Novell NLM (NetWare Loadable Module). Your server may be running an NLM as a print server, CD-ROM driver, an antivirus monitor, backup server and for network management. In fact, every network adapter and disk drive you add to your NetWare server requires an NLM and thus more memory. Figure 5.3 shows a list of some common NLMs running on a NetWare server. You should always check the memory requirements of a network utility before you install it on your server. You may find that you need to add more memory in order to maintain acceptable performance as you add network utilities to your network.

Figure 5.3
You can use the Modules command on your NetWare file server console to see what NLMs are loaded on your system.

```
DPCDROM.DSK
  MICROTEST CD-ROM Driver
  Version 2.52a   May 11, 1994
  Copyright 1993, 1994 Microtest Inc.
MDPDDK.DSK
  Microtest Device Driver
  Version 2.52a   January 13, 1993
  Copyright 1993, 1994 Microtest Inc.
DPTRANS.NLM
  discport (tm) Transport module
  Version 2.52a   May 11, 1994
  Copyright 1993, 1994 Microtest Inc.
DISCPORT.NLM
  discport (tm)
  Version 2.52a   May 11, 1994
  Copyright 1993, 1994 Microtest Inc.
IN2000.DSK
  Always IN-2000/ASPI/NW3.X Driver vcn: 640-012.4(930526)
ASPITRAN.DSK
  Always Dummy ASPITRAN vcn: 683-000.1(930324)
RSPX.NLM
  NetWare 386 Remote Console SPX Driver
  Version 3.12   March 29, 1993
  Copyright 1993 Novell, Inc.  All rights reserved.
<Press ESC to terminate or any other key to continue>
```

You should not even consider installing a network file server without at least 16MB of 70 ns or faster RAM. One rule of thumb to remember is that you need at least 16MB of memory for every one gigabyte of disk space. That 16MB does not take into consideration all of your other add-on utilities and the number of users you have. You can never have too much memory in your file server. Unfortunately, you will probably never have enough money to afford all of that RAM.

Adding Storage Space to Your Network Server

Disk drives are becoming a network commodity. They are inexpensive and no one really worries about them until they fail or fill up. New graphical-based programs take up a lot more disk space than older character-based DOS apps. By the time you add Windows, a Windows-based word processor, spreadsheet, communications program, and database, you can quickly use 150 to 200MB of disk space without storing any data.

Another problem with disk drives is that they break. Besides the fan in your power supply, your hard-disk drive is probably the only other moving part in your PC. As a rule, moving parts break a lot more often than solid state electrical components. Faced with ever-growing storage needs and the chance for failure, a hard-disk drive is a file server component that needs a lot of attention.

There are three major flavors of disk drives, ESDI (enhance small device interface), IDE (integrated device electronics), and SCSI (Small Computer System Interface). All of these drive interfaces have different specifications and were designed to solve specific problems of their day. All three types of drives will work in your network file server, but you should be aware of the advantages and disadvantages of each. I will explain the differences between the three drive types, but I must admit up-front that SCSI is the way to go for your network server.

ESDI Drives   ESDI drives first appeared as a standard interface in 1983 propelled by Maxtor Corporation. ESDI was developed as a high-speed standard to replace the existing ST-506/412 hard disk interface. Not only was ESDI's 24-megabit-per-second transfer rate must faster than existing ST-506/412s, it also included features such as control defect mapping built onto the drive. Except for the added performance and features, the ESDI interface is very similar to the older ST506/412. All of the cables, connectors, drive select jumpers, and terminators are the same on both drive types.

ESDI disk drives originally appeared in high-end systems that needed enhanced performance and where cost was not an issue. Another claim to fame for ESDI drives is their sturdiness. ESDI drives are tanks, you can drop them, kick them, and perform other destructive tasks and they will probably still work. ESDI drives were and are still relatively expensive and have for the most part been replaced by lower-priced IDE and faster SCSI drives. I don't have to worry about telling you to stay away from ESDI drives for your server; chances are you wouldn't be able to find one and they are still more expensive than comparable IDE or SCSI drives.

Don't worry if you do have an existing ESDI drive in your file server. You can probably add a SCSI or IDE drive. However, you will have to be careful of conflicts. I still have a few ESDI drives. They are not fast and they make enough noise to wake the dead, but they have worked for years and I need all the storage I can find.

IDE Drives   Unlike ESDI and SCSI disk drives, which use a disk controller located on the adapter, IDE disks have the disk controller built onto the drive. In fact, IDE is a generic term for any drive that has the disk controller integrated on the disk drive. It is this feature that makes IDE adapters inexpensive. An IDE controller costs approximately $20 compared to around $200 for an ESDI or SCSI controller.

IDE drives are normally used as low-end storage systems for most desktop PCs. Almost every PC you buy today will have an IDE disk drive, unless you specify SCSI. While IDE is the most common drive type, it also has its limitations. The original IDE specification is limited to approximately 500MB of formatted capacity and two drives per controller. A new specification called Enhanced IDE allows for IDE drives with more than a gigabyte of capacity, transfer rates of 10MB per second, and up to four disks on a single controller. If you are concerned with cost and your disk requirements are small, IDE is an acceptable solution for adding more capacity to your file server.

SCSI Drives I prefer SCSI disk drives and controllers for two reasons. First, they provide the best performance and second, you can daisy-chain up to seven SCSI devices on a single card. For example, you can install two SCSI disk drives, three CD-ROMs, and two tape backup drives on a single card in your server. No other specification allows you to mix and match as many different devices on a single card.

Most SCSI disk drives offer a transfer rate of up to 10MB per second, but some of the new SCSI specifications offer faster throughput. There are several different flavors of SCSI including Fast SCSI, Wide SCSI, Fast and Wide SCSI, and SCSI 2. Most of the specifications have to do with the transfer rate and the type of external connectors you use. Fortunately, all of the new specifications are backwards compatible and will work together; you just won't gain the added benefits of the new specifications.

Before you decide on the type of disk drive you are going to put into your server, you need to make sure that you have the proper disk controller drivers for your NOS. If you are using a DOS-based NOS such as LANtastic or POWERLan this is not an issue. However, if you are using a server-centric NOS, such as NetWare or Windows NT, you will need to have the appropriate driver. If the hard disk and controller you purchase do not come with a driver diskette, you are probably in trouble.

Using the Proper Tools

If you are going to perform server hardware upgrades yourself, you need to have the proper tools. I never start a hardware upgrade without three tools: screw drivers, needle nose pliers, and my upgrade bible; *Upgrading and Repairing PCs*, 3rd Edition by Scott Mueller, published by Que Corporation, 1993. It is not hard to take a PC apart and install new hardware if you have the proper hand-tools and a source of information to answer any questions that might pop-up.

Adding Remote Access to Your Server

In Chapter 3, "Prepare for WAN Links and Remote Access," I discussed remote access servers in detail. You may also want to add remote access capability to your file server. If you are upgrading a DOS-based network file server, adding remote access to it is usually as simple as purchasing Symantec's pcAnywhere software and a modem. However, if you are adding remote access to a dedicated non-DOS server, it could be a whole new story.

Fortunately, adding remote access to your Windows NT Server is simple. Microsoft bundles the Remote Access Services (RAS) server with every copy of Windows NT. RAS allows you to dial into your network and establish a remote node connection directly to the server. All you need to add is a modem and a phone line. To make it even easier, Microsoft also bundles the RAS client with both Windows for Workgroups 3.11 and Windows NT Workstation. Once you establish the dial-in connection, you can access all of the network resources the same way you would if you were in the office. However, a dial-in connection is a lot slower than a network cable, so you will have to be careful. Compared to the 10Mbps or greater throughput of a local network connection, a modem connection over a dial-up phone line is limited to 115Kbps, at best.

The Network Operating Software

Novell NetWare is currently the most popular NOS on the market, but it is also the most complicated in terms of adding remote access capabilities directly in the server. Fortunately, Novell offers a product called NetWare Connect that allows you to add remote access to any server running NetWare 3.1X or higher. NetWare Connect retails for approximately $2,000 for eight ports, for the software only, and allows you to dial into the network as a remote node and dial out from any client on the LAN.

Installing NetWare Connect is not as easy as adding a modem to the serial ports on your server. In order to add multiple dial-in and dial-out connections, you have to install a multi-I/O adapter, such as a Digiboard Corp.'s Digiboard in your server. Compared to Windows NT's RAS, NetWare Connect is a lot harder to install.

The most appealing feature of NetWare Connect is the fact that it is an open standard that other vendors can use to develop server-based remote access hardware and software. If Novell continues to hold its place at the top of the NOS stack, it remains important to have a good selection of third-party remote access products.

Upgrading Your Network Cable

I know I have beaten the topic of network cable to death, but your network cable is the chain that keeps your network from crashing to the ground. It's great if you have a fast server, but if you can't connect to it, who will ever know.

Before you can upgrade your existing cable plant, you need to have a diagram of all of the cable runs and the type of connections you are using for your network nodes. If you did not install the existing cable system and cannot get in touch with the person that did, you will probably want to hire a professional cable installer to check out your system. You may be able to use some of the existing cable or at least the conduits it is installed in.

Depending on the type of network you are using, you need to make sure that you install a better grade of cable than what you are currently using. If you are running Token-Ring or Ethernet, you should consider using UTP Level 5 cable. Level 5 is capable of data transfers up to 100Mbps and works with almost every major network topology. You may not need this capability now, but it is best to plan for the future. You may also be able to use the cable for other applications such as telephone or video.

Upgrading Your Cable Hardware

In addition to replacing the cable in your walls, you may want to consider adding new cable hardware to increase your overall network performance. For example, you may want to consider including an Ethernet switching hub. The concept behind an Ethernet switch is fairly simple. On an Ethernet LAN segment, there are packets that don't belong on that segment or that contain corrupted data. Ethernet switches filter and clean off these unneeded packets to provide more room for the necessary packets on that segment.

The two most common filter techniques are called store and forward, and cut through. Store and forward switches check every packet for errors before they allow it to travel to its intended destination. Cut through switches do not provide any error checking; they only determine the destination of the packet. Because store and forward switches have to check every network packet, they have increased latency (delay) and are usually slower than switches that use the cut through technique.

As shown in Figure 5.4, Ethernet switches are designed to provide guaranteed bandwidth to entire Ethernet segments or individual PCs. While Ethernet provides a total bandwidth of 10Mbps, as you add more network PCs, the bandwidth is quickly used up. You can use Ethernet switches to clean off any unneeded network traffic and provide the entire 10Mbps bandwidth pipe to specific workgroups or nodes on the network.

Figure 5.4
You can use an Ethernet switch to provide more bandwidth to specific workgroups or network clients on your LAN. You can connect Ethernet segments to the Ethernet switch ports or individual PCs.

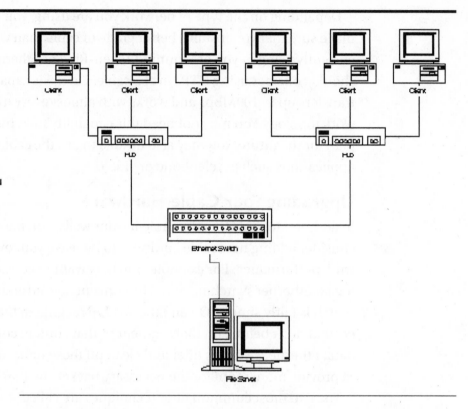

The most common reason you will need to upgrade your cable hardware is the loss of performance. A decrease in network performance is usually pretty easy to troubleshoot. In most cases, you have too many people trying to do too many things across a single cable to a single server at the same time. You will usually see an increase in network performance if you upgrade your network cable, but don't forget to check the other components on your network.

Adding Network Adapters   Another way you can increase the performance of your network cabling system is to add multiple network adapters to your file server. Most server-centric network operating systems will allow you to install up to four network adapters in each file server. You can connect each network adapter to a different LAN segment and evenly distribute the load between your users.

However, each network adapter you add to your server requires additional server memory and could degrade performance.

I recommend that you try adding a network adapter to your server before you invest in an expensive Ethernet switch. If you are considering an Ethernet switch, you will probably have to move your network cable anyway, so why not install an additional network adapter in your server and create a new LAN segment. A network adapter is a lot less expensive than an Ethernet switch and if it doesn't work you can think about a purchasing a switch.

Upgrading Your Network Clients

As Windows continues to gain in dominance over DOS, more people will decide it's time to try out the graphical interface and all of its features including multimedia. PCs that are two years old may work fine for some of your existing DOS applications, but they are not powerful enough to run today's most popular graphical programs. Similar to your file server, the memory and hard disk are the two most common components you will need to upgrade on your client PCs.

Memory

Memory is just as important to your client PC as it is to your file server. The more memory you have in your PC, the faster your applications will run and the more programs you can work in at the same time. I do not even recommend a desktop PC without at least 8MB of RAM. Unfortunately, many new PCs only come with 4MB. While 4MB will run current versions of DOS, Windows, and OS/2, it will not be enough for new operating systems such as Windows 95. To be completely safe, you should give all of your power users at least 8 to 16MB of RAM.

One of the biggest problems with upgrading the memory in your client PCs is finding the space for the new chips. Most new PCs use memory chips called SIMMs (single in-line memory modules). SIMMs are available in different configurations ranging from 256K kilobytes to 16MB. They look like this:

Most motherboards only have four SIMM slots to hold all of your PC's memory. If you want to upgrade a PC from 4 to 8MB of RAM, you may encounter a problem. For example, if your PC only has four SIMM slots configured with four 1MB SIMMs, you will have to remove the four 1MB SIMMs and replace them with two 4MB SIMMs.

The problem comes when you decide what to do with the four 1MB SIMMs. You can't use them anymore, but at $50 a megabyte, you don't want to throw them away. Many people think that because their PC already has 4MB of memory, all they have to buy is four more megabytes to upgrade to 8MB. Before you decide to upgrade, always check your SIMMs. The added cost of the extra 4MB may change your mind, especially if you are upgrading several PCs. To make matters more confusing, not all PCs are alike. Some motherboards may have eight SIMM slots and others only two. Another problem is the size of the SIMM chips. Older PCs use 30-pin SIMMs and newer PCs use 72-pin SIMMs. Unfortunately, the SIMMs are not interchangeable.

Disk Drives

It is always smart to keep your valuable data on the network file server, but you may want to keep your applications on your local hard disk. It takes a lot longer to load Windows from the server than it does to load it from your local drive. As you add more applications, you might find out that you are running out of disk space on your client PCs. This need coupled with the fact that disk drives fail often, may force you to upgrade or replace the drives in your client PCs.

Fortunately, disk drives—especially IDE drives—are inexpensive and fairly easy to install. You can purchase most IDE disk drives for approximately 50 cents a megabyte. A few years ago you would have paid over $1 a megabyte. As I said earlier, disk drives are becoming a commodity and everyone takes them for granted.

If you simply need to add more disk space, you can probably purchase a hard disk and add it to your PC as a second drive. Most new low-end PCs use the IDE hard-disk interface, and you can daisy-chain two disk drives on the same controller. If you have an ESDI disk drive, you can also add a second drive. However, ESDI drives are so expensive it is probably cheaper to switch over to an IDE. If your existing hard disk is an ST-506/412 disk drive, replace it! An ST-506/412 disk drive is too old and too slow to trust for your important network data. The technology behind the ST-506 disk drives has been replaced by faster and more reliable IDE and SCSI disk drives.

If you decide to add a second hard disk to your PC, you will want to make the newer or faster disk the primary boot drive and reserve the other disk for data files. Just because a hard disk is slow doesn't mean it will not work for storing infrequently used data. If you are adding a second IDE drive to your PC, make sure you have the jumper settings for each drive. In order to add a second IDE drive to a single controller, you must configure the first drive as the master and the second drive as the slave. This is not hard unless you don't have the manual. Unfortunately, most new PCs don't come with the hard-drive manual.

Troubleshooting Faulty Drives

Before you replace a faulty drive, always make sure the drive is bad. There are two pieces to a disk-drive marriage, the disk drive and the controller. Just because you can't access a disk drive doesn't mean that it is dead. The controller could be bad or even the cables that connect the two could be the problem. If you don't have another controller to try or a good diagnostic tool, call a consultant. The consultant's hourly rate is probably less expensive than the price of a hard disk you may not even need.

You may also be able to reformat the hard disk. It may turn out that your data is corrupted, not the hardware. If you back up the data off of the hard disk and reformat it, your problem may disappear. Hard disks are inexpensive, but it is cheaper to troubleshoot before you replace them.

Upgrading Your NOS

As I stated earlier, you should not upgrade your software just because a new version is available. Your NOS upgrade should be based on adding key features that will increase your network's productivity or for support. As I mentioned previously, many network vendors stop supporting their software after it gets old. For example, I still have some clients that use NetWare 2.X, but they won't be able to get support from Novell if it breaks. Not every NOS update includes new earth-shattering features and you may not even see a performance increase. If you decide it is time to upgrade your NOS, remember you may also have to upgrade all of your file servers, client PCs, printers, and network peripherals. Don't make the mistake of thinking that you can just install a few diskettes and you will have the latest and greatest version of the software. Treat your NOS upgrade the same as your initial network installation and set aside the same amount of time.

Whenever a vendor introduces a major upgrade to a NOS, there is usually enough hype in the media for you to determine if the added features will benefit your organization's network needs. The following list details some of the more important features to look for in a new version of a NOS.

- Increased performance

- Workgroup e-mail and scheduling

- Network management

- Security

- Improved client support for other NOSs

- Remote access

- Improved user interface

Some of the most worthwhile NOS upgrades include LANtastic 6.0, Windows NT 3.5, and NetWare 4.1. All of these version upgrades included numerous performance increases and features. For example, LANtastic 6.0 added network e-mail and scheduling, and a fax capability. The price of a third-party e-mail package alone could justify the cost of the LANtastic upgrade.

Most new versions retain the same look and feel of their younger siblings, but occasionally this is not the case. With the introduction of NetWare 4.X, Novell introduced a whole new directory structure and replaced most of the network utilities. For example, Syscon, shown in Figure 5.5, was the main utility you used in NetWare 3.X to perform general network tasks such as adding users and configuring network security. However, NetWare 4.X replaced Syscon with a utility called Nwadmin, shown in Figure 5.6. Nwadmin offers a lot more features and has a better interface, but I have been using Syscon for years and I miss it. It is fine when a vendor improves or even adds a new utility, but frustrating when they simply remove the programs you feel comfortable with.

Figure 5.5
The Syscon utility is the major utility you will use in NetWare 3.X to add users, configure security, and customize your login scripts.

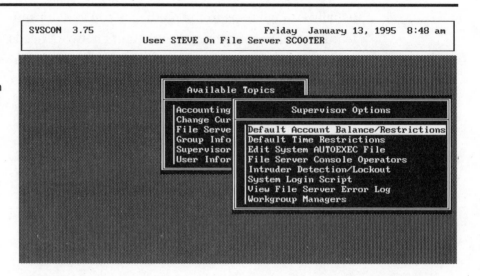

I don't recommend upgrading yor NOS unless you have a valid reason. Valid reasons include new features that will increase your productivity, increased performance, or the need for better technical support. A valid reason to purchase an upgrade to your NOS does not necessarily include a call from a network salesperson or a flier in the mail. Also don't forget that a NOS upgrade can require a lot of time and you may have to totally reconfigure your network file server and client PCs. Plan your upgrade on a weekend or at a time when you can call technical support or a network consultant if you have any problems.

Upgrading for the Future

As new technologies make their way into the market place, you will probably be tempted to upgrade your entire network's infrastructure. The performance and design of most PC-based networks has

Figure 5.6
The Nwadmin utility in NetWare 4.X provides a better interface and more features than Syscon, but it will require time to become familiar with all of the menus and commands.

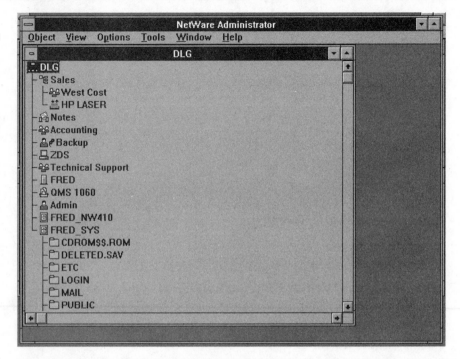

not changed for a few years, so you can expect to see a lot of new technologies on the horizon. Some of these new technologies include 100Mbps Ethernet or Fast Ethernet and ATM (asynchronous transfer mode).

Most people make the decision to upgrade their network for a few basic reasons—to add capacity, to fix a problem, or to increase performance. If you look closely at your network you will probably see a hundred things you could improve. I don't consider an upgrade a major task, I consider it preventive maintenance. A well-functioning and productive network is always in some state of upgrade. However, you need to find a balance between the "bleeding edge" and the "rusty hammer."

CHAPTER

6

Installation

I may seem like a pessimist, but I have installed well over 100 networks and I still get butterflies the night before the big day. I don't doubt my experience or technical knowledge—I doubt the compatibility of the vendor's applications with the network operating system (NOS) and the hardware. While I can't possibly cover every application and every NOS in this chapter, I will discuss the most popular products. I will also discuss the basic tasks you will need to perform and hopefully, provide you with some tricks that will save you time and frustration.

Checking Your Checklist

I hope that you read Chapter 4, "Preparing for the Network." Just in case you didn't, we'll cover the basics here.

Before you install the network, make sure all of the hardware and software has been delivered. Also be certain that you have all of the peripherals you'll need, such as cable, wiring hubs, network adapters, printer cables, and modems. It is amazing how many times I have arrived to do a network installation only to find out that key components, such as the network adapters, have not arrived.

In addition to checking that you have all of your network components, also make sure that the hardware will work with the software and vice versa. Almost every NOS and application vendor has specific hardware requirements. You can't just take for granted that any PC will work with any network software.

The Different Types of Networks

There are several different network operating systems and hundreds of different hardware components and network applications. Every

network is different, but all of them share a few basic similarities. They all use comparable network adapters and cable, and they are all designed for one thing—to share resources. For example, whether you are using Novell NetWare or Artisoft LANtastic, each NOS only offers one way to install the software. The same thing holds true with connecting to printers, mapping network disk drives, and performing other ordinary network tasks. Once you learn the basic menus and procedures for a particular NOS, you will feel comfortable learning and experimenting with other NOSes.

Peer-to-Peer Networks

Most peer networks are 16-bit programs that run on top of DOS. I don't like to call peer networks or small business LANs operating systems because they are usually only programs that run on top of the DOS operating system. This fact limits the performance and robustness of most peer networks. A few peer network vendors, such as Performance Technology and Artisoft, offer an optional 32-bit server program. However, these programs require a dedicated PC, which somewhat defeats the reason you purchased a peer network in the first place.

As I discussed in Chapter 2, a peer-to-peer network allows you to share disk drives and printers between all of the PCs on your network. For example, you can configure each PC to act as either a file server, print server, or both. The most common use of a peer network is to share a printer or eliminate the need for a "sneaker net." It is a lot easier to keep all of your data on a single drive that everyone can access than it is to trade disks all day long if someone needs to access your data. I have some clients who actually stand in line to use a PC. The problem is not due to a limited number of PCs, but the fact that it is the only PC that contains a specific program or set of data.

While there are several applications that you can't run on a network, there is always a way to share the data across the LAN. For example, you could create a DOS batch file that would copy the applications data to everyone's PC at 2:00 A.M. No matter what type of application you use, there is always a way to use a peer network to make your life easier. Peer networks are best suited for companies that have a small number of PCs—less than 20—and need to share files, CD-ROMs, and printers.

There are three major players in the peer network arena: Artisoft's LANtastic, Performance Technology's POWERLan, and Microsoft's Windows for Workgroups, soon to be replaced with Windows 95. While there are other peer network vendors, these three have approximately 80 to 90 percent of the peer market. In the following sections, I will discuss the general procedure for installing each of the three products and list some of the products' features.

Artisoft LANtastic

LANtastic is probably the most popular peer network. In fact, if you start a discussion on peer networks, the word LANtastic will probably pop up within the first sentence or two. LANtastic is a DOS-based application that runs on all of your DOS and Windows-based PCs. Artisoft also offers a version of LANtastic for the Macintosh that you can use to connect your PCs to a Mac and vice versa.

If you run Windows on your PC, make sure you install the proper network Windows drivers. If you don't, you will experience problems if you access any network resources while you are running Windows. Fortunately, the LANtastic installation program is able to detect if you have Windows installed on your PC. When you start the setup program, it will automatically look for Windows. If the install program finds Windows on your system, it will launch Windows and continue the installation. If you don't have Windows on your PC or if you don't want to install the Windows network drivers, you can just run the DOS-based installation program.

Similar to most DOS and Windows-based applications, LANtastic is fairly easy to install. However, you will have to provide the program with certain information during the installation process. For example, you will have to tell the installation program if your PC is going to be a client or a server, the name of your PC, and the type of network adapter you are using. You must also indicate to the program any decisions to install optional products such as e-mail, and scheduling and support for other NOSes. Figure 6.1 shows a sample screen from the LANtastic 6.0 DOS installation program. If you do not provide the correct information, you will have to reinstall the program or manually edit the configuration file.

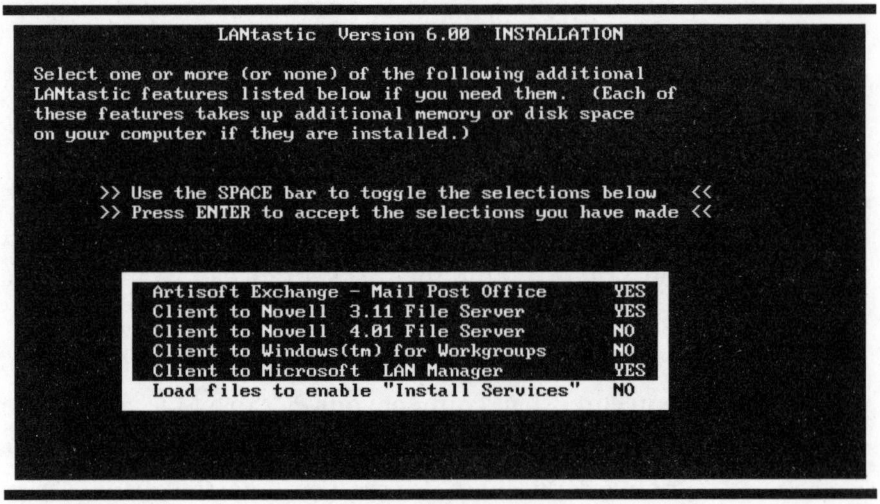

Figure 6.1
The LANtastic installation utility allows you to set up all of your PC's network settings and install other services, such as e-mail, scheduling, and NetWare NCP (NetWare Core Protocol) drivers.

```
                    LANtastic  Version 6.00  INSTALLATION

       Select one or more (or none) of the following additional
       LANtastic features listed below if you need them.  (Each of
       these features takes up additional memory or disk space
       on your computer if they are installed.)


            >> Use the SPACE bar to toggle the selections below   <<
            >> Press ENTER to accept the selections you have made <<


              Artisoft Exchange - Mail Post Office       YES
              Client to Novell  3.11 File Server         YES
              Client to Novell  4.01 File Server         NO
              Client to Windows(tm) for Workgroups       NO
              Client to Microsoft  LAN Manager           YES
              Load files to enable "Install Services"    NO
```

The installation procedure can require between 10 to 30 minutes for each PC, depending on the speed of your PC and the options you choose to install. For example, if you only install the DOS-based program files and not the Windows driver or e-mail and scheduling utilities, the installation program only requires a few minutes. Many people like to install the software across the network, especially if they are upgrading more than 15 PCs. It is a lot faster to copy the programs across the network than it is to walk to each PC and feed it multiple disks. Unfortunately, you cannot install LANtastic across an existing network other than LANtastic. So be aware that if you are upgrading your NetWare, Windows for Workgroups, or POWERLan network to LANtastic, you will have to manually install the new software on every PC on your network.

The Startnet Batch File   In addition to copying files to your hard drive, the LANtastic installation program also creates a startup batch program called startnet. The startnet batch file is placed in the LANtastic subdirectory and you can use any DOS text editor to view or make changes to the file. The startnet batch file performs several tasks including loading your network drivers and connecting to other resources on the network. If your PC is not working properly on the network, startnet is the place to begin looking for problems.

Unfortunately, newer versions of the LANtastic installation program place a lot more information in your startnet file than is needed. In addition to loading the network drivers and making network connections, newer versions of the LANtastic install program insert several lines of Boolean logic. I have found that most of the "if then's" and "go to's" are really not necessary and only work to confuse the novice user who is trying to make a change to the batch file. It is not uncommon for your startnet file to contain 40 or 50 lines of text, when you only need five or six lines. I usually use a text editor to clean out the startnet file in case I need to troubleshoot a network error or add network connections at a later date. However, you should not have to edit the startnet batch file if you perform the installation procedure correctly. I usually only edit startnet when I want to change the name of a PC or add a network redirection to a resource such as a new server or printer.

Software Drivers   LANtastic includes software drivers for most network adapters or you can use the NDIS drivers that come with your card. I recommend that you make sure LANtastic has a built-in

driver for your specific network adapters. If you have to use the NDIS driver that came with your card, you may find yourself spending hours editing your protocol.ini file to make the network work. Even the most experienced network administrator is no match for a complicated protocol.ini. It is a lot easier to call Artisoft and make sure that your adapters will work with LANtastic than it is to find and install the NDIS drivers. Unfortunately, some adapters may include a driver for LANtastic, but only for a specific version. For example, a LANtastic 5.0 adapter driver may not work with LANtastic 6.0.

The Universal Client   One of the most appealing features of LANtasic is the universal client. LANtastic comes with the software you need to interact with a NetWare server using Novell's NetWare Core Protocol (NCP) and IPX (Internet Packet EXchange) with Windows servers using the Server Message Block (SMB) protocol over NetBEUI. The LANtastic 6.0 universal redirector has all the communications tools. For example, you can use the Artisoft redirector in place of the Novell NETX shell program. The LANtastic redirector only loads the specific protocols it needs for the servers it finds on the LAN when it loads. If the NetWare server is turned off when you log on, the LANtastic redirector will not load the NCP drivers and waste your conventional memory. Not only does the universal client make LANtastic a good choice for a peer network, but it is also effective as a client for a server-centric network.

The universal client is great if you work in an office that has multiple heterogeneous networks, but it requires more time to configure. If you want your client PCs to automatically connect to NetWare and Windows file servers, you will have to add the proper syntax in your autoexec or startnet batch file. LANtastic does not allow you to use the NetWare login script so you will have to connect to the network resources using the LANtastic Net commands. The following is an example of a command that connects to a volume named sys on a file server named server: Net Use \\Server\Sys. While this is not a complicated process, it could take you a long time if you use multiple network resources and have multiple network clients.

Memory Requirements Memory requirements are another issue you must face when you install LANtastic or any peer network. The LANtastic drivers can require anywhere from 40K to 90K of conventional memory on your PC. If you run any DOS-based applications, you may not have enough conventional memory after you install the network. If each PC has MS DOS version 5.0 or higher, you can load some, if not all, of the LANtastic drivers into upper memory blocks. MS DOS version 6.X even provides a program called Memaker that will automatically load your network drivers and other programs into upper memory. If you still need more conventional memory, you can use a program such as Helix Software's NetRoom or Quarterdeck System's QEMM to free even more conventional RAM.

The LAN Check Utility LANtastic provides a utility called LAN Check that allows you to see if two or more PCs are communicating across the network. LAN Check will help you diagnose any adapter or cable problems after and during the installation process. Overall, LANtastic is easy to install and maintain. Take your time when you install the software and make sure you read all of your options carefully before you press the Enter key.

Artisoft CorStream If you are using LANtastic as your network, but need to increase performance and capacity, you might want to consider upgrading to CorStream. In a nutshell, CorStream is basically an NLM that runs on NetWare 4.X file server. The CorStream NLMs intercept the Artisoft server message block packets from the LANtastic clients and convert the packets into NetWare service requests. The Artisoft software builds a LANtastic "curtain" around all of the NetWare 4.X file and print services. While all of the NetWare drives and printers appear to LANtastic clients as LANtastic drives and printers, NetWare handles all network requests in its normal fashion. Since conversion takes place, the CorStream server isn't as fast as the native NetWare server.

Because CorStream runs on top of NetWare, it requires a lot of time and effort to install the product. Each package of CorStream contains a full two-user license of NetWare 4.X on a CD-ROM and eight disks that contain a scaled down run-time version of NetWare and the CorStream program. If you are not concerned with disk space and you have a CD-ROM, you will definitely want to use the CD-ROM to install CorStream. It requires about three hours to install the NetWare and CorStream files from the disks compared to less than an hour using the CD-ROM method. As with any NetWare installation, you need drivers for your server's disk drive and network adapter card. I will discuss the NetWare 4.X installation in more detail later in this chapter.

Performance Technology POWERLan

Similar to LANtastic, POWERLan provides both a DOS and Windows-based interface. The DOS-based program is susceptible to the same problems as LANtastic. POWERLan does not have the same large installed base as LANtastic, but it is still a top rate peer network.

The POWERLan installation program will automatically detect the presence of Windows on your PC and install the Windows drivers and program files. Unlike Artisoft, Performance Technology doesn't bundle a network e-mail or schedule utility with the standard POWERLan package. The POWERLan e-mail and scheduling utilities are optional.

The POWERLan installation is even easier than LANtastic's. The only information you have to provide is the PCs name, type of network adapter you have, and whether the PC will act as a dedicated server, nondedicated server, or client. Figure 6.2 shows an example of a screen from the POWERLan installation utility. The installation, with Windows included, only requires approximately 10 minutes. You can also install POWERLan across any type of network connection; LANtastic is limited to LANtastic networks.

Figure 6.2
The POWERLan utility is pretty basic and all you have to know is the type of network adapter you have, your network user name, and whether your PC will act as a server or client.

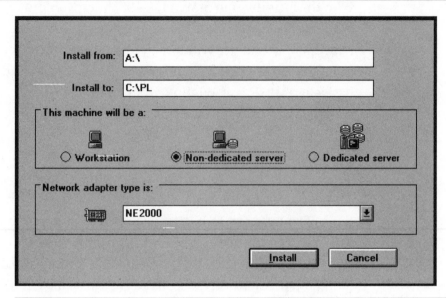

Similar to LANtastic, POWERLan provides built-in drivers for several network adapters. If your adapter is not listed in the installation, you can use the NDIS or Clarkson drivers that come with the card. POWERLan can usually set up your optional NDIS drivers, but occasionally, as with LANtastic, you might have to manually edit your protocol.ini file to set up your network adapter.

The POWERLan installation creates a batch file called plstart to load the network drivers and create your network connections. The plstart file is not as complicated as LANtastic's startnet file, and you can easily edit the file to change your computer's name and add new network redirections. If you are a novice user you shouldn't make changes to your network batch files. I always make a copy of the

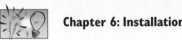

original file in case I make changes that don't work and I need to go back to the original configuration.

Microsoft Windows for Workgroups

With the introduction of Windows 95, Microsoft probably considers Windows for Workgroups to be a dead horse. However, there are still many people that use Windows for Workgroups and they may not immediately upgrade to Windows 95. Windows for Workgroups is basically a version of Windows that has a built-in peer network and a few workgroup applications such as e-mail and scheduling.

The biggest drawback to Windows for Workgroups is you must always run Windows. While many organizations use Windows-based applications, there are still a lot of people that still use DOS-based programs. I use a combination of DOS and Windows-based applications. If you use any DOS-based applications, make sure they will run in a DOS box under Windows for Workgroups. Otherwise, you should stick with a DOS-based peer network such as LANtastic or POWERLan. Microsoft does offer a DOS-based client that can connect to a Windows for Workgroup server. However, the DOS add-on is slow and doesn't even offer an intuitive menu that you can use to make a network connection.

Windows for Workgroups is fairly easy to install. In fact the installation program is identical to a normal Windows 3.X install with the addition of a few network setup menus. Like its DOS-based counterparts, Windows for Workgroups provides built-in drivers for most popular network adapters, if your adapter is not on the list you can use the NDIS drivers that came with the adapter. Windows for Workgroups also works over several different network protocols including TCP/IP, NetBEUI, and IPX/SPX.

Unlike its DOS counterparts, Windows for Workgroups does not use a batch file to start the network and redirect printer ports and disk drives. Windows for Workgroups uses a combination of files to start the network including a Net Start command that resides in your autoexec batch file and several entries in your win, system, and protocol INI files.

Unless you are very familiar with INI file settings, you should not plan on making changes to the network settings unless you use the Windows-based network setup utility, shown in Figure 6.3. Windows for Workgroups is probably the hardest peer network to troubleshoot and tweak unless you really know what you are doing. Whenever I have problems with Windows for Workgroups, I usually just reinstall the program versus trying to wade through the various configuration files.

Figure 6.3
You can use the Windows for Workgroups network setup utility to change the settings on your network hardware and software.

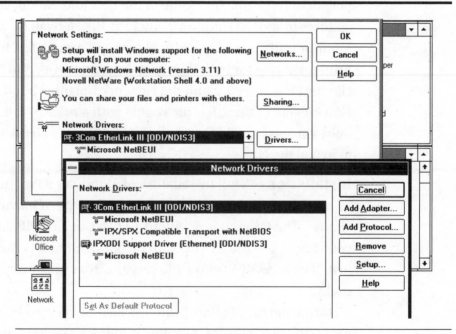

Because Windows for Workgroups includes a full version of Windows, it requires a lot more time to install than LANtastic, POWERLan, or most other DOS-based peer networks. The program comes on eight high-density disks and requires approximately 20 to

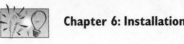

30 minutes to install, depending on the speed of your PC and the number of options you choose.

A major benefit of Windows for Workgroups is its lack of conventional memory usage. Almost all of the network drivers run in extended memory and the Windows for Workgroups network only uses approximately 5K of conventional RAM.

Windows 95

Not only is Windows 95 a new OS (operating system) with a pretty face, it is also a completely new peer network.

Windows 95 offers more network features than any other peer network on the market. Some of the new and enhanced network features found in Windows 95 include the Netwatcher and System Monitor utilities, remote access, network e-mail, fax, file and printer sharing for both Windows-based network and NetWare clients, Plug and Play, and the Network Neighborhood viewer. However, all of these features come with a price. Windows 95 requires at least a 486 PC with 8MB of RAM and at least 40MB just to install the OS.

Installation   A full installation of Windows 95 requires about 30 minutes to an hour depending on the type of installation you choose. The OS comes on about 17 disks or a CD-ROM. If possible, you should use the CD-ROM to install Windows 95. You can also install Windows 95 from a file server across the network, but it's tricky.

During the installation, Windows 95 reboots your PC to test the new settings. If you are installing Windows 95 across the network, the PC must automatically attach to the network in order to finish the install. While you can set up your network connections under the first phase of the installation, if you make a mistake, Windows 95 will not see your server when it reboots.

For example, during the first stage of the installation process, you can configure Windows 95 to connect to either a Windows NT or NetWare file server. However, if you are installing across a network and you don't configure your network settings properly during the first stage, you will not be able to complete the installation. While it is fairly easy to configure the network settings, a novice user may have some problems.

Fortunately, Windows 95 allows you to create a script that will automatically perform the upgrade whenever a user connects to the network or starts an application such as e-mail. You can also copy the 32MB of installation files to a separate subdirectory on your hard disk and install the OS from that directory. If you have the space, copying the files is the fastest and easiest installation.

Windows 95's ability to detect the type of hard disk controller, CD-ROM, sound card, video controller, and network adapter you have in your PCs is impressive even without Plug-N-Play. For example, the installation program can actually determine the type of network adapter you have installed and the adapter's configuration setting. If the program can't get LAN adapter information from a Plug-N-Play, PCI, EISA, or PCMCIA setup file, it looks for existing PROTOCOL.INI or NET.CFG files with adapter setup information.

Maintaining Configuration Information   To make the network administrator's job even more difficult, Microsoft has all but done away with the INI files and uses a new system for keeping configuration information. All of your network hardware and software information is stored in the Windows 95 Registry, shown in Figure 6.4. The registry is basically a database and all of your settings are objects in the database. Microsoft claims that you should never have to edit the registry and you can change all of your network hardware and software settings using the various utilities in the user interface. So far, I haven't had to do more than explore the registry and I hope that doesn't change. Unfortunately, Microsoft does not even provide detailed information on editing the registry so stay away from it if possible.

Figure 6.4
The Windows 95 registry editor, allows you to make changes to your PC's hardware and software settings, including network information.

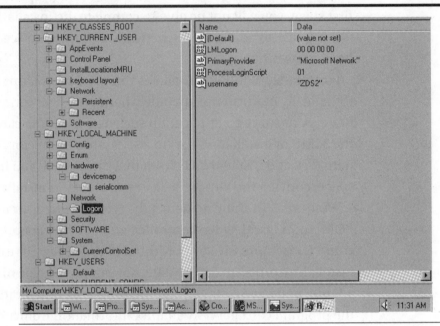

Server-Centric Networks

There are a few common words that I try to avoid when I talk about networks. These include "workstation" and "client-server." While almost everyone calls the network client PCs workstations, PCs are not workstations. A workstation is a UNIX box, not an Intel-based PC. People also frequently refer to server-centric networks as client-server networks. This is misleading because every network is a client-server network—every network has at least one client and one server. I also don't like to use the word "dedicated-server" to denote a server-centric network. You could dedicate your file server using any network. A server-centric network denotes a network that requires you to dedicate a PC to act as the file server. The most popular server-centric networks include Microsoft's Windows NT and Novell's NetWare.

Unlike their peer network siblings, server-centric networks are usually protected-mode 32-bit operating systems and provide better performance and more capacity for data and users. Because server-centric networks are designed for lots of users and data, they are usually more complicated to install and maintain. I have installed NetWare at least 100 times and I still don't claim to know all of the secrets and tips. The secret to learning the tricks to installing a server-centric NOS is to install it multiple times. Unfortunately, a network administrator may not have a chance to perform multiple installations, as would a consultant.

Novell NetWare

NetWare is currently the most popular server-centric network on the market. According to some statistics, NetWare has an installed base of 70 percent of all PC-based networks. Unfortunately, popularity does not mean that the product is easy to install and maintain, only that people trust it and use it. In fact, installing NetWare is a complicated task, and it is a lot different than installing a DOS-based application. I suggest you read the manual before you start loading the software.

The first thing you should remember before installing NetWare is it is not a DOS-based application. NetWare is its own operating system and it only uses DOS to boot the file server. NetWare also uses its own file system, so you can't use a disk drive that has previously been formatted with DOS. The NetWare installation will format the hard disk for you.

It is really amazing how many people are confused about the differences between NetWare and a DOS-based application. I constantly get calls from clients who want to know why they can't use the file server to run a DOS or Windows-based application. Usually, I disconnect the keyboard from the NetWare file server so no one will make that mistake.

Comparing Versions 3.X and 4.X   NetWare 3.X requires a 386 PC with approximately 8MB RAM and a 150MB hard drive. NetWare 4.X needs a 486 PC with 16MB of RAM and approximately a 500MB hard drive. While you can start NetWare 3.X from a bootable disk, NetWare 4.X requires at least a 15MB DOS partition on your hard drive to store the startup files. NetWare 3.X uses a file called server to start the OS, but NetWare 4.X requires multiple files to launch the OS. If I am installing NetWare 3.X I usually create a 5MB to 10MB DOS partition on the hard disk. The server program takes a while to load and it is much faster if you load from your hard disk than from a floppy disk.

Both versions of the NOS require about 30 minutes to an hour to install. You can use disks or a CD-ROM to install the NOS. The disk method takes a lot longer and it can get boring feeding disks into a floppy drive. Even if the target file server doesn't have a CD-ROM drive, I usually borrow one from another PC and install it on the file server. It is usually faster to install a CD-ROM on the file server and install the NOS from the CD than it is to use the disks.

Adapters and Disk Drivers   All of the network adapters and disk drivers for NetWare are called NLMs (NetWare Loadable Modules). If your hard disk controller and network adapter does not come with an NLM on a disk, you will have to use a generic driver or possibly a different card. Even the installation utility, shown in Figure 6.5, is an NLM.

While all of the drivers are called NLMs, the files have different extensions. For example, a NetWare disk driver has a .DSK extension and a network adapter driver uses a .LAN extension. NetWare 3.X requires you to manually load your network adapter and disk drivers, but the NetWare 4.X installation does most of the work for you.

Figure 6.5
The Install NLM, is the main utility you will use to install and configure your NetWare file server. Note that an NCF file is a NetWare configuration file. It is a batch file that is similar to Config.sys and Autoexec.bat for DOS.

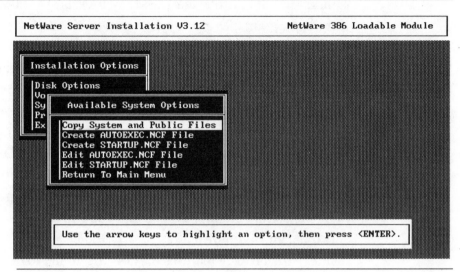

Disk Spanning A very useful feature of NetWare is the ability to span a volume across multiple hard disks. For example, you can use NetWare to create a volume called Vol1, and spread the volume across multiple hard disks. When users connect to that server, they don't know how many drives are in the file server. They only know they are connected to a volume named Vol1. Disk spanning is a lot easier than having multiple volumes and multiple drive letters. You will need to plan your volume names before you attempt the installation if you are going to span multiple disks.

Microsoft Windows NT

Similar to NetWare, Windows NT is also a 32-bit NOS. Windows NT is available in two flavors, NT Server and NT Workstation. Both versions can act as both a network client and a server, but NT Server is designed to offer better performance as a server.

Unlike NetWare, NT doesn't require a dedicated server. You can still use the server as a client PC, but if you dedicate a PC, you will see better performance. Windows NT is also fairly resource hungry. You

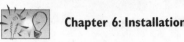

should use a 486 with at least 16MB of RAM and a 500MB hard disk. Just the program files alone can use up to 70MB of hard-disk space.

Windows NT has the same Program Manager user interface as Windows 3.X, but it doesn't run on top of DOS. However, you can run most DOS applications in a DOS window. If you are familiar with Windows, you shouldn't have too much trouble using Windows NT.

The installation program comes on either disk or CD-ROM. It requires about 20 minutes to install the OS using the CD and close to an hour using disks. During the installation, NT will automatically try to detect your network adapter. NT also provides numerous built-in network adapter drivers and you can also use the NDIS drivers that came with the card.

One of my favorite features of NT is the ability to dual boot multiple OSes on the same PC. For example, you can choose to run either NT, Windows 95, or DOS every time you reboot your PC. The dual-boot feature allows you to use your NT machine as a DOS-based client or network file server.

When you install NT, you have a choice of using a standard DOS-formatted disk drive or you can reformat your hard disk with NTFS (NT File System). The NTFS format is faster and supports long file names, but you won't be able to boot DOS if you use NTFS. You need to also make sure that your backup program can recognize and backup files on a NTFS volume. Like NetWare, you can span a volume across multiple hard disks, but only if you are using NTFS.

Overall, Windows NT is a lot easier to install than NetWare, but you should plan on having the manual handy. NT can prove confusing especially if you choose to create a network domain and use TCP/IP as your network protocol.

Tricks to Make Life Easier

There are numerous things you can do to make a network installation easier and faster. One of the most obvious ones is creating batch files to automatically load the network drivers on your client PCs. For example, if all of your client PCs use the same network adapter, you can create a single batch file for all of the different PCs. You can then copy that batch file to each PC without creating it from scratch. In addition to loading the proper network drivers, you can also use batch files and login scripts to automatically connect each PC to network disk drives and printers.

It is also a lot easier if you install the file server software first. If you install the client drivers before the file server is up and running, there is no way to make sure that the settings are correct. I usually install the file server and then one client. Once that client is connected and all of the drive mappings and printer assignments are working, I copy that configuration to a disk and use it to speed up the installation for the rest of the clients.

Any procedure that saves you time is a definite plus and should be remembered for the future. Each network has its own installation procedure so the tricks and techniques you use will vary from NOS to NOS. Most of the techniques simply require common sense and experience.

Cleaning Up After You're Done

When I say "clean up," I don't mean you should pick up any pieces of paper you dropped, I mean you should double-check your work. Not every network installation automatically configures the PC to start the network when you reboot. For example, if use a batch file to start the network, you should make sure you start that batch file when you turn on your PC. Likewise, you need to make sure that all of the other services such as print servers, tape backup, and CD-ROMs are automatically initiated when the server comes up.

If a network is going to go down, it will usually happen within the first week or two. If your file server doesn't go down in the first week, it will probably prove to be a reliable server for months and years to

Field Note: Checking Your Work

This is an embarrassing field note, but I'll use it nonetheless. My consulting company installs a new network almost every week. Recently, we were hired to install a 10-node NetWare network for a condominium. We successfully installed the network, left the bill and were on our way.

A week or two later, I received a call from the client explaining that the power had gone off at the condo and no one could log on to the server. I was worried, because I knew we had installed a UPS for power outages. Even if the battery backup didn't work, the file server PC should automatically restart the network when the power came back on.

When I arrived at the client's office, I was confused when I saw the server asking me to enter a date and time. I looked at the floor and sure enough there was a UPS, but the server wasn't plugged into it. I typed "server" on the file server and the network started. Oops! I guess we forgot to start the server program from within the autoexec batch file. In fact we didn't even create a autoexec batch file.

After I corrected the oversights and was leaving, the client yelled, "Wait, we can't print." I went to the print server and decided to reset it. As the PC acting as the print server was rebooting, it reported an error that it could not find the print server NLM on the file server. I went to the file server, and the pserver NLM was not loaded. I loaded it manually and the printer roared to life. We should have added the Pserver command to the autoexec file so it would load when the server initialized.

It didn't take long to fix these problems, but if we had double-checked our installation on the first day, I would not have had to work on a Saturday. The worst part is we all knew to do these things, but we went too fast and forgot.

come. You don't want your network to have problems during the first two weeks of operation, because you will probably be busy getting rid of all of the kinks and bugs.

All of the network vendors I discussed in this chapter provide excellent documentation and support for their products. If you have any questions or problems, you can probably find the answer in the manual or call technical support. You can also hire a network consultant to help you install your network and fix any problems you encounter after the installation.

Networking Your Printers

Deciding how to network your printers can be a nightmare. You want everyone to have access to the best printers, but do you attach them to the file server, a dedicated print server PC, or should you use an external print server? Your printers are just as important as your data and when they don't work and you can't print an important document, it is just as frustrating as losing your data.

The most common place to install a network printer or printers is on the file server, as shown in Figure 6.6. Unfortunately, you can't always connect all of your printers to the file server and most people keep the dedicated file server in a wiring closet, not out in the open where people would prefer to have their printers. If you are using a peer network, it is much easier to put your printers anywhere you want to. In a peer network, you can configure every PC to act as a file and print server. One drawback to this is everyone must keep their PCs running to allow other users to print to their printer. You must also turn every PC on at approximately the same time so that all of the PCs will see each other and make the proper network connections.

Another popular way to network a printer is to dedicate a PC as a print server. Almost every NOS provides a print server program that will run on an older 286 PC with 1MB of RAM and a small hard disk. Figure 6.7 shows a PC configured as a dedicated print server. The major drawback to this configuration is the added size of a PC. It is usually hard enough to find a good place for a printer without having to also find room for the print server PC.

Most server-centric NOSes, including NetWare, allow you to share a printer attached to a network client PC. For example, you can use a program called Rprinter to configure any client PC on your NetWare LAN as a network print server. Unfortunately, Rprinter is a TSR and requires conventional memory. Also, Rprinter does not work correctly if you install it on a PC that runs Microsoft Windows.

Figure 6.6
The most common place to connect a network printer is directly to the file server.

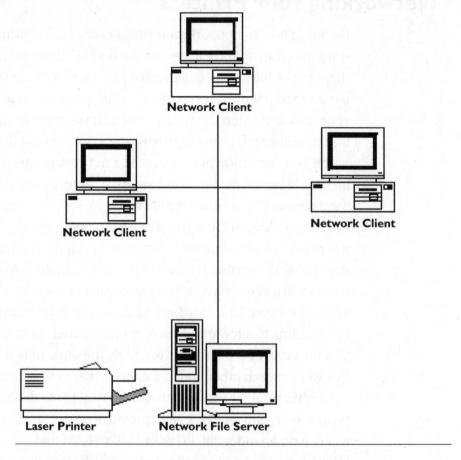

Network Client

Network Client

Network Client

Laser Printer

Network File Server

The best way to network a printer, shown in Figure 6.8, is to use a printer that provides an internal network adapter or to use an external network print server device. Most high-end laser printers include an optional network adapter. You can connect a piece of network cable directly to the printer and place it any where you want. If you can't find an internal network adapter for your printer you can use an external product, such as the Xircom Pocket Print server, to connect any printer directly to the network. These external print servers range in price from $400 to $800, but they are usually cheaper than a dedicated PC and they offer better flexibility.

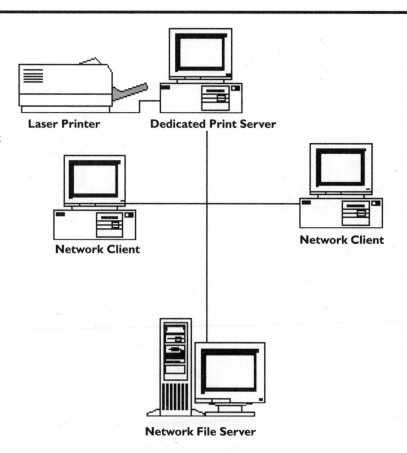

Figure 6.7
You can configure a dedicated PC to act as a print server for all of your network client PCs.

Laser Printer **Dedicated Print Server**

Network Client

Network Client

Network File Server

Managing Your Applications

There has always been disagreement about where you should keep your software applications, on the server or on your local disk drive. After all, the server is backed up every night and usually has a powerful battery backup unit in case of a power outage. However, pulling a lot of data across the network cable every time you launch your word processor can really affect performance.

Obviously, you have to keep your network applications on the file server, but there is not a general rule that tells you where to keep your word processor, spreadsheet, and other stand-alone programs.

Figure 6.8
Several high-
end laser
printers
include an
internal
network
adapter that
you can use
to directly
connect the
printer to
the network,
without using
a PC con-
figured as a
print server.

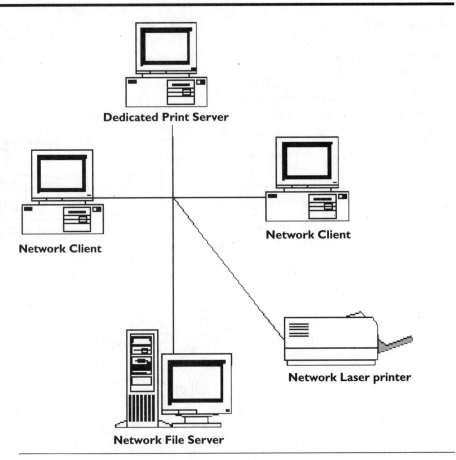

The location of your applications is usually based on how much disk space you have on your client PCs and how you share your software licenses.

I usually prefer to keep my applications on my local PCs and keep all of my data on the file server. I don't worry about losing anything, because I back up both my network clients and my file servers. Not only is it faster if you run your applications locally, it also cuts down on network traffic.

However, not every network client PC has enough disk space to hold all of the applications the user needs to access. Also, if you have

100 PCs or more, it is not really feasible to back up all of your network clients. For these reasons and for other management concerns, many network administrators keep all of their applications and the data on the network file server.

Another reason to store your applications on the network file server is software licensing. In order to take advantage of the concurrent usage agreement of a software license, you may have to install it on the file server. If you install a software package on 10 PCs and only five people ever use that program concurrently, you may still need to purchase 10 licenses. Most new license agreements from large software vendors, such as Microsoft and Lotus, state that if you install a program on your hard disk, you need a license for that PC whether you are using the program or not. The one bright side is that you can use the same software license on your home PC and your office PC, if only one person uses the PCs 80 percent of the time.

If you are a big customer, you may be able to work out an agreement with the software vendors. Unfortunately, most companies will have to install all of their applications on the file server or purchase individual licenses.

If you are using a peer network, you will probably want to keep all of your programs on each PC and only store the data in a central location. Peer servers are not as robust as a server-centric server and if you try to run multiple applications on a DOS-based server you may lock up the PC and bring the network down.

CHAPTER

7

Maintenance and Upkeep

I'm

a firm believer that if you take care of your network it will last a lot longer and provide better performance. In fact, I believe in network maintenance so much that I decided to make a career out of it. All of the different hardware and software components work together to keep your network up and running. Just like a car, if one component quits working, such as your tires or engine, the entire system goes down. You can compare network maintenance to checking the oil in your car's engine and replacing it every 3,000 miles.

Network maintenance is not as technically challenging as installing a new file server or linking two LANs to form a WAN, but it is just as important. Nearly 90 percent of network maintenance is common sense, but there are some tasks that will make your life easier and keep your network healthy and happy.

Maintenance Contracts

Over the years, I have found that most people don't like to maintain their networks or they just forget to maintain them. To combat this problem, I started offering a service I call maintenance contracts. For a set fee every month, I go to my clients' offices and check on their network. As part of the service I do everything from blowing the dust bunnies out of the PCs' power supply and wiping off the monitors and keyboards to designing and maintaining a data backup schedule.

Another reason I like to provide a maintenance contract for some of my clients is that I don't trust their technological skills enough to let them play with their networks. If I left it up to some of them, no maintenance would ever be done or some of them might cause more harm than good. I don't know about you, but I get nervous when a novice PC user begins to delete "unnecessary" files and perform "normal" hard disk maintenance.

Field Note: Beware of Compressing Your Hard Disk

I don't necessarily like to work on the weekend, but many of my clients are open for business then, so I have to be on call. One Saturday morning, I received a call from a panicked client complaining that the hard disk in his LANtastic server was dead. I arrived at the client's office and yep, the LANtastic server was showing a hard disk error. I rebooted the server and the PC still reported a hard disk failure. I removed the case and checked the cables and controller. After I determined that everything was connected properly, I tried to boot from a floppy disk. While the PC did boot from the floppy, I still could not access the hard disk.

I eventually decided that the hard disk had died and I asked the client what he was doing when the hard disk failed. It turned out that he had been compressing his hard disk.He explained that a neighbor had told him about a disk compression utility from Stac Electronics called Stacker. The neighbor had said it was very easy to use, would increase my client's disk space, and because LANtastic was a DOS-based network it would work fine on his file server's hard disk. I asked my client if he knew that the file server's hard disk had already been compressed using MS-DOS's Drive Space utility. He said no, and I proceeded to reformat the failed drive and restore his data from a tape backup. If the client had checked to see if his disk was already compressed before attempting to perform this major task, none of this would have happened.

Checklists for Network Maintenance

While every network installation is different, there are certain components that every PC-based network has, so it is pretty easy to plan a maintenance and upkeep schedule that will work with any network. The following checklist is a good example of some of the maintenance tasks you should perform on your network hardware components at least twice a month.

- Check and if possible defragment the file server's hard disk

- Check and defragment the client PC's hard disk

- Clean off the monitors on all PCs

- Blow out the dust in the floppy disk drives

- Blow out the dust in the PC's power supply

- Wipe off and blow the dirt out of the keyboard

- Check any network error logs or statistics

- Clean the rollers and paper paths on all of the printers

- Clean the rollers and paper paths on the fax machine

- Check the network cables and connectors

- Ask the users about network problems or questions

- Check the free disk space on the file server's hard disk

- Check the backup and verify a tape to make sure the backup is working

- Check any internal or external modems

If you frequently perform all of these tasks it will not take you long to finish your maintenance. For example, it will take less time to defragment a disk if you do it every week as opposed to if you only defragment your disk once every three months. To make sure that I don't forget any of these maintenance tasks, I created what I call a Contract Tick Sheet. Below is an actual tick sheet that I leave at every client's office and fill out whenever I make a contract stop.

Destin Lab Group Contract Tick Sheet

Network Checklist
Chkvol:Y / N Purge All:Y / N
Network Stats: Days Up:
Errors In System Log:
Backups Current:

Desktop Checklist
Chkdsk On Hard Drives:
Disk Drives:
Keyboards:
Printers:
Notes:

Field Engineer:
Date:
Collisions Within Norm:Y / N
Cable Scans Within Norm:Y / N
Notes:

Errors On H. Drive:Y / N Fixed:Y /N
Monitors:
Modems:
UPS Systems:

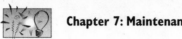

Maintaining Your Hard Disk

While all of the maintenance tasks I listed are significant, maintaining your hard disk drives is probably the most important. After all, why do you own a PC, to create data, right? Sure, you back up all of your data every night, but there are still eight or more hours worth of work that is stored on your hard disk before your nightly backup. While losing a single day's worth of work is not as tragic as losing all of your data, it is still an inconvenience. I don't even like to think about losing a chapter before my nightly backup or until I have sent it to my editor.

Your hard disk drive is one of only a few components in your PC that has moving parts. This is the main reason you should be concerned with its health. Because the hard disk is constantly moving to read and write data, it is not a question of *if* your hard disk will fail, but *when*. Unfortunately, proper maintenance will not prevent your hard disk from failing, but it might slow down the inevitable.

Disk Repair Utilities for DOS

Every desktop operating system provides some type of disk repair utility. The most common one is MS-DOS's check disk (CHKDSK) program. This program does not provide a menu and it is not fool-proof. However, it can detect some common disk errors, such as lost allocation units, lost clusters, and cross-linked files and directories. I usually run CHKDSK on my DOS-based PCs at least once every week or two. Some people are so worried that they actually put the CHKDSK command in their autoexec.bat file, so it will run every time they reboot their PC. I think that is overkill, but it doesn't hurt anything and just takes a few minutes of your time.

Version 6.X of MS-DOS added two disk utilities called ScanDisk and Defrag. ScanDisk, shown in Figure 7.1, can fix more disk problems than CHKDSK, and it provides an easy-to-use menu. ScanDisk also adds a surface scan feature that can locate and mark any bad sectors on your hard disk. The surface scan can take a few minutes to complete, but it's worth doing at least once or twice a month.

Figure 7.1
The ScanDisk utility is available in all versions of DOS 6.X and allows you to fix most common hard disk problems.

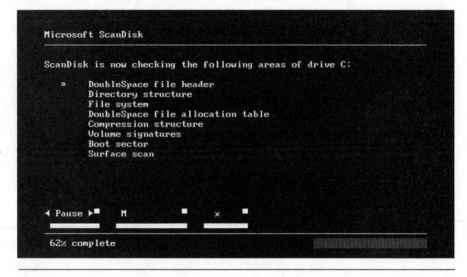

```
Microsoft ScanDisk

ScanDisk is now checking the following areas of drive C:

   »      DoubleSpace file header
          Directory structure
          File system
          DoubleSpace file allocation table
          Compression structure
          Volume signatures
          Boot sector
          Surface scan




◄ Pause ►■    M            ■       ×   ■

62% complete
```

The MS-DOS Defrag utility, shown in Figure 7.2, is not designed to fix any disk problems. Defrag is a utility that optimizes the performance and order of the files and subdirectories on your hard disk. After a period of heavy disk usage, the data on your hard disk is scattered all over the place and whenever you need to access a file, the hard disk has to work extra hard to find the data. The Defrag utility moves all of your files and subdirectories into a logical order. I usually defragment my hard disk once a month or more often if I add or delete a lot of data. Both the ScanDisk and Defrag utilities also allow you to repair and optimize floppy disks and other removable media. Microsoft's Windows 95 provides a graphical version of the ScanDisk and Defrag utilities.

If I encounter a problem that CHKDSK and ScanDisk can't fix, I turn to a third-party utility such as Symantec's Norton Disk Doctor

Figure 7.2
Unlike the MS-DOS ScanDisk utility, the Defrag program does not fix any disk problems. Defrag optimizes your hard disk's performance and places your files and directories in a easily retrievable order.

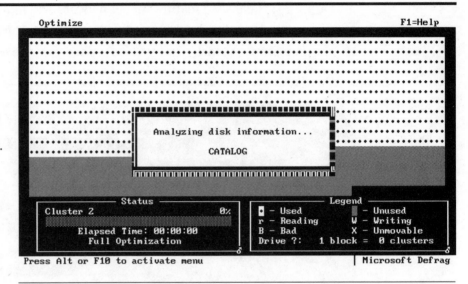

or Calibrate. The Norton Disk Doctor is designed to repair a damaged hard or floppy disk. If I encounter a problem that the Norton utilities can't fix, I usually write the disk off as dead, or in need of reformatting. The Calibrate utility performs a nondestructive format on a damaged disk. I usually try to use Calibrate before I declare a disk dead and perform a standard DOS format. I only throw away a damaged disk after performing a high-level DOS or a low-level (BIOS) format. I have seen dozens of damaged hard disks that worked fine after I reformatted them.

Disk Repair Utilities for Networks

Similar to desktop operating systems, most network operating systems provide some type of disk repair utility. However, if you use a DOS-based peer network, you can use any DOS disk utility to fix system problems. Server-centric NOSes, such as NetWare and Windows NT, provide their own disk utilities. However, server-centric networks like NetWare also perform automatic disk maintenance, so you don't have to use disk repair utilities unless you encounter a problem. The major disk repair utility for NetWare is called Vrepair (volume repair), and allows you to fix disk errors on a NetWare volume. If your server crashes and doesn't automatically come back up, you can use Vrepair to detect and correct a host of different disk errors.

Most server-centric networks also offer some type of hard disk monitor utility. These utilities allow you to see how your hard disk is performing so you can prepare for a failure. The NetWare Monitor utility, shown in Figure 7.3, is a good example of a disk monitor program. The monitor screen doesn't provide a lot of information, but it is a good indicator of how my hard disk is holding up.

Figure 7.3
The NetWare Monitor NLM provides a host of useful information including the status of your file server's hard disk and controller.

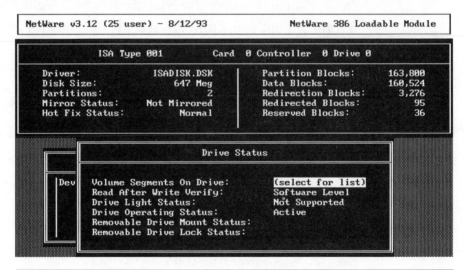

Stocking Your Network Toolkit

I drive a truck, and if you look in the back it won't take you long to determine that I work on PCs for a living. I probably have enough pieces and parts scattered in my truck to install a five node peer network. It wasn't always like that, but over the years I have learned to take everything but the kitchen sink when I go on a service call.

In addition to my disk utilities, screwdrivers, and bottled air, I also make sure that I have extra cables, network adapters, a modem, and some communications software. I also keep a text editor, boot disk, and file viewer on both 5¼- and 3½-inch floppy disks in both a high-density and low-density format. It has taken me several days to create all of my utility disks, but they are great to have. The next section contains a list of items I don't leave home without.

Important Tools for a Network Administrator

In addition to traveling with boot disks for both high- and low-density 3½ and 5¼ floppy-disk drives, be sure to include the following:

- Disk utilities

- A notebook PC

- A modem and communications software

- Screwdrivers and pliers

- Bottled air

- Static wipes

- Cotton swabs

- 25- and 9-pin serial cables

- Parallel printer cables

- Network adapters

- Network cables

- Cable scanner

- Ohm and voltage meter

- Technical support phone numbers for most major vendors

- Soldering iron

- Video adapter

- Monitor

- Keyboard

A lot of the things on the list may seem excessive, but if you bring one of everything, it will help you quickly troubleshoot and fix the problem so the client can get back to work. The best way to stock your toolkit is to keep track of the items that you constantly use. If you never use certain tools, you might not need to keep lugging them around. It is impossible to have every part you might need or use, but experience will teach you about the most important ones.

Storage Management Solutions

Storage management is just a fancy name for tape backup, but it sounds good. I decided to discuss storage management in this chapter because storage management is the most important form of network maintenance. Every time you perform a tape backup, you are maintaining your data on different types of media to ensure that you always have at least one good copy of your information.

Once Burned, Twice Shy

You wear your seatbelts and you carry medical insurance, but do you have an adequate network backup system? Even when the success of a whole business could depend on the stored network data, many people cut corners and gamble on inadequate backup systems if they have any backup systems at all. Corner-cutters might have a surge protector and UPS (uniterruptable power supply) on their new Pentium PC, but their backup system may consist of a few boxes of formatted high-density disks.

Unfortunately, people don't tend to take their backup systems seriously until a disaster happens and they lose all or most of their data. To convince my clients to invest in better backup systems, I came up with a simple list of questions to address this issue: How much is your data worth to you?

- If you lose all of your data and don't have a paper copy of it, how much money would you lose?

- If you lose all of your data, but do have a paper copy of it, how much would it cost you to pay someone to reenter it?

The dollar value of your potential loss should drive the amount of money and effort you invest in a backup system for your network or stand-alone PC.

Whether you have a two node peer network or a 200 node enterprise WAN, there is a product that will guarantee safe storage and retrieval for all of your network data. A storage management system is composed of the software to select the data you want to backup or retrieve, and the hardware used to store it. Sure, the wide range of available backup alternatives makes choosing the right one a tricky job, but if you understand a few facts about the hardware and software the picture becomes clearer.

Storage management solutions range in price and features. In fact, many desktop operating systems including MS-DOS 6.X, OS/2 Warp 3.0, Windows 95 and Windows NT, provide backup software that you can use with disks or tape devices. There are also higher-end products such as Cheyenne's ARCserve, Palindrome's Storage Manager, and Arcada's BackupExec, that offer powerful tape rotation algorithms and support for hundreds of different storage devices.

The Hardware

There are three major types of tape backup media, QIC (quarter inch cartridge), 8mm DAT (Digital Audio Tape), and 4mm DAT. Most of my clients are happy with the 4mm DAT systems. QIC tapes are larger, slower, and usually don't store more than 300MB to 500MB of data. Typically, only low-end tape drives such as Hewlett Packard's (formerly Colorado) Jumbo 120 and 250, use the QIC format. Packages using these drives usually provide software for DOS and Windows, but not for networks. In my experience, the biggest problem with drives that use the QIC tapes is that the tapes are always broken or need reformatting. I only recommend the low-end tape drives and QIC format tapes for people who need to backup a casually used stand-alone PC. In other words, I don't recommend low-end QIC format tape drives for mission-critical data.

High-end autoloaders, systems that physically move tape cartridges into playing position, such as Exabyte's autoloaders, use 8mm DAT cartridges. They can hold from 4G to 50G of data and, depending on the drive, they provide excellent performance. Because the autoloaders are complex mechanical devices, they are fairly expensive and only practical for large networks that need to back up lots of data using a complicated tape rotation system.

The 4mm DAT format is the medium of choice for most tape backup systems. Most 4mm DAT drives provide from 1 Gigabyte to 4 Gigabytes of data storage and can back up up to 30MB of data per minute. If you are looking for a good tape backup device, go with an external or internal 4mm DAT drive from a company such as Conner Peripherals. Most 1G to 2G external DAT drives will cost approximately $1,200 to $1,500 from a mail-order company.

The Software

The hardware can't do its work without backup software. Here again, you have many choices. Software backup packages range from low-end solutions such as Symantec's Norton Backup that can back up data to disks and disk drives, to high-end solutions such as Palindrome's Network Archivist, which includes powerful network backup and tape rotation features.

Products such as Storage Manager and Backup Exec allow you to back up multiple file servers and individual client PCs. This is ideal if any of your network users keep important information on their desktop PCs. Arcada's $695 Backup Exec for NetWare provides an easy-to-use Windows interface and Arcada also offers Backup Exec versions for OS/2 and Windows NT.

High-End Storage Management

Many organizations need more than just a standard storage management solution. They need a better way of storing their existing data without using expensive hard disk drives. Originally designed for mainframes, HSM (hierarchical storage management) systems are designed to reduce storage and administration costs for your systems.

The basic idea of HSM is to provide different categories of data storage with increasingly greater capacity and lower cost, but with longer retrieval time. For example, an HSM system can migrate data that has not been accessed within a specific time period from your server's hard disk to a less expensive media such as an optical juke-box or tape drive. This migration allows you to keep all of your data "on line" and available for network users—it will just take them longer to retrieve data that hasn't been used for a long time.

Cheyenne, Palindrome and Arcada offer an HSM product for Novell NetWare LANs. Palindrome's HSM product, now bundled with Storage Manager (full package is $1,695), works closely with

Network Archivist and allows you to use any kind of storage device you choose for data migration.

HSM is probably overkill for most small to medium size LANs. It can reduce the cost of storage, but first you must have enormous storage needs to see the benefit of an HSM system. If you do need an HSM, Palindrome's HSM is currently the most flexible one on the market.

No matter which storage management solution you choose, you always need to test it to make sure it is working properly. Just because you told it to perform a backup doesn't mean it listened to you. Unless you want to reenter all of your important data or try to run your business without it, *back up now*!

Tape Rotation Methods

I don't trust data cassettes; they are just too small and fragile to be reliable. However, a tape backup system is currently the least expensive and best way to back up your data. To combat my fear, I always use multiple tapes and other media when I perform a backup of my valuable data.

Media rotation methods allow you to use the minimum number of tapes needed to provide sufficient redundancy of your backups. The needs of your organization and the importance of your data will determine the type of rotation method you choose. The method doesn't matter, but make sure you use more than one tape for all of your backups. You also want to replace your tapes every six months or so, depending on the use. A digital tape is similar to a audio cassette. The more times you listen to it, the sooner it will wear out.

No Media Rotation

The term "no media rotation" doesn't mean that you only need to purchase one tape. On the contrary, no media rotation is a method

| **Field Note: Rotate Your Tapes** | Several of my clients use disks to move data from one PC to another and also store the data in case of a hard disk failure. While most of them replace the disks every month or so, they only use a single set of disks at a time. Unfortunately, this is not a very fail-proof method of |

protecting or moving your data.

One of my clients that only used a single set of disks to back up all of his accounting information, found out the hard way about the importance of tape rotation. After a day of work, the client performed a backup of all of his accounting information for that day and subsequently, every day before it. Unfortunately, he did not know that some of the accounting information on the hard disk had become corrupted. When he went to work the next day, the client could not access his information. He tried to restore the data from the previous night's disks but the information on the disks was also corrupted. If this client had used a tape rotation method, he would not have lost all of his information and the hours it took to re-create it from scratch.

of only using a tape once. Most 4mm and 8mm DAT cassettes cost approximately $20 a piece, so some companies simply use a new tape every time they back up. While $20 is not a lot of money for some companies, it can become expensive and you also have to worry about storing all of the tapes. A tape a day for a year can quickly lead to a big stack of tapes.

However, the benefits of the no media rotation are simple. You always have a tape of every workday. If you need to recover lost information from a week ago, you simply find the appropriate tape and you can restore your data.

Grandfather, Father, Son (GFS) Rotation

GFS is the most common tape rotation method. The number of tapes you use for GFS is based on the number of workdays you add data to your network. The GFS method works as follows:

■ You back up your data on a separate tape every working day. You should use a different tape for every daily backup. For example, if your backup cycle is based on a five-day work week, you will need four daily tapes, (the fifth tape comes into play later). You can perform full, incremental or selective backups during the week.

- On the fifth day, you will use a weekly tape. You will need three weekly tapes.

- In the fourth week, you will need a monthly tape. Since there are 13 four-week cycles in a year, you will need to have 14 monthly tapes.

The GFS rotation method is pretty easy to use, if you remember to label your tapes. Also, since the daily tapes are used more frequently than the weekly and monthly tapes, you will need to replace them more often.

Tower of Hanoi Rotation

The Tower of Hanoi tape rotation method is based on a mathematical puzzle of the same name. In the puzzle, a series of rings or disks are stacked in order of descending size on one of three poles. The object of the puzzle is to move all of the rings to the third pole. However, you can only move one ring at a time and you can't place a larger ring on top of a smaller ring. The solution is that the top ring is moved every other time and the bottom ring is moved only once. Every time a ring is added to the puzzle, the required number of moves doubles. Figure 7.4 shows an example of the Tower of Hanoi puzzle using five rings.

Obviously, when you use the Tower of Hanoi as a tape backup rotation method you will replace the rings in the puzzle with digital tapes. The Tower of Hanoi method uses each tape set a different number of times. Each time a new tape set is added, it is used every other rotation. Other tape sets are used every fourth rotation, every eight rotation and so on. You can perform a tape set rotation daily or

Figure 7.4
The Tower of Hanoi rotation method is based on a mathematical problem similar to the one shown in this picture. The object is to move all of the rings to the third pole, but you can only move one ring at a time and you can't place a larger ring on a smaller one.

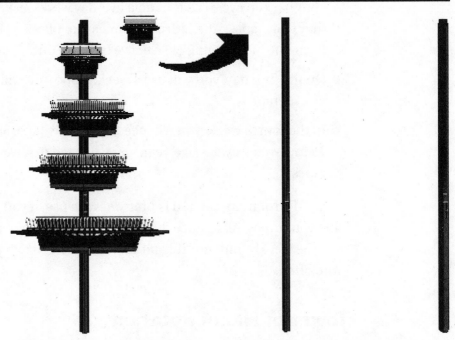

weekly. For example, if you have five weekly tape sets labeled, A, B, C, D, E, your tape rotation would look something like this; A B A C A B A D A B A C A B A E. Each letter represents a full week of tape backups. The following is another graphical example of the Tower of Hanoi rotation.

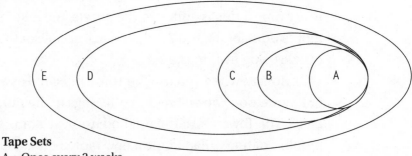

Tape Sets
A = Once every 2 weeks
B = Once every 4 weeks
C = Once every 8 weeks
D = Once every 16 weeks
E = Once every 32 weeks

The Tower of Hanoi method provides several benefits. It allows you to keep several frequent copies of your data, several week-old copies of your data, and a few month or year-old copies of your data. It is not uncommon to have a backup tape that is a year old using several tapes and the Tower of Hanoi method. If you wanted to have the same range of tape backup copies using the GFS method, you would need to use twice as many tapes.

However, the Tower of Hanoi method is complicated and I don't recommend that you try to develop the rotation scheme manually. Fortunately, products such as Palindrome's Storage Manager and Backup Director will keep track of the rotation schedule for you. All you have to do is define the sets and determine how long you wish to keep copies of your data on tape. The Palindrome products also allow you to customize your own tape rotation methods.

Alternative Media

You never want to make the mistake of trusting your tapes or your media rotation scheme. It is always wise to use different types of media and different devices to backup your data. For example, I frequently back up all of my data to a 8mm DAT drive and also to a separate 4mm DAT drive. This doubles my chances of having a good copy of my data. I also keep several copies of my most important data in several locations. For instance, when I finish a chapter in this book, I copy it to two different file servers and I also make a copy on my PC's local hard disk.

Cleaning Your Tape Device

The more you use your tape backup device the dirtier it gets. Most tape backup vendors offer either a head cleaning cartridge or a cleaning kit that includes swabs and a cleaning solution. Ask the vendor how often you should clean your heads, but it is usually a good idea to clean them after every 12 hours of use. If your tape backup device is not working properly, cleaning the heads may even fix the problem. If you take care of your hardware, it will last a lot longer and it is much more likely to work each time you depend on it.

Power Conditioning

I am somewhat of an evangelist when it comes to discussing power conditioning. In Northwest Florida, we usually experience about four power surges or power losses a day during the summer months. I could not get any work done if I didn't have a UPS on my network clients and file servers.

Whether or not you experience a lot of power problems in your area, you still need some kind of power protection for your PCs. Most UPSs for PCs are not designed to let you work through a power loss. The batteries inside only provide power for approximately 10 to 15 minutes. Most UPSs are designed to let you save your work and safely turn off your client or file server PC until the power is restored.

UPSs range in price and features. A bare-bones UPS will cost you approximately $100 for your network clients and $200 for your file server. If you don't have enough money, it is better to buy a UPS for the file server and add a UPS to your client PCs as you get more money or when you think it is necessary.

There is a simple question I ask my clients to convince them that a UPS is worth the money:

If your office suffered a power loss and you lost a document that you had been working on for several hours, how much is your time worth?

If you say your time is worth $20 per hour, if you lose five hours of labor, you could justify spending $100 on a UPS.

Some UPS vendors, such as American Power Conversions, provide software that communicates between your file server and

American's UPS. If you lose power for a certain amount of time, the software will automatically shut down the file server. This is great if the power loss happens at night when you aren't around to take the server down safely. Other UPS vendors include an SNMP (simple network management protocol) agent in their UPS hardware. The SNMP agent allows you to use a network management program, such as Hewlett-Packard's OpenView, to monitor all of your UPSs from a central location. You can gather statistics such as voltage input and output, and current load on the unit. We will take a closer look at SNMP management in Chapter 9.

Most UPSes use gel-cell batteries, similar to those found in motor-cycle batteries, to power your PC when the lights go out. Just like the batteries in a motorcycle, the batteries in a UPS only last for about three to five years. Most UPSs include a test switch you can use to test the strength of your batteries. Even if the UPS passes its self-test, I do not recommend using a UPS that has batteries over five years old.

While most UPSs include some type of surge protection hardware, you may also want to use a second device. A surge protector will not keep your PC running when the lights go out, but it will protect the PC's electronics from power surges.

Protecting Your Investment

Proper network maintenance provides two major benefits. First, it will protect your investment in your hardware, software, and data. Second, it will ensure that you get the best possible performance out of your system. While it is pretty easy to use a calculator to determine how much money you paid for all of your network components, a lot of people don't think about the amount of time and money they have invested in their data. You also don't want your users complaining of slow network performance because the hard disk on your server needs to be defragmented.

If you don't have the time or you don't have the money for the tools to maintain your network, you should consider hiring a consultant. It doesn't take a long time to blow the dust bunnies out of your power supply, but it is just as important as changing the oil in your car. If you write down a schedule and delegate jobs to different users, you will find that all of the maintenance gets done and nobody complains about the extra work. If you don't perform any network maintenance, you will probably hear a lot of complaining, mostly from your boss or your employees.

CHAPTER

8

Management of Servers and Client Computers

Network Management

Software Metering

Software Update and Distribution

Monitoring Your Network Traffic

Keeping Statistical Reports

Protecting Your Network from Viruses

Hands-on Management

If you manage a small network, you probably already know how many PCs are on your network and the type of processor and the amount of memory each one has. However, do you know how much free disk space your client PCs and servers have, the date of their BIOS, and the version of the OS they are running? You could just walk over to each PC and use a few basic DOS or network commands to gather most of this information. You may also wonder why this information is really important and how often you will need to use it.

If you are in charge of a medium to large network, the reasons for keeping track of the components on your network are pretty obvious. If your boss calls in a rush and needs to know how many 486 PCs the company owns and the amount of money you spent on hardware upgrades last year, you may not have time to run around and count PCs or look for old receipts. No matter what size network you have, properly managing your network is not only important, it is also smart. You have spent a lot of money and time installing and maintaining your hardware and software, shouldn't you at least know what kind of resources you have.

Network Management

Network management is the practice of keeping track of all of the hardware and software components on your network. There are several different methods you can use to gather and store this information. You can use existing network management application suites that will automatically gather information from all of your network PCs, or you can design your own manual methods. The method you choose should be based on the size of your network, how much money you want to spend, the type of information you need, and how often you need to access this information. In this chapter, I will discuss the different methods you can use to gather information about your network, and make sure that everything is running smoothly.

There are several reasons why you should be concerned with keeping track of and managing your network components. One reason is convenience. Almost every software program you purchase is going to have certain hardware requirements. For example, some programs may require a sound board, a specific amount of memory, a specific version of DOS, or a minimum amount of disk space. The ability to open a spread sheet or refer to a piece of paper to see this configuration information for all of your PC's can be a real time saver when you are planing a software purchase or any other upgrade.

Another reason for proper management is to maintain the health of your network. If you have a handle on all of your network resources you will be able to quickly troubleshoot any network problems. For example, if you know that you are almost out of disk space on your server, you won't have to wait for an end-user to experience a disk space error before you solve the problem.

Keeping an Inventory of Your Network Hardware

Keeping an inventory of your network hardware is probably the most common network management task. Every network administrator needs to know exactly what type of hardware they have and where it is located. A good hardware inventory will help you in several different ways. The most obvious advantage of an up-to-date hardware inventory is asset control. You need to know how much hardware you have so you can keep good financial records. Similar to any other kind of inventory, your network hardware is important in determining your company's net worth. An inventory of your network hardware will also help you create a thorough diagram of your network. This diagram will help you troubleshoot problems (such as overloaded LAN cable segments) and plan for network upgrades.

Obviously, maintaining an inventory of your network hardware may seem more important and complicated if you have hundreds of network components scattered across multiple LANs, but it is just as important for a 10-node peer network. However, the only difference between a network hardware inventory for a large network and for a small network is how you gather the information.

Gathering the Information

There are dozens of network management programs on the market that will automatically gather and maintain an inventory of your hardware. Most of these programs, including Frye's FUN (Frye's Utilities for Networks) and Saber's LANWorkstation, are fairly easy to learn and use. These programs also perform other network management tasks, such as software inventory, application metering, and software distribution, which we will discuss later on in the chapter. Unfortunately, these programs can cost several thousand dollars depending on the number of client PCs and file servers you have on your network. While this may not seem like a lot of money to a large corporation, it may prove to be too much for a small company with a small network.

Starting Small   Almost every desktop and network OS includes some type of utility you can use to gather hardware information on your client PCs and file servers. If you only have 10 to 20 PCs, you may decide to use these built-in utilities to create and maintain your own hardware inventory. Some of the most popular bundled utilities include MSD (Microsoft Diagnostics) for PCs running MS-DOS version 5.0 and higher, and the Monitor NLM and other utilities for your NetWare servers. Other NOSes including Windows NT also offer utilities you can use to gather hardware information.

I use MSD whenever I need to quickly view the hardware configuration on a DOS-based PC. MSD, shown in Figure 8.1, is not the most exciting utility in the world, but it allows you to gather important hardware information including the type of processor, amount of RAM, the number and type of I/O ports, disk drive information, and memory usage. You can also use MSD to create a detailed report that you can print out or save as a text file. I use the report generator a lot whenever I want to provide a client with a list of all of his or her PC configurations.

Figure 8.1
The MS-DOS MSD utility offers you a quick way to gather basic hardware information about your PC.

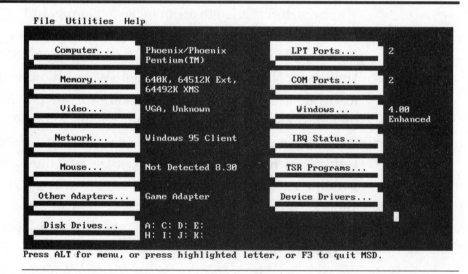

In addition to gathering hardware information, you can also use MSD to view the most common software configuration files, including your autoexec.bat, config.sys, and your Windows INI files. Because MSD is a DOS-based utility, you can use it to gather information on any DOS-based network client or file server. The MSD utility has saved me several hours diagnosing a problem on days that I left the office without my normal utilities.

If you need a more powerful utility to gather hardware information and perform other diagnostic tasks, you should consider an optional program such as Symantec's Norton Utilities. The Norton Utilities software retails for approximately $200 and allows you to gather hardware information on any DOS or Windows-based PC. While Norton Utilities doesn't really provide much more detailed information than MSD, it does allow you to run diagnostic tests on individual components.

Novell's NetWare provides several different utilities that you can use to gather hardware information on your file servers. Unfortunately, you can't use the built-in utilities in NetWare to gather in-depth hardware information, such as the date and type of BIOS, the processor speed, and information about your serial and parallel ports. The Monitor NLM provides the most hardware information of all of the built-in NetWare utilities, but it is basically limited to disk drive information and memory usage. You can also use a high-end network management package, such as FUN, to gather information on your NetWare servers. However, if you need to gather more in-depth hardware information on your NetWare server, but you can't afford an expensive management package, you can always down the server, boot DOS, and use a program such as MSD or the Norton Utilities.

Getting Bigger   While utilities, such as MSD and Norton Utilities will provide you with a basic hardware inventory, they are not really feasible for keeping an inventory of a large network. If you need to keep track of a large number of network client PCs and file servers, you should consider a network management package. Products such as FUN and LAN Workstation are designed specifically to allow you to maintain a network hardware inventory and they also provide other management features.

Most high-end network management utilities use one of two methods for gathering information on your network hardware. The software can include a scan utility that you can run from a login script or a TSR that you can load on every PC that you want to monitor. The scan utility will automatically interrogate your PC's BIOS and network software to gather information on your PC's processor, video adapter, RAM, disk drives, BIOS, I/O ports, and network adapter. The scanner then sends this information to a common database located on the file server.

The TSR approach performs the same tasks, but requires some conventional memory and may conflict with other TSRs and device drivers on your PCs. The one benefit of a TSR is the ability to constantly scan the hardware for changes. However, not many people remove a hard-disk drive without powering off the PC.

While almost every high-end network management utility can perform a hardware scan of your client PCs, not all of them can gather hardware information on your non-DOS servers. For example, FUN uses a NLM to gather hardware information on your NetWare file servers, but LAN Workstation does not provide any hardware information on your file server. Because your file server's hardware doesn't change very often a server-based hardware scanner may not be important to some people. However, you need to take this fact in to consideration before you purchase a network hardware inventory utility. Also, most of these high-end packages are NOS specific so make sure that the program you purchase will work with your network.

The most appealing feature of hardware inventory utilities is not how they scan your hardware, but what they do with the information once they gather it. If you have hundreds of PCs, you don't want to see a 100-page report on all of your PC's hardware. A good network management package will let you sort the inventory information and generate numerous canned and custom reports. Products such as FUN, shown in Figure 8.2, even allow you to predefine what type of inventory information you wish to gather. For example, you can configure FUN to list only the network PCs that have a Pentium processor, 16MBs of RAM and a Super VGA video adapter.

Figure 8.2
You can use the FUN utility to customize your inventory search. For example, you can gather information on all PCs that have a Super VGA adapter.

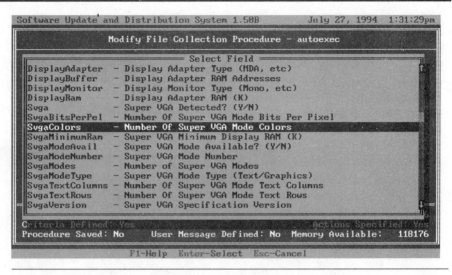

Some of the custom hardware inventory reports you can create using these network management utilities are a bean counter's dream. You can use LAN Workstation, shown in Figure 8.3, to associate additional information with each of the hardware items. For example, you can add warranty information, pricing, date of purchase, and other information to all of the hardware items in your inventory. This is ideal if you want to know exactly how many PCs you bought in a certain period of time, how much you paid, and their configurations.

You can also use some of these hardware inventory utilities to provide security and prevent theft of your equipment. You can configure the software to automatically notify you if an item is missing from an individual PC, or if the number of PCs has changed. This is a good deterrent for preventing someone from walking away with one of your CD-ROMs.

Whether you use a low-end utility such as MSD or a high-end solution such as FUN, you should keep some type of hardware inventory. It is always frustrating when I try to troubleshoot a problem

Figure 8.3
In addition to using LAN Workstation to gather information, this program can also be used to add notes to your inventory.

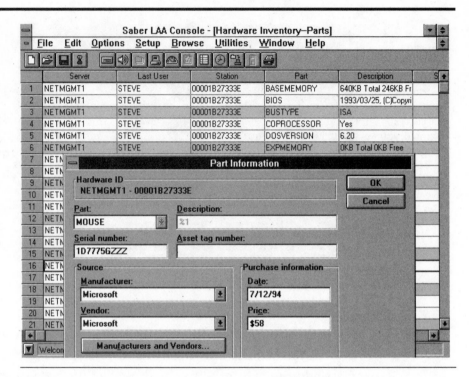

Checklist for Basic Hardware Inventory

❑ BIOS manufacturer, version, and date
❑ CPU model and speed
❑ Amount of conventional and extended memory
❑ Hard-disk type and size
❑ Disk types and density
❑ Number of serial ports
❑ Number of parallel ports
❑ Video adapter
❑ Network adapter
❑ Type of BUS (that is, ISA, DCI, EISA, or MCA)

If you can gather the above information, it will help you and it will help anyone who needs to work on your network or provide technical support over the phone. It will also come in handy when you need to order a new software package and the salesperson asks you about your hardware configurations.

over the phone and the caller doesn't even know how fast his or her PC is or how much memory is installed. You don't have to gather in-depth information, but you should at least have a list of your basic hardware components. The following is a list of the most important hardware items.

Keeping an Inventory of Your Network Software

The idea behind a software inventory is very similar to the concept of a hardware inventory. You need to know what software programs are installed on your PCs, their version numbers, and where they are located. If you only use a few applications you can probably keep track of all of your software by hand. However, if you have several software applications installed on several client PCs and file servers, it is a lot harder to keep track of them.

Unlike hardware diagnostic utilities, most desktop and network operating systems do not include a built-in software inventory program. If you want to know what software is installed on each of your client PCs and file servers, you will need to use a file listing utility such as the DOS Dir command or the File Manager in Windows. Unfortunately, not all software applications use file names that reflect the names of the program. For example, I know that that the file called winword.exe is the executable for Microsoft's Word for Windows application, but a novice user may not pick that up.

If you need to keep track of a large number of applications, you should invest in a network management utility. Products like FUN and LAN Workstation provide excellent software inventory features in addition to hardware inventory.

Similar to hardware inventory utilities, software inventory programs also use a scanner or memory resident program to keep track of all of the software installed on your network clients and file servers. However, some programs can only inventory the software on your file servers and others can only inventory the software on your clients. If you keep your applications in both places, you need a utility that can scan and inventory the software on your file server and your network clients.

In addition to keeping tabs on all of your applications, a software inventory utility can help you keep unwanted files and directories off your file server and client PCs. Many Windows-based applications install support files, such as DLLs and INIs, in your Windows subdirectory. When you upgrade an application or get rid of it, you don't want to keep all of these support files laying around. Most software inventory utilities have a database of thousands of existing software applications and their support files. These utilities can determine if a driver belongs to a specific application and allow you to delete it if you no longer need the application.

A good way to evaluate a software inventory utility is by the number of applications it can recognize. For example, FUN can currently recognize 6,000 different applications installed on your file server or client PCs. As shown in Figure 8.4, FUN can also determine the version of most applications, the vendor name, and a brief description of the program.

Figure 8.4
The FUN utility can detect specific information about many of your applications— including vendors name, version number, and a brief description of the program.

```
The Frye LAN Directory 1.50E                          July 27, 1994  1:25:20pm
  Software: Files                                                   NETMGMT1
 SOL.EXE          Windows Solitaire Game 3.1         Microsoft Corporation
 SOUNDREC.EXE     Windows Sound Recorder 3.1         Microsoft Corporation
 SOUNDREC.EXE     Windows Sound Recorder 3.1         Microsoft Corporation
 SUDS.EXE         ?Software Update & Distribution Syst  Frye Computer Systems, Inc
 SYSCON.EXE       ?NetWare                           Novell, Inc.
 SYSCON.EXE       ?NetWare                           Novell, Inc.
 SYSCON.EXE       ?NetWare                           Novell, Inc.
 SYSCON.EXE       ?NetWare                           Novell, Inc.
 SYSEDIT.EXE      Windows System Files Edit 3.1      Microsoft Corporation
 TAPEDC00.NLM     ?Tape drive support NLM            Novell
 TAPEDC00.NLM     ?Tape drive support NLM            Novell
  07/27/94 13:22:54                                  1    :005150AB:000000000001

 File: TAPEDC00.NLM  Size: 18,796       Date: 02/13/91  Time: 16:37:54
 Path: SYS:\NETWARE\NETWARE.312\NETWARE.312_____\C
 Product name: Tape drive support NLM                     Version:
 Manufacturer: Novell
 Serial #1:                            Serial #2:
 Total Copies: 0

            F1-Help  F9-Options  Esc/Tab-Unzoom  Enter-Edit
```

Similar to hardware inventory utilities, software inventory products must be able to create detailed reports. The inventory information is useless if you can't view it and manipulate it to your needs. Fortunately, most products allow you to create detailed reports of your software or save the information as a spreadsheet, database, or text file. McAfee's $55 per node Brightworks network management utility is one of the best products on the market in terms of generating detailed inventory reports. You can use Brightworks to create reports based on vendor name, application and even the name of the file server or client PC that the program is installed on.

Some products, including Brightworks, will alert you if any of the applications on your file servers move or change. This notification is ideal if you are concerned with your users copying licensed software to their desktop PCs. The notification feature in Brightworks can send you an e-mail, fax, and even an alphanumeric page if any software has changed since your last inventory.

Software inventory is only important if you are managing a large network with multiple applications. Most small networks only use a few applications and almost any user could tell you the names of the applications and where they are installed. At the very least, you should write down the names and versions of all of your applications in case a consultant or technical support engineer needs this information to help you solve a problem.

Software Metering

Occasionally, a client will call me to say that they want to purchase a new software package, but they don't know how many user licenses they need. Instead of trying to remember the number of nodes on this client's network, I explain what a license agreement means. Most software vendors base their license agreements on concurrent usage, not on the number of desktops on your network. For example, if you have 80 users, but only 60 of them ever use Microsoft Word at the same time, you can safely purchase 60 Word licenses. While this news usually makes the caller happy, it can also lead to frustrating guesses about how many people ever use the same application at the same time.

Fortunately, there is a solution that allows you to monitor software usage and stay in-line with the license agreement. Several vendors, including Saber Software, Microsystems Software, and McAfee Associates, offer products that meter or monitor the software on all of your network servers. These products are designed to help you determine the exact number of software licenses your company really needs and to help you stay legal.

Software metering is a pretty straightforward process. A piece of software, known as the monitor, resides on either your file server or network clients and keeps track of the number of users that open and close an application. You can use the reports from the monitor to determine the proper number of licenses to purchase or you can configure the monitor to restrict access to an application after a pre-defined number of users start-up the program.

Software metering utilities can help you before you buy a new software package and after you install it. You can use a software metering utility to monitor software usage for a month or two before you purchase your new application or update. This "software audit" will help you determine how many licenses of a product you should purchase and could save you a lot of money. Similar to hardware and software inventory utilities, most software metering utilities can generate excellent reports that you can view on screen, print, or export to another program. Most of these reports are also approved by the SPA (Software Piracy Association) and are a great defense if you ever go through a legal audit of your software.

Even if you are not planning to purchase a new application, software metering utilities can help you determine if you purchased too many licenses and should consider asking the vendor for a refund. If you can't get your money back, at least you will know how many licenses to buy the next time you upgrade the application.

You can also use software metering to determine who is using what applications and for how long. With the help of multitasking, many people will launch an application and keep it running all day without even using it. Every morning, I usually open my word processor, e-mail, address book, and spreadsheet, but I don't necessarily use all of them every day.

Most products, including McAfee's SiteMeter, use a monitor that runs on your NetWare file server as a NLM. This server-based metering is nice because it doesn't require you to load a TSR on each client PC, but it is limited to NetWare networks. If you use a different NOS, such as Windows NT, Banyan VINES, or IBM LAN Server, you may want to consider Microsystems Software's $595 Software Sentry. Software Sentry uses a TSR to meter your network applications. Unfortunately, TSRs require memory, take a lot of time to install on each client, and could possibly cause a conflict with some of your other programs. The best solution is to use a server based monitor and an optional TSR.

If you have thousands of clients and hundreds of servers stretched across a WAN, don't worry, there are several metering utilities that will work across your enterprise-wide network. Saber's $695 SEAM (Saber Enterprise Application Metering) and SiteMeter, which retails for $400 for up to 10 nodes, allow you to monitor and control your applications on multiple networks from a central location.

Both SEAM and SiteMeter also allow you to share your licenses across multiple networks. For example, if your office in New York reaches the limit on its Word licenses, it can borrow extra licenses from your Los Angeles office. The software metering utility does not transfer the program across the WAN link, only the license information. This sharing allows you to purchase a company-wide license for a product versus purchasing individual license agreements for each location.

SiteMeter, shown in Figure 8.5, takes the concept of enterprise-wide metering to another level. If one location is constantly borrowing licenses from another location that constantly has extra licenses, SiteMeter can permanently move those licenses to a new location. SiteMeter calls this "load balancing" and it basically divides the licenses into as many parts as you need. The software vendors may not like load balancing, but according to McAfee it does not break any current agreements.

Software metering is probably only worth the cost and effort if you have well over a hundred network clients and multiple servers. Software piracy is a major problem and it is probably going to get worse. The software vendors are not going to lose money because of

Figure 8.5
You can use SiteMeter to create a customized usage graph of all of your network applications on multiple servers.

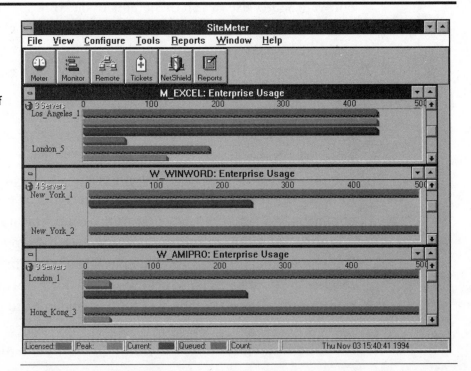

piracy, they will just raise the price of their software and recoup the money from you. Networks are a great place to share information, just make sure that you are not using yours to share products illegally.

If you can't afford a software metering utility, you should do your best to manually monitor how many people are using a application at the same time. Some network applications even provide their own metering capabilities. For example, if you own a five user license of a accounting package and user number six tries to gain access, the application will restrict them from the program. It doesn't matter how you control access to your applications, but it could save you money and you will sleep better if you adhere to the license agreement.

Software Update and Distribution

If you have ever installed a large program such as Windows or OS/2 on a few dozen PCs, you will really appreciate the benefits of software update and distribution utilities. Even if you only install small updates and drivers, software distribution can be a real time saver.

A software distribution utility is one of the newest functions found in some of the most popular network management packages, including Brightworks, FUN, and LAN Workstation. As the number of networked nodes grows, the job of updating the software on each user's hard disk gets tougher and tougher. Centralized software distribution programs use special programs and TSRs loaded onto each node that draw updates from the server. These centralized software distribution products make good use of the network to increase your productivity.

The concept behind software distribution is pretty simple. You just bought a new network printer and now you are faced with the task of installing a new printer driver on 100 PCs. A software distribution utility would allow you to automatically send the new printer driver to all of the PCs and make any other changes in the user's configuration

Field Note: Automating Your Software Distribution

One of my customers has approximately 150 client PCs connected to two NetWare servers. Recently, he decided to upgrade his NetWare 3.11 servers to version 3.12. The main reason for this upgrade was to get the added performance boost of NetWare's packet burst. Packet burst allows you to send multiple network packets across the wire without waiting for an acknowledgment for each packet. Older versions of NetWare that did not offer packet burst would send an acknowledgment after it received each packet. Packet burst definitely increases performance so I agreed with my customer's plan to upgrade.

Because packet burst requires new software on each of the clients, I recommended that my customer consider purchasing a network management package that provided automatic software distribution and update. Sure, we could walk to all 150 PCs and install the software, but that would take a long time. My customer decided to do the client upgrades by hand and use his existing MIS staff to save money.

Unfortunately, the MIS staffers were constantly fielding help desk problems and they did not have time to perform the client upgrades. I was happy for the job, but none of my employees, not to mention myself, were looking forward to the task of manually upgrading 150 PCs.

After two days we were almost half-way done and we had had enough. I approached my customer and showed him my bill for the last two days with three people working. I then showed him the price of a software distribution utility—the prices were about the same. Fortunately, my customer conceded and purchased the software. The package arrived the next day and by the end of the day we had upgraded the rest of the client PCs.

files the next time they log on to the network. For example, if you are using Windows, you need more than just a new printer driver, you also need to make changes to your INI file to reflect the new printer and where it is connected on the network. Most software distribution utilities can copy the new driver and edit the user's INI files to set up the new printer on their desktop.

Another unique feature of software distribution utilities such as Brightworks, FUN, and LAN Workstation is the ability to schedule software distribution. If you are installing a large program, you don't want to tie up the user's PC if they are busy. You can use the utilities to give the user the option of performing the distribution when they first log on to the network or you can allow them to delay it to another time or day. You can also force an update if you need a program installed quickly.

All of the bells and whistles of the software distribution utilities, such as scheduled updates and automatic file editing, are usually performed using scripts. Most of the scripts use the same language as Microsoft BASIC, but if you are unfamiliar with a scripting language, you will have a hard time creating your own. Fortunately, most of these vendors provide several canned scripts that you can use as examples or modify to meet you own needs.

If you have a medium to large network and you frequently add software to some or all of your network clients, a software distribution utility is a must for your business. The ability to automatically distribute software applications, updates, and file changes from a single location is a great idea.

Monitoring Your Network Traffic

In addition to all of the other utilities, many network management packages, including FUN and LAN Workstation, also include a network traffic monitor. While these monitors are not as sophisticated as a network protocol analyzer, such as Network General's Sniffer, or Novell's LANalyzer, they do provide you with basic traffic information.

Network traffic monitors are useful if you want to keep track of packet collisions and other statistics. Traffic monitor utilities don't perform neat tasks such as distributing software or metering applications, but they are a good tool for troubleshooting. For example, if a user complains of a slow network connection, you can use a traffic monitor to check for collisions or other errors between the client PC and the file server. Most basic traffic monitors don't let you capture and filter packets so you won't be able to tell if the problem is caused

Figure 8.6
The LAN
Workstation
server
manager will
allow you
to monitor
individual
server
performance
features, such
as disk
usage, CPU
utilization,
and network
traffic.

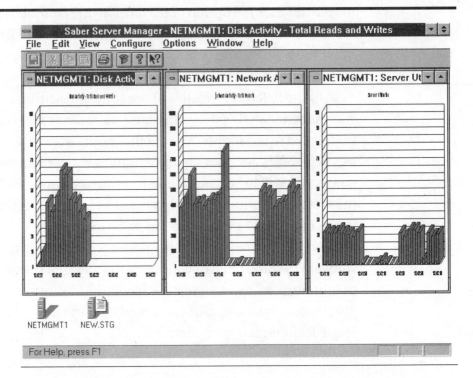

by a particular application or adapter, but you will be able to get a general idea of your network traffic patterns.

I usually use a network traffic monitor to confirm my theory that there is a lot traffic on a network. Unfortunately, you usually can't keep a history of traffic statistics using these low-end monitors so if you see a lot of errors it could just be a fluke, not a recurring problem. Traffic monitors are a nice tool to have, but you probably won't get much use out of them.

Keeping Statistical Reports

Almost all high-end network management utilities, including FUN and LAN Workstation, will allow you to keep statistical reports on information such as software usage, hardware and software inventory, and network and server usage. While the ability to gather all of this information is nice, it is useless if you can't keep a report. A statistical report is even better, because it allows you to keep track of the changes over time.

The two most common uses of a statistical report are to monitor network and server usage. For example, a statistical report, like the one shown in Figure 8.6, will allow you to monitor your server's disk usage, processor utilization, and network packet information over a set period of time. You can use these reports to determine when your network server is experiencing a big workload and when your network is quiet. This will help you determine if you should think about upgrading your server or adding an additional LAN cable segment.

The ability to keep a statistical report of network usage will allow you to see what individuals are doing on your network. For example, you could create a statistical report, like the one shown in Figure 8.7 on an individual client PC to see how many network packets they transmitted over a certain period of time. This report would help you troubleshoot a faulty adapter in one of your network clients or file server PCs.

Figure 8.7
The FUN utility allows you to monitor network statistics for all of your network clients and file servers.

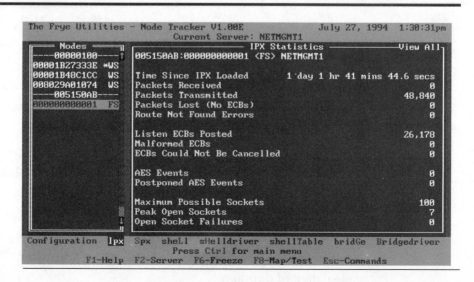

There are two reasons to keep statistical reports, the first is for troubleshooting, and the second is for planning. A statistical report is a better tool for troubleshooting network traffic or file server performance than a real-time monitor. If you use a real-time monitor, you are only seeing a small piece of the overall work day. For example, you could be monitoring your file server's performance at a time when several users are compiling large print jobs. The results will look like your server is overworked, but as soon as the print jobs are done the server's performance may return to normal.

As a tool for designing your upgrades, statistical reports can show you where your network cable is the most saturated and allow you to plan new cable segments. Statistical reports can also tell you when it is time to add more memory to your server or perform some other type of upgrade.

Gathering detailed reports can require a lot of time and effort to get exactly the information you are looking for. I don't recommend that a manager of a small network take the time to create statistical reports of network performance. In a small environment it is just as easy to walk over and manually monitor each PC on the network.

Protecting Your Network from Viruses

I don't doubt that viruses are a problem; I have encountered the little buggers several times and I did not enjoy it. However, I think the fear of viruses especially on the network, are overblown. Most viruses attach to your PC using the DOS interrupt 21. When you load most network requesters, including NetWare's, the requester uses that same interrupt and disables the virus. The virus is still there but it is harmless. By using many of the same interrupts as DOS, most network requesters prohibit the virus from ever finding its way onto your network. However, they can still infect your client PCs and cause a lot of damage.

Unfortunately, hackers are creating new types of viruses every day so you probably need to be careful. If you are constantly adding new programs to your network or downloading files from an on-line service or BBS, you should probably consider adding a network antivirus utility to your LAN. Products such as Symantec's $995 Norton Anti-Virus for NetWare will monitor your file server and prevent any viruses from deliberately or accidentally infecting your network.

Network antivirus utilities can provide two types of protection. Almost all of them provide a memory resident program, such as a NLM for NetWare, that resides on your file server and scans every file and program for a virus. Some antivirus utilities also use a TSR or executable program on each of the client PCs to protect them from receiving an infected file from the network. The ideal solution is to have an antivirus scanner running on both your file servers and your network clients.

Unfortunately, every memory resident program you load requires more memory on both the file servers and the client PCs. Some virus scanners can also degrade performance due to the fact that they take the time to scan every file you access. If your network operates in a semiclosed environment and you don't frequently exchange files with other people, you will probably be safe if you just run a weekly or monthly virus scan on all of your PCs. A network antivirus utility is a nice feature to have, but they can be expensive and unnecessary for many LANs.

Hands-on Management

All of the utilities and tasks that I mentioned in this chapter are examples of what I refer to as "hands-on" management. Many people consider network management to consist of high-end management consoles monitoring routers and mainframes across a WAN. That is another type of network management and I will discuss it in

Chapter 9. However the management utilities that I discussed in this chapter are designed to help even the smallest LANs.

Network utilities such as hardware and software inventory, application metering, and software distribution provide you with tangible information that you can see and use on a day-to-day basis to manage your network. True network management entails keeping track of all of your network components and making sure that they perform the tasks they are designed for. Not only do these utilities help you keep your network up and running they can also make your life a lot easier.

CHAPTER

Managing Backbone Systems

There are two types of network management programs; desktop or LAN management utilities and backbone or enterprise management utilities. Desktop management utilities, like the ones I discussed in Chapter 8, provide features such as hardware and software inventory, application metering, and software update and distribution. Desktop network management utilities are usually all you need to manage the day-to-day tasks on a small to medium LAN. Backbone management utilities are designed to track your critical internetwork links and their components. To use an analogy from the plumbing industry, desktop management takes care of the sinks and showers, and backbone management takes care of the pipes that hook everything together.

In this chapter I will discuss some of the products and methods you can use to manage your enterprise-wide network and the hardware components that form the links. I will also look at some network specific management platforms that allow you to track and gather detailed information on all of your network clients and servers from a central management console.

Using SNMP to Manage Your WAN

Most enterprise management platforms rely on the Simple Network Management Protocol (SNMP) and other standards to provide you with management information. This data typically consists of detailed reports and maps of all of the communication devices on your network. You can combine these backbone network management platforms with the application and system management utilities in the desktop management suites to provide complete control of your network.

What Is SNMP?

The SNMP was developed by the same government and university committees that developed the TCP/IP network protocol. The SNMP consists of three parts; the management console, the management agents, and the MIB (Message Information Base). All of these parts work together to allow the network manager to monitor and control multiple network components from a central location.

The SNMP management console is a software program that runs on a PC or a UNIX workstation and gathers management information from the SNMP agents. The SNMP agents are hardware and/or software processes that run on most high-end network communication components, including bridges, routers, and wiring concentrators. The agents send the management information to the console in a MIB format. The MIB is a standard that defines the type of information that the agent gathers and how the information is stored. There are two standard MIBs, MIB I and MIB II. These standard MIBs define certain information variables that every SNMP console must monitor. For example, if you are using a SNMP console to manage a wiring hub, the MIB will contain information on the status of the ports, that is, are the ports active or inactive. Vendors that provide SNMP management for their products, usually include the standard MIBs and proprietary MIBs that provide management information specific to their product.

The biggest benefit to SNMP is the fact that it is a standard, and in theory, a SNMP agent from one vendor can communicate with a SNMP management console from another vendor. Unfortunately, this is not always the case because different vendors adhere to the standard in different ways. Another problem is the standard MIB I and MIB II are limited in the amount of information they gather from your network component. To add functionality and better management, SNMP vendors create their own MIBs to gather more information from the hardware. However, be aware that if the management console does not know about the proprietary MIB, it can not gather the information.

Fortunately, most SNMP management consoles provide a MIB compiler that can interrogate the contents of a vendor's proprietary MIB. The compiler allows the management console to gather specific information from that vendor's hardware. As a rule, SNMP is the closest thing possible to a universal management standard, but don't take for granted that your management console will talk to the SNMP management agent.

SNMP Management Products

Backbone SNMP network management platforms, such as Hewlett Packard's OpenView and IBM's NetView, were originally written for UNIX workstations on large TCP/IP networks. They query the MIBs of statistical data in network devices, gather the reported information, and present it in highly graphical reports.

These programs have recently been ported over to the Windows platform and work with other protocols including IPX. While there are several Windows-based network management platforms on the market, the three most popular are Novell's NetWare Management System (NMS), VisiSoft's VisiNet, and OpenView for Windows. All of the packages allow you to create a graphical map of your entire network, monitor individual nodes, receive reports and alarms, and control backbone devices that respond to the SNMP protocols.

These three network management platforms allow you to keep an inventory of all of your network clients, servers, and other network devices such as routers and hubs. They do not offer the same detailed inventory information as desktop management utilities. Unless you have a SNMP or some other agent installed in all of your client PCs, the only information you can gather using these platforms is the Ethernet and MAC layer addresses of each client and server.

Because most SNMP-based management products use TCP/IP to manage and control your SNMP agents, you need to be familiar with all of your TCP/IP address, domain, and host names. Compared to the desktop management utilities, these management platforms require more time to install and configure. It will easily take you a week or more before you are completely comfortable with the product.

However, SNMP has generally been accepted as the true network management standard for most high-end communication devices. You may even find an SNMP agent in other components on your network including UPSs and even network clients and file servers. In fact, Windows 95 includes a built-in SNMP agent in the OS. If you have any network clients running Windows 95, you can use a management console such as OpenView to monitor and control individual network PCs.

Although the management software suites have grown, no single solution provides in-depth hardware and software inventory, application metering and distribution, and SNMP management and control. Until there is a single solution, you can start with the LAN management suites and add enterprise SNMP reporting as your network expands beyond local connections.

Until SNMP becomes as useful and inexpensive as desktop management utilities, I do not recommend it for most small networks. Sure it would be nice to gather information from your hub, but couldn't you just walk down the hall to the wiring closet and see if the ports are active. Unless you are in charge of a large network or need to centrally manage multiple communication devices scattered across a large geographical location, it may prove cheaper and easier to walk down the hall.

OpenView, NMS, and VisiNet are discussed below.

Hewlett Packard's OpenView   The most popular of the Windows-based SNMP management products is HP's OpenView. OpenView for Windows Workgroup Node Manager version 1.0 retails for $1,495 and accepts data over both IPX and TCP/IP networks. You can run OpenView on any PC running Windows 3.X or Windows NT. OpenView for Windows is integrated with all of HP's management platforms and you can pass management information to UNIX-based workstations running OpenView.

You can use OpenView to automatically search and map all of the IPX and IP devices on your network and to create a graphical map of all of your networks. Each map, like the one in Figure 9.1, can contain submaps that depict individual cities or even floors or rooms of an office building. In addition to the standard SNMP management features such as mapping, automatic discovery, SNMP management, and trap management, HP's Node Manager adds enhanced alarm notification, remote control, and Visual OpenView for creating your own OpenView modules.

Figure 9.1
HP's OpenView allows you to create a graphical map of your entire enterprise network. You can create a map representing different countries, cities, or even floors in your office.

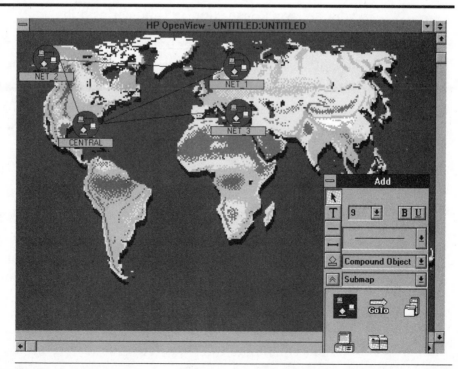

Workgroup Node Manager also comes bundled with other TCP/IP network utilities, including FTP Software's PC/TCP, Intel's LANDesk Desktop Remote, and Ex Machina's Notify Connect. PC/TCP is a full Winsock and WinSNMP complaint TCP/IP protocol stack that includes utilities such as ftp, telnet, and SLIP and PPP dial-up connections. Desktop Remote allows you to remotely control any local or remote PC on the network. You can configure Notify to page the network administrator when OpenView detects any conditions you set up. Workgroup Node Manager also offers a MIB compiler that you can use to create your own MIBs.

HP is considered to be one of the leaders in designing backbone management applications for both small and enterprise-wide networks. The workgroup products are ideal for a small to medium LAN that includes SNMP aware network components. OpenView will allow you to track and monitor information from everything from your desktop PCs to your UPS and wiring hubs.

Novell's NetWare Management System (NMS)   Similar to HP's OpenView line of products, the goal behind the design of Novell's NMS is to provide a scalable management platform for both small and large networks. NMS version 2.0 retails for $2,495 and contains many of the same features found in OpenView. Like OpenView, NMS also creates a graphical map of your network and uses an automatic discovery feature to list of all the IPX and IP nodes on the network. If you add the $2,495 NetWare Analyzer Agent and the $495 NetWare Management agent, you can monitor all of your NetWare 3.X and 4.X file servers and monitor network traffic on several LAN segments. Combined, all of the modules provide the same information you would normally have to use a backbone management program and a network cable sniffer to gather.

VisiSoft's VisiNet   While VisiNet does not have the same popularity as OpenView and NMS, it offers several features not found in the other two products. VisiSoft provides several different VisiNet

modules that work over several different protocols, including
TCP/IP, IPX, and NetBIOS. For example, you can use VisiNet to manage LANtastic, NetWare, and Windows for Workgroups networks.

VisiNet version 2.5 retails for $795 for a single network license. Like its competitors, VisiNet uses the Windows graphical interface to display discovered network nodes and to create a graphical map of your network. The VisiNet SNMP module retails for $1495 and allows you to monitor and control the SNMP agents on your network. VisiNet does not offer all of the alerting and remote control features found in other products, but it is less expensive and fairly easy to use.

Reporting and Controlling Network Problems

As with any network diagnostic utility, if an enterprise management utility cannot alert the network administrator or take steps to fix the problem it is almost useless. A good diagnostic and backbone management platform should be able to generate a report when a problem occurs, alert the administrator to the problem, and possibly take some steps to fix the error.

Most enterprise management products include some method of reporting and notification. For example, you can use a SNMP management console, such as OpenView to set up thresholds for error conditions based on statistics such as port activity, network activity, disk usage and even the temperature in your wiring closet. If a threshold is exceeded, the SNMP agent will automatically create an alert for the network administrator. Some management utilities can even take action against a few different errors, such as resetting the port on a hub if a connection is broken.

Enterprise management products provide different levels of notification. Almost every enterprise management program will create an alert on the management console if an error occurs on any of the managed hardware. The alert is necessary but not very helpful if the network administrator is away from her desk. Some network management programs provide notification via e-mail, fax or even an alphanumeric or digital pager. For example, if the network server goes down on a Saturday, the management console will automatically page the network administrator to advise him or her of the problem.

Monitoring Traffic with Network Analyzers

Network analyzers do not completely fall into the category of enterprise network management products because you probably wouldn't use them to track network traffic across a WAN link. However, they are similar to SNMP and other enterprise management platforms because they track and manage information regarding your network's plumbing.

Network/protocol analyzers are available as software programs, such as Novell's LANalyzer and Triticom's LANdecoder. You install them on a dedicated PC or a portable computers, such as Network General's Sniffer, which you attach to your network. There are different protocol analyzers available for most types of network topologies, including ARCnet, Ethernet, and Token Ring. Once you attach a protocol analyzer to your network cable, it captures data packets as they pass across the wire.

As the protocol analyzer captures network protocols, it uses special software to decode them. All network protocols allow you to filter and sort network protocols to make them easier to process. It would take you a long time to sift through all of the protocols on the network, especially if you were looking for an individual MAC address of a network client PC. To make your life easier, most protocol analyzers including Triticom's LANdecoder, shown if Figure 9.2, provide an English-language identification of the protocols you are viewing. However, if you do not know the network protocol lingo and acronyms, the English version may not help you any more than the hexadecimal numbers.

Field Note: Analyzing Your Protocols	

Field Note: Analyzing Your Protocols

I have all of the tools of the network administrator's trade, but I usually count on basic DOS commands and common sense to fix most network problems. When one of my clients called to inform me that his network was constantly locking up, I took my trusty cable scanner, DOS utilities, and screwdrivers to fix the problem. After I arrived at the client's office, the network was functioning fine, so I called the problem a fluke and asked him to call me if it happened again.

The network continued to lock up every other day for approximately a month. Over that period, I spent several hours replacing network connectors, swapping out network adapters and hubs, and constantly scanning the cable. There are approximately 75 PCs on this network, so I did not have the time to check each network adapter.

One day, during the network crisis, one of my employees asked me if we should try a protocol analyzer on the network. I thought this idea was overkill, but we had tried everything else so I agreed.

We installed the protocol analyzer on the network and configured the software to look for network collisions. We set the filter to capture packets for as long as the disk space would allow, and we went to lunch. When we returned, we saw that the majority of network collisions were happening whenever a particular MAC address, network PC, was broadcasting information. We used the MAC or Ethernet address to find the PC and we replaced the network adapter.

After a week of no complaints, I called the client and was glad to hear that all network problems had disappeared. If I had used the tools that were available to me, I could have solved the problem much faster and I would have learned a few things along the way.

You can configure most protocol analyzers to display the captured packets selectively in real time, or to store them in a buffer so you can view them later. For example, you could configure an analyzer to only capture packets from a specific network file server for a set period of time. You can even set up more detailed information such as the type of protocol you want to capture and the specific errors that you are looking for. If you don't want to use any filters, you can configure the analyzer to capture as many packets as it can hold and then filter out the unwanted data at a later time. Either way, you will need to learn how to set up filters if you want to capture specific data and troubleshoot specific network errors.

Figure 9.2
The LANdecoder protocol analyzer can convert network data packets into English so you understand what you are viewing.

```
┌Frame─Time Stamp────Destination─Source────────Summary─(APP)───────Frm─7─of─136┐
         4 08:04:25.1502 Imagen100F71 Vend?-3935CE NCP Rep Service Queue Job (No..
         5 08:04:25.3213 Artsft218FF5 MicroT4015B4 NCP ?
         6 08:04:27.3459 Vend?-3935CE Imagen100F71 NCP Cmd Service Queue Job
         7 08:04:27.3462 Imagen100F71 Vend?-3935CE NCP Rep Service Queue Job (No.
┌Frame Detail──────────────────────────────────────────────────────────────────
▲IPX
 NCP *** NetWare Core Protocol ***
 NCP
 NCP     Response Type: 3333 (Response)
 NCP   Sequence Number: 241  Connection: 1  Task: 1
 NCP
 NCP     Response Code: 23, Sub-code 113 (Service Queue Job)
 NCP                  — Response to Frame 6
▼NCP   Completion Code: D5 (No Queue Job)
┌────Hexadecimal─────────────────────────────────────────ASCII──────────────
 0000  08 00 86 10 0F 71 00 20  AF 39 35 CE 00 26 FF FF   .....q. .95..&..
 0010  00 26 00 11 00 00 00 01  08 00 86 10 0F 71 40 00   .&.........q@.
 0020  00 00 55 67 00 00 00 00  00 01 04 51 33 33 F1 01   ..Ug.......Q33..
 0030  01 00 D5 00 40 00 00 00  00 00 00 00 36 38 00 00   ....@.......<8..
                       ─────Frame Source: CAPTURED─────
   Use Tab to Move Summary Cursor; ↑↓, PgUp/PgDn, Home/End to Move Detail Cursor
                 Use + or - to Scroll Hex; Esc to Hide Detail
   F2-ID  F3-Time  F4-Scan  F5-Jump  F6-Load  F7-Save  F8-Lvl  F9-Search  F10-Ftr
```

Figure 9.3
The LANdecoder protocol analyzer can keep track of network utilization and other important information such as packets sent and received.

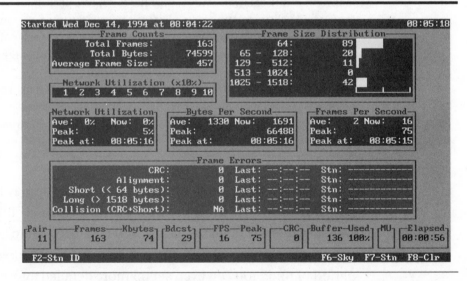

In addition to capturing network protocols, most protocol analyzers also let you monitor network statistics, such as the number of packets transmitted and received. Products such as LANdecoder, shown in Figure 9.3, even allow you to monitor network utilization and throughput, percentage of bad packets and a measurement of the peak load experienced by the network since the analyzer was activated. Some high-end protocol analyzers can also generate network traffic and even test your network cable for a break or short.

Protocol analyzers perform some very sophisticated processing to decipher a network protocol into English. Because of this, they are usually expensive and range in price from $1,000 to $2,000 for a software-only product and up to $10,000 for a hardware and software solution.

Because protocol analyzers can capture all of your network protocols as they travel across the wire, you don't want to leave them unattended. Anyone could use an analyzer to view your important network data. Most network operating systems encrypt information such as user names and passwords, but they don't encrypt your data.

Protocol analyzers are every technowizard's favorite toy. Whether you understand all of the information that they capture and generate, you have to admit that they look high-tech. I am always impressed when I walk into a network wiring closet and see a protocol analyzer working away in the corner.

NOS-Specific Management Tools

Not surprisingly, most major network vendors, including Microsoft and Novell, provide their own network management utilities that perform both desktop and enterprise management tasks. Novell has taken the lead with the introduction of NDMS (NetWare Distributed Management Services). NDMS is the name of Novell's suite of network management products, that include a network analyzer, SNMP agent, and an SNMP management console. NDMS is an open system for distributed management that is designed to provide complete network management for every hardware and software component on the network. In fact, both VisiSoft and Hewlett Packard have announced plans to support NDMS.

One of the key components of NDMS, is NMS, discussed earlier in this chapter, NMS is a SNMP management platform that allows you to monitor and control your NetWare file servers and SNMP manageable hardware on your network. The NMS suite of products also includes the LANalyzer protocol analyzer and a product called AppWare. AppWare is a suite of development tools that vendors can use to write management applications that work over NetWare networks.

While NDMS and NMS sound like a nice set of utilities, the key point is that they are designed to help manage ever single aspect of your NetWare network. Because they were developed as an open standard, others can use them to create additional products that will help you manage your LAN.

Microsoft has also thrown its hat into the ring with a suite of network utilities that provide both enterprise and network management, MSM (Microsoft System Management) formerly, SMS (System Management Services), is a product that provides management features including, software and hardware inventory, software distribution, remote client management and network protocol analysis. While Novell's NDMS and NMS are targeted toward NetWare LANs, MSM is designed to work with other network operating systems including NetWare, Windows NT, and Digital's PATHWORKS.

Managing Your Investment

A high-speed, or for that matter a low-speed, network link is fairly expensive. Depending on the throughput of the link a company may spend as much as $3,000 a month to connect their networks across a WAN. If the communication hardware is not working and your networks are not connected, you still have to pay the bills for the link.

Enterprise management products are designed for several tasks. They help you keep tabs on your expensive network connections and they allow you to monitor multiple hardware components from a central location.

Enterprise management suites are not something that a manager of a small network should consider purchasing. While products such as a protocol analyzer may seem like the ideal tool to solve any problem, they are more than you need to troubleshoot a five node peer to peer network. However, as your network grows, you should be aware that there is a network tool for every size network and every size problem.

CHAPTER

10

Troubleshooting

You have designed, installed, and maintained your PC-based network, but now the darn thing keeps breaking. You have exhausted your software and hardware manuals and the network never seems to break at the same time. Now you are faced with accepting the fact that your network is never going to work properly or you are eventually going to have to track down the problem and fix it.

In this chapter, I will give you some pointers on troubleshooting specific components and problems on your network. I can't possibly cover every network error you will encounter, but I can show you some of the common steps you need to take to find the offending hardware and software and how to fix them.

There will always be software and hardware problems that no one can explain. Sometimes the problem disappears, other times you learn to live with it and work around it. If an end-user is constantly complaining about problems, but you can never re-create the problems, make sure they know how to use the system. Some end-users don't like to admit that they are hitting the wrong keys or skipping steps, so you have to be patient when they call you for help.

Finding the Problem

I like to compare troubleshooting most PC and network problems to diagnosing a problem with your car. How many times have you driven your car to a mechanic to diagnose a grinding noise, only to have the noise stop when you pull into the parking lot? You try to explain the noise to the mechanic, but without actually hearing it, it's hard for a professional to determine what the problem is. When the mechanic pops the hood and looks around, everything may look fine. After you leave the shop and get close to home, the grinding noise starts again with renewed vigor.

Unfortunately, diagnosing your car or your PC is not an exact science. Sure, some mechanics have a fancy computer that they can plug into your car's engine, but the computer can't check everything. Along those same lines, there are dozens of desktop and network diagnostic software utilities that you can use to help you troubleshoot the problem, but these also are not foolproof. However, once you find the problem with your network, it will be pretty easy to fix. It may involve replacing the faulty hardware component or reconfiguring your software. One of the hardest jobs a network manager has to do is finding the problems, not fixing them.

You can spend years reading books and going to classes and seminars, but until you spend some time maintaining a network you will have a hard time tracking down problems. Network troubleshooting combines detective skills and common sense with experience. While a novice network manager will eventually get to the root of the problem, an experienced network manager will do so more quickly and with less effort.

Troubleshooting Network Clients

The most common and frequent network problems occur on your network client PCs. While these problems may not always affect or relate to any network issues, if your clients are not working properly then your network is not working properly. The most common client problems include memory conflicts, hardware conflicts, application errors, disk drive errors, and the always present operator errors, which I like to call "cockpit problems."

The one rule you must remember is to not treat your client PCs as standalone desktops. Every change you make to your individual PCs could affect the performance and health of your network. You want your end-users to experiment with their PCs so they will learn how to use them, but you don't want them adding new software and hardware every time you turn your back.

Dealing with Software Problems

In my experience, 70 percent of all software problems that occur on a network are related to adding new software or upgrading your existing applications. Whether it's adding a new version of DOS or Windows, a virus scanner, or a memory manager, you need to be careful that the new software will work with your existing network software and hardware on your client PCs. While many software upgrades will not conflict with your network, it is always best to be careful.

Before you add any software to your network clients or file servers, you need to perform a full backup and verification of all of your important data. In addition to a full backup, I always print out copies of all of my configuration files, including autoexec.bat, config.sys, and all of my Windows .INI files. It is always useful to have a working copy of these files that you can use to troubleshoot a problem.

In addition to helping you identify the causes of software problems, the tasks described below will also help you determine if your network is causing trouble with your applications. For example, there are several applications that you can't run across a network and several that will not launch if the network drivers are resident in your PC's memory. If you are not able to use an application after you install your network, try removing the network drivers and see if the problem goes away.

Troubleshooting software problems on your network is not an exact science. If you can't solve the problem on your own, don't be surprised if you have to call the software vendor's technical support line. You can attempt the tasks I mention below to determine if the network software is having a problem with your applications.

Unfortunately, you then will have to determine how to solve the problem and/or switch applications or network operating systems. This is the main reason why you should initially make sure that all of your network components will work with your business applications.

Checking for Compatiblity and System Requirements

If you are adding a new software application to your PCs, you will want to check with the software vendor to make sure that the program is compatible with your network. While you are checking with the software vendor about network compatibility, you should also find out all of the system requirements, such as memory and disk space, that the program needs. If the program requires 600K of conventional memory, but you only have 520K left on your PC after you load the network drivers, you will probably experience some problems. If the program requires 10MB of available disk space on each PC, but some of your clients PCs don't have enough space, you will not be able to use the program. It is not enough to determine if the program is compatible with your network, you must also make sure that your network clients have enough resources to run the program.

Some of the most common problems you will encounter with software on your network clients are based on the version of DOS and Windows you are using. For example, if you upgrade your NetWare client PCs from DOS version 5.0 to DOS 6.2X, you may receive an error when you try to load the NetWare Netx client software. Some versions of Netx do not work with DOS 6.X because the driver was developed before DOS 6.X. You can solve this problem by using the DOS Setver (set version) command in your config.sys file, but this requires additional conventional memory and may cause other problems.

Most people use the newer NetWare VLM (Virtual Loadable Module) drivers on their client PCs. VLMs are faster than the older Netx drivers and they are not tied to a specific version of DOS.

However, depending on the configuration you use, the VLM drivers may require more conventional memory than the Netx drivers. After you upgrade all of your PCs from Netx to VLMs, you may find that some of your DOS-based applications issue an out of memory error.

Taking Advantage of Diagnostic Utilities

There are several diagnostic utilities for DOS and Windows, including Symantec's Norton Utilities, that can help you troubleshoot hardware problems. Unfortunately, these utilities usually can't diagnose software problems. If you do experience problems on your network clients after you install a new software program, there are some simple tasks you can perform to determine if the new software is causing the problem or if it just happens to be a coincidence.

Uninstalling New Programs

If you suspect that a new program is causing problems on your network, the easiest troubleshooting task is to uninstall the program. However, most programs don't include an uninstall utility so you can't be positive that you removed all of the files if you simply delete the program's subdirectory. If you can't successfully remove the program, you should look for any changes the program made to your configuration files. For example, a new program may make changes to your autoexec.bat, config.sys or Windows .INI files. If you have a backup of these files, you should restore them and see if the problem goes away. If you want to know what changes caused the problem, you can print out both copies of the files and perform a line by line comparison.

Loading the Autoexec.bat and Config.sys Files

In an effort to make your life easier, the developers at Microsoft added a neat tool in MS DOS 6.X that allows you to load your autoexec.bat and config.sys files line by line. For example, when you boot your PC, you can hit the F8 key and DOS will prompt you to load each line in your autoexec.bat and config.sys files. This feature allows you to bypass certain TSRs or device drivers without removing them from your configuration files and constantly rebooting your PC to try out the new configuration.

Taking Care of Hardware Problems

If you could just connect your network clients to the network and never touch them again your life would be much simpler. Unfortunately, people are always adding new hardware to their desktop PCs to increase productivity and/or play games. The first question you should ask when an end-user calls you to trouble-shoot a problem, is whether any new hardware has been added to the PC. While software does not usually conflict with other programs unless in is resident it memory, hardware devices are always prime candidates for conflicts.

Resources for Hardware Devices

Most hardware devices you put in your PC require specific resources. For instance, most internal adapters require an IRQ (interrupt), I/O address, and in some cases, a memory address. Unfortunately, your PC only has a set number of these resources, so the more hardware you add the better your chance for a hardware conflict. For example, older XT PCs only provided eight IRQs and newer PCs only 16. The following list details some common hardware devices in your PC and the IRQs they commonly use.

IRQ	Hardware Device
0	System Timer
1	Keyboard Controller
2	Second IRQ Controller
3	Serial or Com Port 2

4	Serial or Com Port 1
5	Parallel Port 2
6	Floppy Disk Controller
7	Parallel Port 1
8	Real Time Clock
9	Available (Same as IRQ2)
10	Available
11	Available
12	Mouse Port
13	Math Coprocessor
14	Hard Disk Controller
15	Available

While you may not have all of these hardware devices in your PC, it is important to know which IRQs and other resources are available whenever you are installing or troubleshooting a new hardware device. While it is pretty easy to change the IRQ, I/O, and memory setting on most adapters, you may still encounter some unexplained problems when you add a new hardware device. The most common problem is with network adapters or other cards that use a memory address.

Using Memory Managers Most people use a memory manager to access the extended memory above 640K. When you install a memory manager such as Microsoft's EMM386, the manager grabs all available memory locations. If your network adapter needs a memory address, you may have to exclude that range of memory from use by your memory manager. For example, if your adapter is set to use a memory address of CC000, you will need to exclude the area around CC000 to CCFFF to give your adapter room to load. While this may sound complicated, there are several diagnostic utilities that will show what memory is available on your PC. I usually use Microsoft's MSD, because it is easy to use and comes with every version of MS DOS version 5.X and later. Figure 10.1 shows you how to use MSD to determine if you have a memory address available for use.

Figure 10.1
In this MSD screen shot, I can see that I have a possible free memory address available from C400 to CFFF, but that the C000 memory address is in use by ROM (read-only memory).

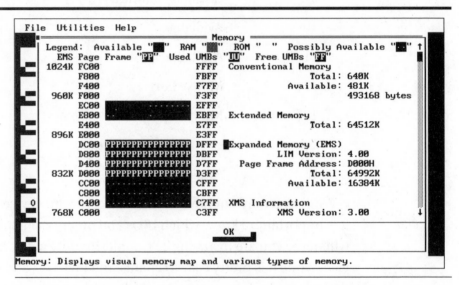

If your network adapter does require a memory address, the vendor usually supplies a diagnostic utility with the card, or you will receive "a memory in use" error when you try to load the network drivers. If you can't find a free memory address, or can't seem to exclude a certain address, you should try removing the memory manager from your config.sys file and then loading the network adapter drivers.

Removing Excess Adapters

Another way to troubleshoot a hardware problem is to remove all of the internal adapters that are not necessary for normal operation, such as a sound card, CD-ROM adapter, and serial or parallel ports.

If your problem goes away, you can start replacing the adapters until you find the one that was causing a problem. The problem is not always a conflict between system resources; sometimes a card gets damaged and seems to work fine until you add a new piece of hardware.

Troubleshooting Network File Servers

Troubleshooting the hardware in your PC is usually no different from diagnosing a problem in your network client PCs. All PCs use the same resources whether they are running DOS or Novell NetWare. However, a hardware error in your file server is usually more important, because you have to bring the network down to troubleshoot and fix the problem.

While you don't have to learn new procedures to troubleshoot your file server's hardware, the software could be a different story. Most high-end NOSes, such as NetWare, LAN Server, and Windows NT, do not run on top of DOS, they include their own OS. Just because you can boot your PC under DOS and make everything work, doesn't not mean that it will work with your network server software. This means that all of those great DOS tricks you use on your network clients might not work on your file server. Fortunately, most NOSes include some basic diagnostic software that will give you an idea of where the problem lies.

Diagnosing Your NetWare Server

NetWare may be the most poplar server-centric NOS on the market, but it is also one of the most complicated. If you have ever tried to use the system console commands, you would probably agree with me. While competing products such as LAN Server and Windows NT provide you with an easy to use graphical interface for loading software and configuring your server, NetWare limits you to unintuitive load and set commands from a colon prompt on the system console. While you do get used to these commands, only a few people really master them.

If you are experiencing problems such as lost connections or slow performance on your NetWare LAN, you will probably turn to the Monitor NLM to look for answers. While the Monitor utility does not provide you with all of the answers, it is a good place to monitor statistics. For example, if a user can connect to the file server, you can use the Monitor utility to see how many users are currently connected and see if you have reached your user license maximum.

If a user complains of slow performance, you can also use the Monitor LAN Information menu, shown in Figure 10.2, to see if the network adapter in your file server is sending or receiving bad packets or collisions across the cable. If the network adapter is receiving bad packets, but only when a certain user tries to access the network, you can be pretty sure that you need to check the adapter in that user's PC.

In addition to the Monitor utility, NetWare also includes several detailed error logs that you can view to determine why your file server locked up or a host of other problems. If the file server experiences a serious error, the OS will allow you to copy detailed error codes to a floppy disk so you can better determine what caused the problem.

My biggest complaint with software problems on a NetWare file server is the fact that certain NLMs and other drivers just seem to stop working. One day, your backup program loads and works fine and the next day you to try to load the backup NLM and you receive a "call to undefined variable" or some other NetWare specific error message.

Diagnosing Your Windows NT Server

Similar to NetWare, Windows NT provides device drivers for specific hardware. If you do not have the proper device drivers for your hardware, NT will not recognize it and it probably will not work.

Figure 10.2
The Monitor LAN Information menu allows you to monitor all of the packets that travel to and from the network adapter in your file servers. If you network is slow, you can use this utility to determine if the performance lag is caused by lost packets or collisions.

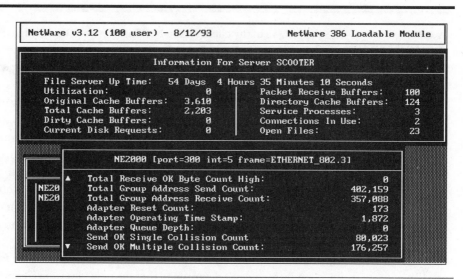

Furthermore, if your hardware causes problems, you can always reboot the file server using DOS or any other OS to troubleshoot the problems.

As with NetWare, software problems under Windows NT are harder to diagnose than hardware problems. Fortunately, Windows NT provides several different utilities to help you diagnose software errors. Every time you restart the file server, Windows NT keeps a log of all of the services that did initialize and any that didn't. The Event Viewer, shown in Figure 10.3, is a great place to start looking for problems. For instance, if your tape backup device did not initialize, the Event Viewer will alert you to the problem before you try to perform your daily backup. While the Event Viewer does not provide you with all of the information you might need to solve the problem it does show you where to start looking.

Similar to NetWare's Monitor utility, the Windows NT Performance Monitor, shown in Figure 10.4, is useful if you need to track down a faulty network adapter on the file server or on a network client. Unlike NetWare's Monitor, the NT Performance Monitor presents this information in a graphical format and also allows you to set up

Field Note: It Worked Just Fine Yesterday

One of my clients has a NetWare network that I honestly believe is possessed. All of the hardware and software on the network is top rate, but no matter what software you try to load, nothing will work without hours and hours of troubleshooting and kicking and screaming. Even when we do make things work, we aren't sure exactly what we did to fix the problem.

The biggest problem we encountered was with the client's network backup software. The software runs as a NLM on the server and seemed to work fine for several months. We decided to add a CD-ROM to the file server and of course this caused the backup software to refuse to load. We removed the CD-ROM software but the backup NLMs would still not load. After spending several hours on the phone with a technician, we were told that we needed to download a newer version of some of our NetWare NLMs.

We downloaded the new NLMs and they worked and so did the tape backup software, but only for a day. I determined that the new files were corrupted so I downloaded them again and put them on a diskette to take to the client. The NLMs would load fine from the diskette, but not if we copied them to the file server's hard disk. We decided not to press our luck and left everything alone from fear of breaking it again.

I still don't know why the drivers would not load from the hard disk and I still don't understand why our old drivers decided to expire. Fortunately, Novell is constantly offering free updates to most of their drivers, but I still wonder why my old drivers decided to quit working without any warning.

It is hard to put the blame on Novell because so many other factors could cause the same problems. However, do not be surprised when a server-based application quits working and you have to download some new NetWare drivers to solve the problem.

alerts if a certain event takes place. You can set up an alert threshold to notify you if the processor utilization reaches 90 percent or for any other event that you wish to monitor.

Other Troubleshooting Tips

Software and hardware doesn't always stop working for no reason; occasionally they have help. In addition to checking for the obvious,

Figure 10.3
The Windows
NT Event
Viewer keeps
a log of every
service as it
loads or fails
to load on
your file
server.

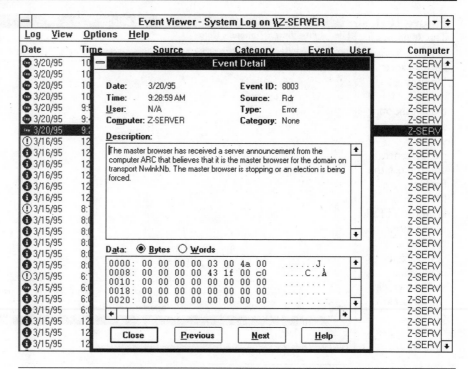

make sure you perform a virus scan on any file server or client PC that is not working properly. You also want to check for faulty network cables, loose connections, and other problems such as faulty power supplies.

If you plan your network installation carefully and perform frequent maintenance tasks, you will save yourself a lot of time when it comes to troubleshooting problems. Throughout this book I emphasize the importance of planning and maintenance. I make my living installing and troubleshooting PC-based networks. It is a lot easier to diagnose and repair a well-designed network versus an ad hoc system that is held together with bandages and a lot of good intentions.

Figure 10.4
The Windows NT Performance Monitor is a great tool for troubleshooting your file server's performance. You can use the Performance Monitor to keep track of all of the major hardware components in your file server, including the CPU, hard disk, and network adapter.

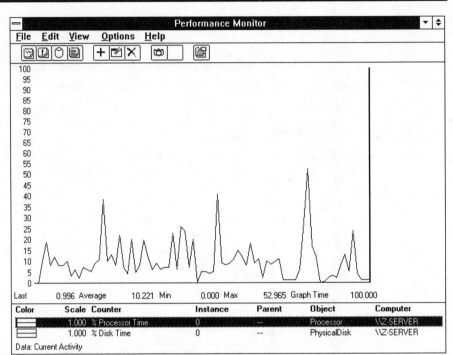

APPENDIX

A

Directory of Vendors

The list of vendors in this appendix was compiled with the help of Computer Select, a comprehensive computer products database for buyers of hardware, software, and other computer-related products and services.

Computer Select is a CD-ROM product that is updated each month and is available in annual subscriptions. The database contains information on more than 12,000 vendors of computer products and includes information about more than 70,000 hardware and software products. Finally, Computer Select features more than 70,000 articles from over 140 computer, technical, and business periodicals.

Computer Select is a product of Ziff Communications. For more information about Computer Select, or to subscribe, please call 212-503-4400.

Drawing Programs

Product	**Visio (V.3.0)**
Company	Shapeware Corp. 520 Pike St., Ste. 1800 Seattle, WA 98101-4001 800-446-3335; 206-521-4500 FAX: 206-521-4501 Tech support: Use main no.
Specs	Mfr. suggested list price: $249 Release date: 1994 Application: Graphics-Paint & Draw Compatible with: Windows 3.X Minimum RAM required: 4MB Additional hardware/software required: Windows 3.X Source language: C Customer support: 90-day free phone support
Summary	Intelligent drawing program designed for non-artist business and technical users who need to create drawings or diagrams. Provides collection of 22 stencils and more than 750 SmartShapes. Features Switchable User Interface, connector tool shapes for total quality management and support for Lotus Notes and OLE 2.0.
Product	**SysDraw (V.7.1)**
Company	Microsystems Engineering Co. (division of Freedom Solutions Group, Inc.) 2500 Highland Ave., Ste. 350 Lombard, IL 60148 800-359-3695; 708-261-0111 FAX: 708-261-9520 Tech support: 708-261-0355 Tech support BBS: 708-261-9604
Specs	Mfr. suggested list price: $995 Release date: 1994 Application: Documentation Generators/Aids Compatible with: PC-MS/DOS; DEC VAX/VMS; AT&T UNIX System V Customer support: Maint. fee $200 per yr.

	Site licensing available: Yes
Summary	Allows system managers to prepare detailed documentation of entire system. Includes more than 750 pieces of clip art including hardware and communication devices. Compatible with MASS-11 Classic Document Processor, MASS-11 Draw and WiziWord.
Product	**SysDraw for Windows (V.7.1)**
Company	Microsystems Engineering Co. (division of Freedom Solutions Group,Inc.)
	2500 Highland Ave., Ste. 350
	Lombard, IL 60148
	800-359-3695; 708-261-0111
	FAX: 708-261-9520
	Tech support: 708-261-0355
	Tech support BBS: 708-261-9604
Specs	Mfr. suggested list price: $995
	Release date: 1994
	Application Documentation Generators/Aids
	Compatible with Windows 3.X
	Minimum RAM required: 8MB
	Additional hardware/software required: Windows 3.X
	Customer support: Maint. fee $200 per yr.
	Site licensing available: Yes
Summary	Allows system managers to prepare detailed documentation of entire system. Includes more than 2,000 replicas of Digital, IBM, HP, Sun, SynOptics and Cisco hardware, network and communications equipment, printers, workstations, terminals and scanners.

Network Operating Systems

Product	**CorStream (V.1.0)**
Company	Artisoft, Inc.
	2202 N. Forbes Blvd.
	Tucson, AZ 85745
	800-233-5564; 602-670-7100
	Direct sales: 800-846-9726
	FAX: 602-670-7101
	Tech support: 602-670-7000
	Tech support BBS: 602-884-8648
Specs	Mfr. suggested list price: $950 (5-user standalone); $1,149 (5-user network); $5,699 (100-user standalone); $6,999 (100-user network)
	Release date: 1994
	Application: Network Resource Sharing
	Compatible with: PC-MS/DOS
	Network compatibility: Novell; LANtastic
Summary	Server for LANtastic OS that combines LANtastic NLM and Novell NetWare US. Provides fault tolerance, file system/media management, mission-critical reliability and applications capability. Built on 32-bit multitasking, multithreaded OS and seeks data across multiple disk drives. Allows user to install as much memory as needed for optimal throughput. Available in French, German, Spanish and Italian.
Product	**LANtastic Network Operating System (V.6.0)**
Company	Artisoft, Inc.
	2202 N. Forbes Blvd.
	Tucson, AZ 85745
	800-233-5564; 602-670-7100
	Direct sales: 800-846-9726
	FAX: 602-670-7101
	Tech support: 602-670-7000
	Tech support BBS: 602-884-8648
Specs	Mfr. suggested list price: $119 (PC); $139-$4,999 (OS/2)
	Number sold: 1,800,000
	Release date: 1994
	Application: Network Operating Systems
	Compatible with: PC-MS/DOS; OS/2

Minimum RAM required: 41K
(client); 70K (server)
Disk storage required: 700K
Network compatibility: NetBIOS;
Token-Ring; Ethernet; ARCnet;
LANtastic
Source language: Assembly
Customer support: Unlimited free
phone support; tech support via BBS
Site licensing available: Yes

Summary   Provides printer, disk, CD-ROM and
file sharing, e-mail and local and network disk backup. Supports
NetBIOS-compatible adapters, chat
and voice mail with sounding board
adapters on each PC. Includes resource caching and despooling feature. Available in Japanese.

Product   **Microsoft Windows for Workgroups
(V.3.11)**
Company   Microsoft Corp.
One Microsoft Way
Redmond, WA 98052-6399
800-426-9400; 206-882-8080
Direct sales: 800-MSPRESS
FAX: 206-635-6100
Tech support: 206-454-2030; 206-
637-7098 (Windows)
Tech support BBS: 206-936-6735

Specs   Mfr. suggested list price: $100-$250
Release date: 1993
Application: Network Operating
Systems
Compatible with: Windows 3.X
Minimum RAM required: 3MB
Disk storage required: 9.5MB
Additional hardware/software re-
quired: Windows 3.X
Network compatibility: NetBIOS;
Banyan; TCP/IP; NetBEUI

Summary   Peer network OS which extends basic
Windows utilities including File
Manager, Clipboard and Print
Manager. Includes e-mail, scheduling, ClipBook, WinMeter which
graphically shows percentage of CPU
time used for local applications and

resource sharing and NetWatcher
which shows names of users connected to local PC, directories connected to and files opened. Includes
point-to-point server.

Product   **Microsoft Windows NT Server (V.3.5)**
Company   Microsoft Corp.
One Microsoft Way
Redmond, WA 98052-6399
800-426-9400; 206-882-8080
Direct sales: 800-MSPRESS
FAX: 206-635-6100
Tech support: 206-454-2030; 206-
637-7098 (Windows)
Tech support BBS: 206-936-6735

Specs   Mfr. suggested list price: $700
(server); $27-$40 (per client)
Release date: 1994
Application: Network Operating
Systems
Compatible with: Windows NT
Minimum RAM required: 16MB
Disk storage required: 9MB
Additional hardware/software re-
quired: Network adaptor card
Network compatibility: DEC
Pathworks; LAN Server; Windows for
Workgroups; AppleTalk; Novell;
TCP/IP; NFS; LAN Manager;
IPX/SPX; SNA

Summary   Supports all features of Advanced
Server plus provides NetWare gateway that allows NT clients to use file
and print resources on Novell servers
and includes migration tool for net
managers who want to switch from
NetWare to NT. Accommodates 256
dial-up links. Links remote TCP/IP
users to SLIP or PPP. Encapsulates
IPX within IP. Includes built-in IP
routing software and built-in support
for IP over ISDN.

Product   **NetWare (V.4.1)**
Company   Novell, Inc.
122 East 1700 South
Provo, UT 84606-6194

Specs
800-453-1267; 801-429-7000
FAX: 801-429-5155
Tech support: 800-638-9273
Mfr. suggested list price: $1,395-$47,995
Release date: 1994
Application: Network Operating Systems
Compatible with: PC-MS/DOS; Apple Macintosh; Sun SPARCstation/SunOS; HP Apollo; IBM RS/6000/AIX; SCO UNIX; NeXT
Additional hardware/software required: CD-ROM drive
Site licensing available: Yes

Summary
Incorporates all features of previous versions of NetWare plus adds new capabilities. Includes transparent directory service installation option and administration utilities. Added features are file compression that doubles size of server hard drives and disk block suballocation. File server can act as print server for up to 256 printers attached either to servers or clients. Service agents allow customers to backup DOS, Windows and OS/2 clients and NetWare servers. Available on CD-ROM.

Product **OS/2 LAN Server (V.4.0)**
Company IBM (International Business Machines)
Old Orchard Rd.
Armonk, NY 10504
800-426-3333; 914-765-1900
Direct sales: 800-426-7695 (IBM PC Direct)
Tech support: 800-237-5511
Tech support BBS: 919-517-0001; 800-847-7211 (OS2)

Specs
Mfr. suggested list price: $715-$2,065
Release date: 1994
Application: Network Operating Systems
Compatible with: OS/2
Minimum RAM required: 2.5MB
Disk storage required: 7.2
Additional hardware/software required: OS/2 2.1
Network compatibility: Token-Ring; Ethernet

Summary
IBM no. 15F7138, 15F7139, 04G1051, 04G1052, 04G1055, 04G1056. Supports OS/2 LAN Requestor portion of IBM's OS/2 Extended Edition version 1.2.Includes most of Microsoft LAN Manager's capabilities. Supports 16– and 32–bit OSs. Provides double byte character set, Windows support and OEM enabling. Provides disk mirroring/duplexing and local server security. CD-ROM version available.

Product **Powerlan (V.3.1)**
Company Performance Technology, Inc.
800 Lincoln Center, 7800 I-Hwy. 10, W, Ste. 800
San Antonio, TX 78230
800-443-LANS; 210-979-2000
Direct sales: 800-327-8526
FAX: 210-979-2002
Tech support: 210-979-2010
Tech support BBS: 210-979-2012

Specs
Mfr. suggested list price: $198 and up (2-users); $99 (each addl.user)
Number sold: 30,000
Release date: 1994
Application: Network Operating Systems
Compatible with: PC-MS/DOS; OS/2
Minimum RAM required: 13K (workstation); 11K (server)
Disk storage required: 2MB
Network compatibility: NetBIOS; Token-Ring; Ethernet; ARCnet
Customer support: phone support; tech support via BBS; tech support via fax; tech support via on-line access Site licensing available: No

Summary
Peer-to-peer network OS that supports up to 255 users. Features printer sharing and network disk sharing, low memory requirements,

administrative tools and printing capabilities.

Product	**VINES (V.5.54)**
Company	Banyan Systems Inc. 120 Flanders Rd. Westboro, MA 01581-1033 800-222-6926; 508-898-1000 FAX: 508-898-1755 Tech support: Use main no. Tech support BBS: 508-836-1834
Specs	Mfr. suggested list price: $1,495 and up Release date: 1994 Application: Network Operating Systems Compatible with: PC-MS/DOS; OS/2; Apple Macintosh Minimum RAM required: 4MB (server); 256K (client) Disk storage required: 4MB (server) Network compatibility: Banyan; 3Com; Ungermann-Bass; Token-Ring; Ethernet; PC-Net; ARCnet; AT&T StarLAN; LANSTAR; ProNET; VistaLAN Source language: C Customer support: phone support; on-site support avail. Site licensing available: No
Summary	Integrated, distributed network OS for local or global internetworking and management of PCs, minicomputers and mainframes. Creates enterprise-wide multi-vendor networks. Support available for DOS, Windows, OS/2 and Macintosh.

Remote Access

Remote Control

Product	**Close-Up/LAN-The Network Remote (V.2.5)**
Company	Norton-Lambert Corp. P.O. Box 4085

Santa Barbara, CA 93140
805-964-6767
FAX: 805-683-5679
Tech support: Use main no.

Specs	Mfr. suggested list price: $395-$1,995 Release date: 1990 Application: Network Resource Sharing Compatible with: PC-MS/DOS Minimum RAM required: 9K (Novell); 13K (all other networks) Network compatibility: Novell; 3Com; Banyan; Ungermann-Bass; AT&T StarLAN; LANtastic; CBIS; NetBIOS; IPX Customer support: Free phone support; tech support via on-line access. Site licensing available: Yes
Summary	Allows users to view and control one, many or all PCs on LAN or WAN. Accesses DOS, runs any application, share files, computers and printers with others on LAN. Used for teaching, network supervision and conferencing. Supports dialog windows, password security and self-installation.

Product	**Close-Up 6.0 Host & Remote for Windows and DOS**
Company	Norton-Lambert Corp. P.O. Box 4085 Santa Barbara, CA 93140 805-964-6767 FAX: 805-683-5679 Tech support: Use main no.
Specs	Mfr. suggested list price: $199 Number sold: 900,000 Release date: 1994 Application: PC Communications Utilities Compatible with: Windows 3.X; PC-MS/DOS Minimum RAM required: 42K Disk storage required: 1.4MB Additional hardware/software required: Windows 3.X; Modem

Network compatibility: Novell;
NetBIOS; Windows for Workgroups;
IPX
Customer support: Free phone support; tech support via on-line access
Site licensing available: Yes

Summary Remote control program. Allows user to control PCs by modem that are miles away. Features remote access to PCs and networks, file transfer, remote printing in Windows, roaming dialback and general communications.

Product **Norton pcANYWHERE (V.5.0)**
Company Symantec Corp.
10201 Torre Ave.
Cupertino, CA 95014-2132
800-441-7234; 408-253-9600
FAX: 408-253-3968
Tech support: 415-892-1424
Tech support BBS: 503-484-6669

Specs Mfr. suggested list price: $179; $599 (network)
Release date: 1994
Application: PC Communications Utilities
Compatible with: PC-MS/DOS
Minimum RAM required: 512K
Disk storage required: 1.5MB
Network compatibility: Novell; NetBIOS; Banyan
Source language: C
Customer support: tech support via on-line access; tech support via BBS; fax on demand phone/fax support; unlimited 90-day phone support; PriorityCare, PremiumCare support agreement avail.
Site licensing available: Yes

Summary Offers PC-to-PC remote computing via serial or modem connection. Allows user to remotely control one PC from keyboard of another. Off-site remote PC, laptop or PC terminal controls distant host PC as if user were seated in front of it. Includes remote driver mapping, security features, bi-directional gateway and user-definable modem.

Product **Norton pcANYWHERE for Windows (V.2.0)**
Company Symantec Corp.
10201 Torre Ave.
Cupertino, CA 95014-2132
800-441-7234; 408-253-9600
FAX: 408-253-3968
Tech support: 415-892-1424
Tech support BBS: 503-484-6669

Specs Mfr. suggested list price: $199
Release date: 1993
Application: PC Communications Utilities
Compatible with: Windows 3.X
Minimum RAM required: 2MB
Disk storage required: 5MB
Additional hardware/software required: Windows 3.X
Network compatibility: Novell; NetBIOS
Source language: C
Customer support: tech support via on-line access; tech support via BBS; fax on demand phone/fax support; unlimited 90-day phone support; PriorityCare, PremiumCare support agreement avail.
Site licensing available: Yes

Summary Offers PC-to-PC remote computing via serial or modem connection. Allows user to remotely control one PC from keyboard of another. Off-site remote PC, laptop or PC terminal controls distant host PC as if user were seated in front of it.

Product **ReachOut/Network (V.4.0)**
Company Stac Electronics
12636 High Bluff Dr.
San Diego, CA 92130-2093
800-522-7822; 619-794-4300
FAX: 619-794-4570
Tech support: 619-929-3900
Tech support BBS: 619-431-5956

Specs Mfr. suggested list price: $295

Number sold: 300,000
Release date: 1994
Application: Network Management
Compatible with: Windows 3.X; PC-MS/DOS
Minimum RAM required: 640K
Disk storage required: 3MB
Additional hardware/software required: Windows 3.X
Network compatibility: Novell; NetBIOS; Banyan; LAN Manager; TCP/IP
Source language: Assembly; C
Customer support: support agreement avail.
Site licensing available: Yes

Summary   Remote control application that allows administrator to monitor and control client. Allows user on one PC to connect to another PC and control that PC as if user were local. Pinpoints and fixes problems on user's PC without leaving desk. Features include remote mouse support, chat window, pull-down point and shoot menus and context-sensitive help.

Product   **ReachOut/ACS**
Company   Stac Electronics
12636 High Bluff Dr.
San Diego, CA 92130-2093
800-522-7822; 619-794-4300
FAX: 619-794-4570
Tech support: 619-929-3900
Tech support BBS: 619-431-5956

Specs   Mfr. suggested list price: $295
Number sold: 10,000
Application: PC Communications Utilities
Compatible with: Windows 3.X; PC-MS/DOS
Additional hardware/software required: Windows 3.X
Network compatibility: Novell; NetBIOS; Banyan

Customer support: Free phone support; tech support via BBS; tech support via on-line access
Site licensing available: Yes

Summary   Remote control for Asynchronous Communications Servers. Works with modem-sharing software such as Telebit, NASI/NACS and INT-14 to allow any PC on network to perform remote communications using any available modem from modem pool. Dialing into LAN, user can remotely monitor or take control of another PC running Windows or DOS, as if at PC.

Product   **ReachOut/Modem (V.4.0)**
Company   Stac Electronics
12636 High Bluff Dr.
San Diego, CA 92130-2093
800-522-7822; 619-794-4300
FAX: 619-794-4570
Tech support: 619-929-3900
Tech support BBS: 619-431-5956

Specs   Mfr. suggested list price: $199
Number sold: 200,000
Release date: 1994
Application: PC Communications Utilities
Compatible with: Windows 3.X; PC-MS/DOS
Minimum RAM required: 640K
Disk storage required: 2MB
Additional hardware/software required: Windows 3.X
Source language: Assembler; C
Customer support: tech support via BBS; addl. support agreement avail.
Site licensing available: Yes

Summary   Allows users to remotely operate and take control of PC over telephone line. Allows user to create network gateway and gain access to any available workstation running ReachOut/Network. Provides support for industry standard NASI, NCSI, Interrupt 14 and Telebit API interfaces for modem pools.

Remote Node

Product
: **LANexpress Remote LAN Access System (V.2.0)**

Company
: Microcom, Inc.
500 River Ridge Dr.
Norwood, MA 02062-5028
800-822-8224; 617-551-1000
FAX: 617-551-1021
Tech support: Use main no.
Tech support BBS: 617-255-1125 (Modems); 617-762-5134 (Carbon Copy)

Specs
: Mfr. suggested list price: $3,499-$4,399 (2-port server); $4,999-$5,899 (4-port server); $7,999-$8,899 (8-port server)
Release date: 1994
Application: PC Communications Utilities
Compatible with: Windows 3.X
Additional hardware/software required: Windows 3.X
Network compatibility: Token-Ring; Ethernet

Summary
: Hardware/software package that lets mobile users dial into their host LANs via cellular or land lines and launch remote nodes and remote control applications on one call from Windows interface. Includes LANexpress Remote, LANexpress Server, 8 built-in DeskPorte Fast or TravelPort modems, expressWatch, SNMP-based management software and Microcom's Carbon Copy for Windows.

Product
: **NetWare Connect (V.1.0)**

Company
: Novell, Inc.
122 East 1700 South
Provo, UT 84606-6194
800-453-1267; 801-429-7000
FAX: 801-429-5155
Tech support: 800-638-9273

Specs
: Mfr. suggested list price: $595 (2-port); $2,195 (8 port); $5,995 (32-port)
Release date: 1993
Application: Network Resource Sharing
Compatible with: PC-MS/DOS
Minimum RAM required: 12MB
Disk storage required: 20MB
Additional hardware/software required: Novell Netware
Network compatibility: Novell

Summary
: Provides remote-node access, remote-control connections and dial-out connection for NetWare, AppleTalk and LAN Workplace clients on NetWare 3.X and 4.X networks. Supports asynchronous, X.25 and ISDN connections. Includes security features and auditing function that tracks connections, services accessed, time of day, amount of data transferred and outbound numbers.

Product
: **Remote Office (V.1.3)**

Company
: Stampede Technologies, Inc. (subsidiary of International Software Services, Inc.)
78 Marco Lane
Dayton, OH 45458
800-763-3423; 513-291-5035
FAX: 513-291-5040
Tech support: Use main no.

Specs
: Mfr. suggested list price: $395 and up
Release date: 1994
Application: Network Gateways, Interfaces, Switching
Compatible with: PC-MS/DOS
Minimum RAM required: 24K
Network compatibility: Novell; LANtastic; Banyan; LAN Manager; Windows for Workgroups; Token-Ring; Ethernet; TCP/IP; NetBIOS; IPX

Summary
: Remote LAN access system. Performs as multi-port bridge/router, simultaneously controlling point-to-point connections with every remote client. Allows each user to dial into corporate LAN for access to desktop files, network

servers, network printers or mainframe gateway.

Product **Remote Office for Windows (V.1.3)**

Company Stampede Technologies, Inc. (subsidiary of International Software Services, Inc.)
78 Marco Lane
Dayton, OH 45458
800-763-3423; 513-291-5035
FAX: 513-291-5040
Tech support: Use main no.

Specs Mfr. suggested list price: $395 and up
Release date: 1994
Application: Network Gateways, Interfaces, Switching
Compatible with: Windows 3.X
Minimum RAM required: 24K
Additional hardware/software required: Windows 3.X
Network compatibility: Novell; LANtastic; Banyan; LAN Manager; Windows for Workgroups; Token-Ring; Ethernet; TCP/IP; NetBIOS; IPX

Summary Remote LAN access system. Performs as multi-port bridge/router, simultaneously controlling point-to-point connections with every remote client. Allows each user to dial into corporate LAN for access to desktop files, network servers, network printers or mainframe gateway.

Product **Remote Office Gold (V.2.0)**

Company Stampede Technologies, Inc. (subsidiary of International Software Services, Inc.)
78 Marco Lane
Dayton, OH 45458
800-763-3423; 513-291-5035
FAX: 513-291-5040
Tech support: Use main no.

Specs Mfr. suggested list price: $895 (8-port); $1,790 (16 port)
Release date: 1994
Application: Network Gateways, Interfaces, Switching

Compatible with: PC-MS/DOS
Minimum RAM required: 28K
Network compatibility: Novell; TCP/IP; Ethernet; Token-Ring; IPX

Summary Designed to provide remote LAN access capabilities to variety of third party point-to-point protocol routers and communication servers. Allows users to access databases, e-mail and Internet. Provides security, modem lights, ExeGuard warning feature and RCViewer remote control utility. Includes multi-protocol drivers and supports NDIS, ODI, Packet Drivers, IEEE 802.3/IEEE 802.2 frame types and V.32bis.V.42bis modems.

Product **Remote Office Gold for Windows (V.2.0)**

Company Stampede Technologies, Inc. (subsidiary of International Software Services, Inc.)
78 Marco Lane
Dayton, OH 45458
800-763-3423; 513-291-5035
FAX: 513-291-5040
Tech support: Use main no.

Specs Mfr. suggested list price: $895 (8-port); $1,790 (16-port)
Release date: 1994
Application: Network Gateways, Interfaces, Switching
Compatible with: Windows 3.X
Minimum RAM required: 28K
Additional hardware/software required: Windows 3.X
Network compatibility: Novell; TCP/IP; Ethernet; Token-Ring; IPX

Summary Designed to provide remote LAN access capabilities to variety of third party point-to-point protocol routers and communication servers. Allows users to access databases, e-mail and Internet. Provides security, modem lights, ExeGuard warning feature and RCViewer remote control utility. Includes multi-protocol drivers and supports NDIS, ODI, Packet Drivers,

IEEE 802.3/IEEE 802.2 frame types and V.32bis.V.42bis modems.

Remote Node Servers/Routers

Product	**ViewBlazer**
Company	Telebit Corp. One Executive Dr. Chelmsford, MA 01824 800-989-8888; 508-441-2181 FAX: 508-441-9060 Tech support: 408-734-5200
Specs	Mfr. suggested list price: $995-$4,995 Release date: 1994 Application: Network Management Compatible with: Windows 3.X Minimum RAM required: 4MB Disk storage required: 10MB Additional hardware/software required: Windows 3.X Customer support: Unlimited toll-free phone support Site licensing available: No
Summary	Windows-based network management system. Provides device configuration, access security management and monitoring features which allows operator to fine-tune system to needs of network. Provides templates to facilitate configuration process and minimize operator error. Operator-defined event severity levels permit are supported. Extends management to dial and leased line facilities.

Product	**500-CS Communication Server**
Company	Cisco Systems, Inc. 170 W. Tasman Dr. San Jose, CA 95134-1706 800-553-6387; 408-526-4000 FAX: 408-526-4100 Tech support: Use toll-free no.
Specs	Mfr. suggested list price: $3,295 Number installed to date: 4,500 Date announced: 1992 Product classification: Router

Description: Combines multiprotocol terminal server, async routing, gateway server and telecommuting server functions
Local or remote: Remote
Configuration: Standalone
Number of LAN interfaces: 1
Network compatibility: Ethernet
IEEE standard: IEEE-802.3
LAN speed: 10 Mbps
Protocols supported: TCP/IP; LAT; IP; IPX; OSPF; IGRP; RIP; EGP; BGP; SLIP; ARAP
Number of WAN interfaces: 8; 16
WAN services supported: X.25
Serial interfaces supported: RS-232; V.35
Network management standards: Telnet

Product	**Model 3800A Multimedia Router**
Company	Bay Networks, Inc. 4401 Great America Pkwy., P.O. Box 58185 Santa Clara, CA 95054 800-776-6895; 408-988-2400 FAX: 408-988-5525 Tech support: 800-473-4911
Specs	Mfr. suggested list price: $5,995 Date announced: 1994 Product classification: Router Description: Ethernet multimedia router Local or remote: Remote Number of LAN interfaces: 1 Network compatibility: Ethernet IEEE standard: IEEE-802.3 10BaseT Media type: UTP LAN speed: 10 Mbps Protocols supported: XNS; DECnet; AppleTalk; IP; IPX Number of WAN interfaces: 1 WAN services supported: X.25; ISDN; Frame Relay; SMDS; PPP Serial interfaces supported: RS-232

Product	**Dr. BonD-B**

Company   NEC America, Inc. (Data
Communications Systems Division)
1525 Walnut Hill Lane
Irving, TX 75038
800-222-4NEC; 214-518-5000
FAX: 214-518-5572
Tech support: 800-538-8166

Specs   Mfr. suggested list price: $3,405
Date announced: 1992
Shareable devices: Remote access to
TCP/IP, SPX/IPX, and AppleTalk pro-
tocols via 4 V.42 bis/V.32 bis Modem
Network compatibility: Ethernet
IEEE standard: IEEE-802.3 10Base2;
10Base5; 10BaseT
LAN speed: 10 Mbps
Interfaces supported: 4 DB-25; 1 AUI;
1 BNC; 1 RJ-45

Product   **LANRover/2E Plus**
Company   Shiva Corp.
63 Third Ave., Northwest Park
Burlington, MA 01803
800-458-3550; 617-270-8300
FAX: 617-270-8852
Tech support: 617-270-8400
Tech support BBS: 617-273-0023

Specs   Mfr. suggested list price: $2,799
Standard warranty included: 1 yr.
Date announced: 1994
Shareable devices: Remote access to
IPX, AppleTalk, ARA, TCP/IP, or
NetBEUI protocols via 2 external
Modem
Network compatibility: Ethernet
IEEE standard: IEEE-802.3 10Base2;
10Base5; 10BaseT
LAN speed: 10 Mbps
CPU compatibility: Apple Macintosh
Interfaces supported: 4 DB-25; 1 AUI;
1 BNC; 1 RJ-45

Product   **LANRover/4E Plus**
Company   Shiva Corp.
63 Third Ave., Northwest Park
Burlington, MA 01803
800-458-3550; 617-270-8300
FAX: 617-270-8852

Tech support: 617-270-8400
Tech support BBS: 617-273-0023

Specs   Mfr. suggested list price: $4,299
Standard warranty included: 1 yr.
Date announced: 1994
Shareable devices: Remote access to
NetWare, TCP/IP, or NetBEUI
protocols via 4 external Modem
Network compatibility: Ethernet
IEEE standard: IEEE-802.3 10Base2;
10Base5; 10BaseT
LAN speed: 10 Mbps
CPU compatibility: Apple Macintosh
Interfaces supported: 4 DB-25; 1 AUI;
1 BNC; 1 RJ-45

Product   **LANRover/8E Plus**
Company   Shiva Corp.
63 Third Ave., Northwest Park
Burlington, MA 01803
800-458-3550; 617-270-8300
FAX: 617-270-8852
Tech support: 617-270-8400
Tech support BBS: 617-273-0023

Specs   Mfr. suggested list price: $4,999
Standard warranty included: 1 yr.
Date announced: 1994
Shareable devices: Remote access to
NetWare, TCP/IP, or NetBEUI
protocols via 4 external Modem
Network compatibility: Ethernet
IEEE standard: IEEE-802.3 10Base2;
10Base5; 10BaseT
LAN speed: 10 Mbps
CPU compatibility: Apple Macintosh
Interfaces supported: 8 DB-25; 1 AUI;
1 BNC; 1 RJ-45

Product   **PortMaster IRX**
Company   Livingston Enterprises, Inc.
6920 Koll Center Pkwy., Ste. 220
Pleasanton, CA 94566
800-458-9966; 510-426-0770
FAX: 510-426-8951
Tech support: Use toll-free no.

Specs   Mfr. suggested list price: $2,395-
$3,250
Standard warranty included: 1 yr.

Date announced: 1991
Product classification: Router
Description: Attaches Ethernet to remote sites via T1/E1 facilities
Local or remote: Remote
Configuration: Standalone
Number of LAN interfaces: 1
Network compatibility: Ethernet
IEEE standard: IEEE-802.3 10Base2; 10Base5; 10BaseT
Media type: Thick coax; Thin coax; UTP
LAN speed: 10 Mbps
Protocols supported: TCP/IP; IP; IPX; HDLC/LAPB; RIP; UDP; ARP; PPP
Number of WAN interfaces: 1
WAN services supported: T1; E1
Serial interfaces supported: RS-232; RS-449; V.35
Network management standards: SNMP; Telnet
Additional functions: Flash memory for upgrades

Product **PortMaster PM-2**
Company Livingston Enterprises, Inc.
6920 Koll Center Pkwy., Ste. 220
Pleasanton, CA 94566
800-458-9966; 510-426-0770
FAX: 510-426-8951
Tech support: Use toll-free no.
Specs Mfr. suggested list price: $2,495
Standard warranty included: 1 yr.; depot
Date announced: 1992
Network compatibility: Ethernet
Number of ports: 10 serial; 1 parallel
Port expansion architecture: Fixed capacity
Protocol(s) supported: TCP/IP; IPX
Serial interface(s): RS-232
Type of connectors: DB-25
Max. throughput per port: 38.4 Kbps
IEEE standard: IEEE-802.3 10Base2; 10Base5
Network discipline: Baseband
Media type: Thick coax; Thin coax
Microprocessor: 80386-DX

Clock frequency: 25 MHz
RAM installed: 1MB
Additional features: SLIP; CSLIP; PPP; SNMP MIB II

Product **BReeze 1000**
Company Networks Northwest, Inc.
3633 136th Place, SE, Ste. 100
Bellevue, WA 98006
800-835-9462; 206-641-8779
FAX: 206-641-8909
Tech support: Use main no.
Specs Mfr. suggested list price: $2,695
Standard warranty included: 3 yr.
Date announced: 1992
Product classification: Bridge/Router
Description: Multiprotocol Ethernet bridge/router
Local or remote: Remote
Configuration: Standalone
Number of LAN interfaces: 1
Network compatibility: Ethernet
IEEE standard: IEEE-802.3 10Base2; 10Base5; 10BaseT
Media type: Thick coax; Thin coax; UTP
LAN speed: 10 Mbps
Host interfaces supported: Ethernet
Protocols supported: TCP/IP; LAT; OSI; IP; IPX; SPX; NETBIOS; OSPF; RIP; PPP
Number of WAN interfaces: 1
WAN services supported: T1; ISDN; Frame Relay
Serial interfaces supported: RS-232; V.35
Packet filtering rate: 14,880 pps
Data compression supported: Yes
Error correction supported: Yes
Network management standards: SNMP; Telnet
Additional functions: V.32 bis 14.4K or V.fast modem

Product **BReeze 2000**
Company Networks Northwest, Inc.
3633 136th Place, SE, Ste. 100
Bellevue, WA 98006

Specs
800-835-9462; 206-641-8779
FAX: 206-641-8909
Tech support: Use main no.
Mfr. suggested list price: $2,695
Standard warranty included: 3 yr.
Number installed to date: 200
Date announced: 1994
Product classification: Bridge/Router
Description: Ethernet bridge router
Local or remote: Remote
Configuration: Standalone;
Rackmount
Number of LAN interfaces: 1
Network compatibility: Ethernet
IEEE standard: IEEE-802.3 10Base2;
10Base5; 10BaseT
Media type: Thick coax; Thin coax;
UTP
LAN speed: 10 Mbps
Protocols supported: TCP/IP; IPX;
SPX
Number of WAN interfaces: 2
WAN services supported: T1; E1;
ISDN; Frame Relay; PPP
Serial interfaces supported: RS-232;
V.35
Data compression supported: Yes
Error correction supported: Yes
Network management standards:
SNMP

Network Printing

Product **Pocket Ethernet Print Server IIPS**
Company Xircom, Inc.
26025 Mureau Rd.
Calabasas, CA 91302
800-438-9472; 818-878-7600
Direct sales: 800-874-7875
FAX: 818-878-7630
Tech support: 800-874-4428
Tech support BBS: 818-878-7618
Specs
Mfr. suggested list price: $599
Standard warranty included: lifetime
Date announced: 1994
Shareable devices: Printer

Network compatibility: Ethernet
IEEE standard: IEEE-802.3 10Base2;
10BaseT
LAN speed: 10 Mbps
Interfaces supported: BNC; RJ-45

Network Management Utilities

Product **Brightwork Utilities for Netware (V.1.0)**
Company McAfee Associates, Inc.
2710 Walsh Ave., Ste. 200
Santa Clara, CA 95051
800-866-6585; 408-988-3832
FAX: 408-970-9727
Tech support: 408-988-4181
Tech support BBS: 408-988-4004
Specs
Mfr. suggested list price: $495 (50-user)

Application: Network Management
Compatible with: Windows 3.X
Minimum RAM required: 2MB
Disk storage required: 5MB
Additional hardware/software required: Windows 3.X; Novell Netware
Network compatibility: Novell
Customer support: Unlimited toll-free phone support
Site licensing available: No
Summary Suite of applications for small and medium-sized LANs. Tracks network software and hardware. Allows user to support and troubleshoot Windows or DOS workstations on LAN. Monitors system performance, security, capacity and configuration. Provides LAN user with access to printers attached to any PC on network.

Product **Frye Utilities for Networks— NetWare Management (V.2.0)**
Company Frye Computer Systems, Inc.
19 Temple Place
Boston, MA 02111-9779

800-234-3793; 617-451-5400
FAX: 617-451-6711
Tech support: Use toll-free no.
Tech support BBS: 617-426-1910

Specs Mfr. suggested list price: $495 (initial server license, 395 each addl. server)
Release date: 1994
Application: Network Management
Compatible with: PC-MS/DOS
Minimum RAM required: 640K
Disk storage required: 400K
Network compatibility: Novell
Source language: C
Customer support: toll-free phone support; tech support via BBS
Site licensing available: No

Summary Allows user to retrieve and edit information needed to troubleshoot, diagnose and manage network. Edits and updates Syscon, Pconsole, Fconsole, Printcon, Printdef, Volinfo and Filer information. Provides detailed explanations of all errors and terms and recommendations for solutions. Provides single-screen to show all server's user activity in real-time graphic, numeric and text formats.

Product **Frye Utilities for Networks— Software Metering and Resource Tracking for Netware (V.1.5)**

Company Frye Computer Systems, Inc.
19 Temple Place
Boston, MA 02111-9779
800-234-3793; 617-451-5400
FAX: 617-451-6711
Tech support: Use toll-free no.
Tech support BBS: 617-426-1910

Specs Mfr. suggested list price: $495 (100-user server license); $995 (250-user server license); $3,795 (1,000-user server license)
Release date: 1994
Application: Network Management
Compatible with: PC-MS/DOS; Apple Macintosh; OS/2
Minimum RAM required: 250K

Additional hardware/software required: Novell Netware
Network compatibility: Novell
Source language: C
Customer support: Unlimited toll-free phone support; tech support via BBS
Site licensing available: No

Summary NLM that allows user to monitor and control use of all software on network. Provides graphical display to show cumulative and daily usage. Checks for potential security breaches including virus intrusions. Provides customizable reports that allow for current and historical activity to be gathered. Features local drive monitoring and ability to find file without requiring its path.

Product **Frye Utilities for Networks— Software Update and Distribution System (V.1.5)**

Company Frye Computer Systems, Inc.
19 Temple Place
Boston, MA 02111-9779
800-234-3793; 617-451-5400
FAX: 617-451-6711
Tech support: Use toll-free no.
Tech support BBS: 617-426-1910

Specs Mfr. suggested list price: $995 (initial license, 895 per addl. license)
Release date: 1994
Application: Network Management
Compatible with: PC-MS/DOS
Minimum RAM required: 640K
Disk storage required: 1.5MB
Network compatibility: LAN Manager; Novell; LAN Server; Banyan; DEC Pathworks; AT&T StarLAN
Source language: C
Customer support: toll-free phone support; tech support via BBS
Site licensing available: No

Summary LAN software distribution system. Can be set to automatically replace entire application with new one.

Designed for remote distribution of shrink-wrapped packages as well as network drivers, tools and utilities. Works across bridges and routers. Includes distribution lists and user menu procedures, alarm options, master procedures, procedure retry and per user log summary.

Product **Frye Utilities for Networks—SUDS Wide Area Network Distribution Module (V.1.0)**

Company Frye Computer Systems, Inc.
19 Temple Place
Boston, MA 02111-9779
800-234-3793; 617-451-5400
FAX: 617-451-6711
Tech support: Use toll-free no.
Tech support BBS: 617-426-1910

Specs Mfr. suggested list price: $1,495 (initial server license, 1,295 per addl. server license)
Release date: 1994
Application: Network Management
Compatible with: PC-MS/DOS
Minimum RAM required: 640K
Disk storage required: 640K
Additional hardware/software required: Novell Netware; Frye Utilities for Networks—Software Update and Distribution: System V.1.5 or higher
Network compatibility: Novell
Source language: C
Customer support: toll-free phone support; tech support via BBS
Site licensing available: No

Summary Extends range of Software Update and Distribution System by letting network manager create set of procedures at one server to be automatically copied to any or all installations of SUDS on WAN. Includes package inspection security feature, ability to define and save target lists and report writing.

Product **LANWatch Network Analyzer (V.4.0)**

Company FTP Software, Inc.
100 Brickstone Sq., 5th Fl.
Andover, MA 01810
800-282-4FTP; 508-685-4000
Direct sales: 508-685-3300
FAX: 508-794-4488
Tech support: 800-382-4FTP

Specs Mfr. suggested list price: $1,200
Release date: 1994
Application: Network Management
Compatible with: PC-MS/DOS
Minimum RAM required: 512K
Disk storage required: 2.0MB
Network compatibility: Token-Ring; Ethernet; Novell; Banyan; SNA; IPX
Source language: C
Customer support: Free phone support
Site licensing available: Yes

Summary Network analyzer for LANs. Useful for developing and debugging protocols and for installing, troubleshooting and monitoring networks. Provides background, view, save, load, trigger, alarm and search filters and can filter packets by protocol, address or content.

Product **LT Stat (V.3.0)**

Company Blue Lance, Inc.
1700 West Loop South, Ste. 1100
Houston, TX 77027
800-TKO-BLUE; 713-680-1187
FAX: 713-622-1370
Tech support: Use main no.

Specs Mfr. suggested list price: $295
Release date: 1991
Application: Report Management
Compatible with: PC-MS/DOS; OS/2
Minimum RAM required: 256K
Disk storage required: 680K
Additional hardware/software required: Novell Netware.
Network compatibility: Novell
Source language: C
Customer support: Unlimited free phone support
Site licensing available: Yes

Summary Report generator which allows user to create, view, save and print 36 detailed statistical reports on system configuration, file server disk utilization, security, server performance and workstation usage. Designed for Network Installers, Network Administrators and Systems Engineers who install, configure and maintain NetWare LANs and WANs. Reads/reports bindery, disk utilization and server performance information using Novell-like interface or through command line interface

Product **Monitrix—The Network Manager (V.3.0)**
Company Cheyenne Software, Inc.
3 Expressway Plaza
Roslyn Hgts., NY
11577 516-484-5110
Direct sales: 800-243-9462
FAX: 516-484-3446
Tech support: 800-243-9832
Tech support BBS: 516-484-3445
Specs Mfr. suggested list price: $495
Release date: 1994
Application: Network Management
Compatible with: PC-MS/DOS
Minimum RAM required: 80-135K (server); 512K (workstation)
Disk storage required: 46-150K (server); 400K (workstation)
Network compatibility: Novell
Source language: C
Customer support: toll-free phone support; tech support via BBS
Site licensing available: Yes
Summary Provides wide range of activities for network managers including complete set of inventory, point-to-point connectivity tests and performance analysis.

Product **Norton Utilities (V.8.0)**
Company Symantec Corp.
10201 Torre Ave.
Cupertino, CA 95014-2132
800-441-7234; 408-253-9600
FAX: 408-253-3968
Tech support: 415-892-1424
Tech support BBS: 503-484-6669
Specs Mfr. suggested list price: $179
Release date: 1994
Application: Disk/Tape/File Utilities
Compatible with: Windows; PC-MS/DOS
Minimum RAM required: 640K (DOS); 4MB (Windows)
Disk storage required: 8MB
Additional hardware/software required: Windows 3.X
Network compatibility: Novell
Source language: C
Customer support: tech support via online access; tech support via BBS; fax on demand phone/fax support; unlimited 90-day phone support; PriorityCare, PremiumCare support agreement avail.
Site licensing available: No
Summary DOS utilities. Provides Norton Disk Doctor which repairs and recovers file system damage and detects media defects early to prevent data loss. Includes Speed Disk which defragments files for disk access and data recovery. Provides 400 DOS commands. Includes suite of Windows-specific utilities and troubleshooting tools.

Product **Saber LAN Management System for NetWare (LMS)**
Company Saber Software Corp.
5944 Luther Lane, Ste. 1007
Dallas, TX 75225
800-338-8754; 214-361-8086
Direct sales: 800-338-8754, ext. 41
FAX: 214-361-1882
Tech support: 800-526-8086
Tech support BBS: 214-361-1883
Specs Release date: 1995
Application: Network Management

Compatible with: PC-MS/DOS;
Apple Macintosh
Additional hardware/software re-
quired: Novell Netware
Network compatibility: Novell

Summary Combination of Saber LAN
Workstation, Saber LAN Workstation
for Macintosh Computers, Saber
Enterprise Application Manager,
Saber Server Manager and SDK.
Features menuing, centralized file
and software distribution, scripting
languages, automatic software/hard-
ware inventorying, remote control,
disk/print management, real-time
information viewing and management and event manager to track,
prioritize and queue pre-defined activities.

Product **Saber LAN Workstation (V.5.0)**
Company Saber Software Corp.
5944 Luther Lane, Ste. 1007
Dallas, TX 75225
800-338-8754; 214-361-8086
Direct sales: 800-338-8754, ext. 41
FAX: 214-361-1882
Tech support: 800-526-8086
Tech support BBS: 214-361-1883

Specs Mfr. suggested list price: $199 ($49
add'l node licenses)
Release date: 1994
Application: Network Management
Compatible with: Windows 3.X; PC-
MS/DOS
Minimum RAM required: 1MB
Disk storage required: 5MB
Additional hardware/software re-
quired: Windows 3.X
Network compatibility: Novell;
Banyan; LANtastic; LAN Server; MS-
NET; Microsoft Windows NT
Advanced Server
Source language: C
Customer support: phone support;
tech support via BBS
Site licensing available: Yes

Summary Integrated set of network utilities.
Provides tools for designing customized menus, tracking software licenses, managing disk space and
catching potential trouble spots.
Offers graphical and object-oriented
front-end to Windows. Features help
function. Includes printer management utilities for DOS and Windows,
DOS file management and security.

Product **Transcend Network Management**
for Windows
Company 3Com Corp.
P.O. Box 58145, 5400 Bayfront Plaza
Santa Clara, CA 95052-8145
800-638-3266; 408-764-5000
FAX: 408-764-5001
Tech support: 800-876-3266
Tech support BBS: 408-980-8204

Specs Release date: 1994
Application: Network Management
Compatible with: Windows 3.X
Minimum RAM required: 4MB
Disk storage required: 40MB
Additional hardware/software re-
quired: Windows 3.X
Network compatibility: Token-Ring;
Ethernet; Windows for Workgroups

Summary Allows network managers to inte-
grate administrative tasks on their
choice of computing environments
and management platforms.
Transcend Enterprise Manager for
Windows environment covers multiple types of network devices and
technologies and Transcend
Workgroup Manager handles administration of Ethernet LANs. User can
move from workgroup to enterprise
management as needed. Features
SmartAgent, hierarchical map, bit-
mapped hub view, password protection, alarm notification and activity
monitoring and thresholding.

Network/Protocol Analyzers

Product **Network General Reporter**

Company Network General Corp.
4200 Bohannon Dr.
Menlo Park, CA 94025-1097
800-764-3329; 415-473-2000
Direct sales: 800-846-6601
FAX: 415-321-0855
Tech support: 800-395-3151

Specs Mfr. suggested list price: $4,995
Release date: 1994
Application: Network Management
Compatible with: Windows 3.X
Minimum RAM required: 4MB
Disk storage required: 500MB
Additional hardware/software required: Windows 3.X
Network compatibility: Windows for Workgroups

Summary Application designed to help network administrators organize data collected by Sniffer network monitoring and analysis tools. Features 20 automated reports for displaying multiple views of collected RMON data. Reports can be used to track network traffic patterns, baseline performance and error trends for diagnosing network problems.

Product **Expert Sniffer Internetwork Analyzer**

Company Network General Corp.
4200 Bohannon Dr.
Menlo Park, CA 94025-1097
800-764-3329; 415-473-2000
Direct sales: 800-846-6601
FAX: 415-321-0855
Tech support: 800-395-3151

Specs Release date: 1993
Application: Network Management
Compatible with: PC-MS/DOS
Minimum RAM required: 8MB
Disk storage required: 130MB
Site licensing available: No

Summary Allows companies to directly manage expert systems-based problem solving for router-based internetworks. Finds network bottlenecks and offers recommendations. Offers features for analyzing/monitoring data traffic across internetworks including expert analysis of internetworks for automatic problem identification and analysis of LAN protocols over WANs.

Product **Distributed Sniffer System with Expert Analysis Application**

Company Network General Corp.
4200 Bohannon Dr.
Menlo Park, CA 94025-1097
800-764-3329; 415-473-2000
Direct sales: 800-846-6601
FAX: 415-321-0855
Tech support: 800-395-3151
Category: Software, Communications Networking Software

Specs Mfr. suggested list price: $7,495-$8,495
Release date: 1993
Application: Network Management
Compatible with: PC-MS/DOS
Site licensing available: No

Summary Gives organizations way to leverage network management resources across multiple locations and ability to address complexity crisis created by rapid network growth, shortage of skilled personnel and shrinking budgets. Allows users to troubleshoot and monitor internetwork from centralized locations.

Product **Distributed Sniffer System (V.2.2)**

Company Network General Corp.
4200 Bohannon Dr.
Menlo Park, CA 94025-1097
800-764-3329; 415-473-2000
Direct sales: 800-846-6601
FAX: 415-321-0855
Tech support: 800-395-3151

Specs Mfr. suggested list price: $4,995-$10,995
Release date: 1994
Application: Network Management
Compatible with: PC-MS/DOS
Minimum RAM required: 8MB
Disk storage required: 120MB
Network compatibility: Novell; Banyan; Token-Ring; Ethernet; DECnet; AppleTalk; NFS; TCP/IP
Source language: C
Site licensing available: No

Summary Network analysis system. Analyzes/processes information on individual network segments. Communicates through network to multiple central consoles. Provides text at 7 layers of protocol stack. Analyzes over 140 protocols and communicates across topologies connected by bridges/routers. Contains Sniffmaster/X which accesses SunNet Manager and HP OpenView network management from anywhere on network. Provides pager support.

Product **LANalyzer**
Company Novell, Inc.
122 East 1700 South
Provo, UT 84606-6194
800-453-1267; 801-429-7000
FAX: 801-429-5155
Tech support: 800-638-9273

Specs Mfr. suggested list price: $1,495
Release date: 1994
Application: Network Management
Compatible with: UnixWare
Minimum RAM required: 4MB
Disk storage required: 5MB
Network compatibility: Novell; NFS; AppleTalk; SNA; UnixWare
Site licensing available: No

Summary Provides protocol analysis to mid-sized networks. Captures network packet data on NetWare 3.X LANs and performs limited amount of decoding. Troubleshoots IBM mainframes and AS/400 computers, networked applications running on IBM equipment and related front-end devices.

Product **LANdecoder/e (V.2.1)**
Company Triticom
P.O. Box 444180
Eden Prairie, MN 55344
612-937-0772
FAX: 612-937-1998
Tech support: Use main no.
Tech support BBS: 612-829-0135

Specs Mfr. suggested list price: $945
Release date: 1993
Application: Network Management
Compatible with: PC-MS/DOS
Minimum RAM required: 512K
Disk storage required: 300K
Network compatibility: Novell; Ethernet; Banyan; TCP/IP; AppleTalk; Token-Ring; ARCnet; DECnet; NetBIOS; IEEE
Customer support: phone support
Site licensing available: Yes

Summary Captures and decodes data on Ethernet LANs. Diagnoses and solves network communication problems and allows user to monitor and tune network usage and performance. Features filtering and triggering.

Software Metering

Product **Saber Enterprise Application Manager (SEAM) (V.5.0)**
Company Saber Software Corp.
5944 Luther Lane, Ste. 1007
Dallas, TX 75225
800-338-8754; 214-361-8086
Direct sales: 800-338-8754, ext. 41
FAX: 214-361-1882
Tech support: 800-526-8086
Tech support BBS: 214-361-1883

Specs Mfr. suggested list price: $695; $19 (each addl. workstation)

Release date: 1994
Application: Network Management
Compatible with: Windows 3.X
Minimum RAM required: 512K
Disk storage required: 22K (client)
Additional hardware/software required: Windows 3.X; Novell Netware; Saber LAN Workstation
Network compatibility: Novell
Source language: C
Customer support: support agreement avail.
Site licensing available: Yes

Summary   NLM add-on to Saber LAN Workstation. Provides metering for NetWare 3.X or higher users by tracking applications across servers and on local hard drives and additional metering for DOS and Windows applications. Allows workgroups to share licenses. Maintains license compliance by locking out users who try to access applications whose copies are all in use. Able to meter DOS or Windows applications running under Windows without any TSR requirements.

Product   **SiteMeter (V.5.0)**
Company   McAfee Associates, Inc.
2710 Walsh Ave., Ste. 200
Santa Clara, CA 95051
800-866-6585; 408-988-3832
FAX: 408-970-9727
Tech support: 408-988-4181
Tech support BBS: 408-988-4004

Specs   Mfr. suggested list price: $495 (100-user); $995 (250-user)
Number sold: 60,000
Release date: 1994
Application: Network Management
Compatible with: PC-MS/DOS
Minimum RAM required: 2MB
Disk storage required: 8.5MB
Additional hardware/software required: Novell Netware
Network compatibility: Novell; PC-LAN; TCP/IP

Source language: C; Assembler
Customer support: Free unlimited phone support; tech support via BBS
Site licensing available: Yes

Summary   Provides network software control for NetWare LANs. Provides virus protection. Limits simultaneous use of software programs to insure compliance with license agreement. File server VAP/NLM module interacts with small TSR on each workstation to provide secure environments. Includes software metering capabilities under Windows.

Product   **Software Sentry (V.2.0)**
Company   Microsystems Software, Inc.
600 Worcester Rd.
Framingham, MA 01701-5342
800-489-2001; 508-879-9000
FAX: 508-626-8515
Tech support: 508-626-8513
Tech support BBS: 508-875-8009

Specs   Mfr. suggested list price: $295 per server (50-user); $595 per server (100-user); $895 per server (250-user)
Release date: 1994
Application: Network Management
Compatible with: PC-MS/DOS
Network compatibility: Novell; Banyan; DEC Pathworks; LAN Server; LANtastic
Source language: C; C++
Customer support: 120-day free phone support; tech support via BBS
Site licensing available: Yes

Summary   License-metering and network management tool for LANs with Windows and DOS clients. Manages application license use on LAN and on local PC hard drives. Monitors standalone applications and suites of applications to let administrators manage applications by usage, rather than by number of users. Provides application version control across network.

Virus Software

Product	**Norton AntiVirus (V.3.0)**
Company	Symantec Corp.
	10201 Torre Ave.
	Cupertino, CA 95014-2132
	800-441-7234; 408-253-9600
	FAX: 408-253-3968
	Tech support: 415-892-1424
	Tech support BBS: 503-484-6669
Specs	Mfr. suggested list price: $129
	Release date: 1993
	Application: Security/Auditing Software
	Compatible with: Windows 3.X; PC-MS/DOS
	Minimum RAM required: 512K
	Additional hardware/software required: Windows 3.X
	Network compatibility: Novell; 3Com; LAN Manager; Banyan; LAN Server; LANtastic
	Customer support: tech support via on-line access; tech support via BBS; fax on demand phone/fax support; unlimited 90-day phone support; PriorityCare, PremiumCare support agreement avail.
	Site licensing available: No
Summary	Program designed to detect and intercept more than 1,500 PC viruses and repair files damaged by viruses. Includes memory-resident virus intercept feature to check applications and files loaded into memory. Features password protection option. Detects and destroys Michelangelo virus. Includes both Windows and DOS interfaces.

Storage Management

Product	**ARCserve for NetWare DOS Edition—The Backup Solution (V.4.02)**
Company	Cheyenne Software, Inc.

	3 Expressway Plaza
	Roslyn Hgts., NY 11577
	516-484-5110
	Direct sales: 800-243-9462
	FAX: 516-484-3446
	Tech support: 800-243-9832
	Tech support BBS: 516-484-3445
Specs	Mfr. suggested list price: $295-$7,295
	Release date: 1994
	Application: Disk/Tape/File Utilities
	Compatible with: PC-MS/DOS
	Minimum RAM required: 640K (workstation); 200K (server)
	Disk storage required: 600K (workstation); 150-180K (server)
	Additional hardware/software required: Novell Netware
	Network compatibility: Novell
	Source language: C
	Customer support: toll-free phone support; tech support via BBS
	Site licensing available: Yes
Summary	NLM integrated data management service for Novell networks, provides continuous backup and restore capabilities to wide range of local hard disk, optical or tape devices. Data verification capabilities can supply confirmation of successful, complete backup jobs. Requires Novell NetWare 3.X or higher.

Product	**ARCserve for NetWare Windows Edition (V.5.01)**
Company	Cheyenne Software, Inc.
	3 Expressway Plaza
	Roslyn Hgts., NY 11577
	516-484-5110
	Direct sales: 800-243-9462
	FAX: 516-484-3446
	Tech support: 800-243-9832
	Tech support BBS: 516-484-3445
Specs	Mfr. suggested list price: $395-$9,295
	Release date: 1994
	Application: Disk/Tape/File Utilities
	Compatible with: Windows 3.X
	Minimum RAM required: 4MB
	Disk storage required: 10MB

Additional hardware/software required: Windows 3.X; Novell Netware
Network compatibility: Novell
Customer support: toll-free phone support; tech support via BBS
Site licensing available: Yes

Summary Integrated data management service for Novell networks. Provides continuous backup and restore capabilities to wide range of local hard disks, optical or tape devices. Data verification capabilities can supply confirmation of complete backup jobs.

Product   **ARCserve for Windows NT (V.1.0)**
Company   Cheyenne Software, Inc.
3 Expressway Plaza
Roslyn Hgts., NY 11577
516-484-5110
Direct sales: 800-243-9462
FAX: 516-484-3446
Tech support: 800-243-9832
Tech support BBS: 516-484-3445

Specs   Mfr. suggested list price: $895
Release date: 1994
Application: Disk/Tape/File Utilities
Compatible with: Windows NT
Source language: C
Customer support: toll-free phone support; tech support via BBS

Summary   Provides peer-to-peer backup of Windows NT and Windows for Workgroup clients. Provides continuous backup and restore capabilities to wide range of local hard disk, optical or tape devices. Data verification capabilities can supply confirmation of successful, complete backup jobs.

Product   **Backup Director (V.4.0) NLM**
Company   Palindrome Corp. (subsidiary of Seagate Technology, Inc.)
600 E. Diehl Rd.
Naperville, IL 60563-1476
800-288-4912; 708-505-3300
FAX: 708-505-7917
Tech support: Use main no.

Specs   Tech support BBS: 708-505-3336
Mfr. suggested list price: $995-$1,595
Release date: 1995
Application: Network Management
Compatible with: PC-MS/DOS
Minimum RAM required: 640K
Additional hardware/software required: Novell Netware
Network compatibility: Novell
Customer support: phone/fax support; tech support via BBS

Summary   NLM that allows network administrator to backup files automatically, customize and schedule backup functions and select individual files for backup. Provides GUI, automatic tape labeling, file tracking and file finder utility. Prompts network administrator for correct tape to insert for restore or backup. Requires Novell NetWare 3.X or higher. Workgroup version available.

Product   **Backup Exec for Windows NT Server**
Company   Arcada Software, Inc.
37 Skyline Dr., Ste. 1101
Lake Mary, FL 32746
800-3ARCADA; 407-333-7500
FAX: 407-333-7770
Tech support: Use toll-free no.
Tech support BBS: 407-444-9979

Specs   Mfr. suggested list price: $795
Release date: 1994
Application: Disk/Tape/File Utilities
Compatible with: Windows NT
Customer support: toll-free phone support; tech support via BBS
Site licensing available: Yes

Summary   Full-featured, 32-bit backup application created specifically for Microsoft Windows NT Server. Features global network view, data compression, disk grooming, e-mail notification, file versioning, multi-drive concurrent backup, Windows NT file system support, scheduled/unattended backup, open/skipped file processing, multiple verification methods and optional loader support.

Product	**Backup Exec for NetWare—Windows Workstation Edition**
Company	Arcada Software, Inc.
	37 Skyline Dr., Ste. 1101
	Lake Mary, FL 32746
	800-3ARCADA; 407-333-7500
	FAX: 407-333-7770
	Tech support: Use toll-free no.
	Tech support BBS: 407-444-9979
Specs	Mfr. suggested list price: $149
	Release date: 1994
	Application: Disk/Tape/File Utilities
	Compatible with: Windows 3.X; PC-MS/DOS
	Minimum RAM required: 640K (DOS); 2MB (Windows)
	Disk storage required: 2MB
	Additional hardware/software required: Windows 3.X
	Network compatibility: Novell; Windows for Workgroups
	Customer support: phone support; tech support via BBS; tech support via on-line access
	Site licensing available: Yes
Summary	Backs up NetWare 2.X or 3.X server to Windows or DOS workstation. Backs up drive of workstation on which it resides but does not cover hard drives of other client PCs.

Product	**Conner HSM (V.3.0)**
Company	Arcada Software, Inc.
	37 Skyline Dr., Ste. 1101
	Lake Mary, FL 32746
	800-3ARCADA; 407-333-7500
	FAX: 407-333-7770
	Tech support: Use toll-free no.
	Tech support BBS: 407-444-9979
Specs	Mfr. suggested list price: $7,500
	Release date: 1993
	Application: Network Management
	Compatible with: PC-MS/DOS
	Minimum RAM required: 4MB
	Disk storage required: 1MB

Additional hardware/software required: Novell Netware; Adaptec SCSI controller: optical jukebox; tape library
Network compatibility: Novell
Customer support: Unlimited toll-free phone support; tech support via BBS
Site licensing available: Yes

Summary	System designed to reduce storage requirements of NetWare file servers. Allows network administrator to create system that automatically migrates least-used files to dedicated server and combination of hard drives, magneto-optical media and tape drives. Enables administrators to specify amount of time files remain unused before they are moved off file server onto HSM hard drive.

Product	**HSM Software (V.3.1)**
Company	Palindrome Corp. (subsidiary of Seagate Technology, Inc.)
	600 E. Diehl Rd.
	Naperville, IL 60563-1476
	800-288-4912; 708-505-3300
	FAX: 708-505-7917
	Tech support: Use main no.
	Tech support BBS: 708-505-3336
Specs	Mfr. suggested list price: $2,995
	Release date: 1993
	Application: Network Management
	Compatible with: PC-MS/DOS
	Additional hardware/software required: Novell Netware
	Network compatibility: Novell
Summary	Hierarchical Storage Management software. Automates identification and migration of infrequently used data to secondary storage and automatically recalls migrated files to primary storage when they are accessed.

Product	**Jumbo 250 DJ-20 (Data Compression)**

Company   Colorado Memory Systems, Inc.
          (subsidiary of Hewlett-Packard Co.)
          800 S. Taft Ave.
          Loveland, CO 80537-9929
          800-845-7905; 303-669-8000
          Direct sales: 800-451-4523
          FAX: 303-667-0997
          Tech support: 303-635-1500
Specs   Mfr. suggested list price: $199
          Standard warranty included: 1 yr.
          Date announced: 1990
          Product classification: Mini-
          Cartridge
          Capacity: 250MB
          Streaming tape unit: Yes
          Data transfer rate: 125K/sec.
          Recording density: 14700 bpi
          Recording tracks: 28
          Serpentine tracking: Yes
          Tape width: 1/4 in.

Product   **Network Archivist (V.4.0) NLM**
Company   Palindrome Corp. (subsidiary of
          Seagate Technology, Inc.)
          600 E. Diehl Rd.
          Naperville, IL 60563-1476
          800-288-4912; 708-505-3300
          FAX: 708-505-7917
          Tech support: Use main no.
          Tech support BBS: 708-505-3336
Specs   Mfr. suggested list price: $1,895-
          $3,295
          Release date: 1995
          Application: Network Management
          Compatible with: PC-MS/DOS
          Minimum RAM required: 640K
          Disk storage required: 1MB
          Additional hardware/software re-
          quired: Novell Netware
          Network compatibility: Novell
          Customer support: phone/fax sup-
          port; tech support via BBS
          Site licensing available: No
Summary   Manages all tapes. Maintains short-
          term back-ups and long-term
          archives by updating tapes. Selects
          and performs all archiving functions.
          Manages all tape rotations and up-

dates. Backs up and restores all
Novell extended attributes, directory
trustees and bindery files. Handles
file server grooming.

Product   **Network Archivist DOS (V.3.1)**
Company   Palindrome Corp. (subsidiary of
          Seagate Technology, Inc.)
          600 E. Diehl Rd.
          Naperville, IL 60563-1476
          800-288-4912; 708-505-3300
          FAX: 708-505-7917
          Tech support: Use main no.
          Tech support BBS: 708-505-3336
Specs   Mfr. suggested list price: $1,695-
          $2,895
          Release date: 1994
          Application: Network Management
          Compatible with: PC-MS/DOS
          Additional hardware/software re-
          quired: Novell Netware
          Network compatibility: Novell
          Customer support: Unlimited toll-
          free phone/fax support; tech support
          via BBS
Summary   DOS version of Palindrome's
          Network Archivist tape backup soft-
          ware. Manages all tapes. Maintains
          short-term backups and long-term
          archives by updating tapes. Selects
          and performs all archiving functions.
          Manages all tape rotations and up-
          dates. Backs up and restores all
          Novell extended attributes, directory
          trustees and bindery files. Handles
          file server grooming.

Product   **Norton Backup (V.2.2)**
Company   Symantec Corp.
          10201 Torre Ave.
          Cupertino, CA 95014-2132
          800-441-7234; 408-253-9600
          FAX: 408-253-3968
          Tech support: 415-892-1424
          Tech support BBS: 503-484-6669
Specs   Mfr. suggested list price: $149
          Number sold: 25,000
          Release date: 1993

Appendix A

Application: Disk/Tape/File Utilities
Compatible with: PC-MS/DOS
Minimum RAM required: 512K
Disk storage required: 2MB
Network compatibility: Novell;
3Com; NetBIOS; Banyan; PC-LAN;
LAN Manager; LANtastic
Source language: C; Assembler
Customer support: tech support via
on-line access; tech support via BBS;
fax on demand phone/fax support;
unlimited 90-day phone support;
PriorityCare, PremiumCare support
agreement available.
Site licensing available: Yes
Summary   Backup and restore facility. Protects
against loss of data due to hard disk
crash, virus-related file damage or
user error. Includes graphic-like user
interface, pop-up menus, simultaneous reading/writing of disk data to
speed backup, 3 levels of data verification and 3 levels of data compression.

Product   **Norton Backup for Windows (V.3.0)**
Company   Symantec Corp.
10201 Torre Ave.
Cupertino, CA 95014-2132
800-441-7234; 408-253-9600
FAX: 408-253-3968
Tech support: 415-892-1424
Tech support BBS: 503-484-6669
Specs   Mfr. suggested list price: $149
Release date: 1993
Application: Disk/Tape/File Utilities
Compatible with: Windows 3.X
Minimum RAM required: 2MB
Additional hardware/software re-
quired: Windows 3.X
Network compatibility: Novell;
3Com; LAN Manager
Customer support: tech support via
on-line access; tech support via BBS;
fax on demand phone/fax support;
unlimited 90-day phone support;
PriorityCare, PremiumCare support
agreement available.

Site licensing available: No
Summary   Utilizes Windows 3.X multitasking
capabilities to allow users to backup
files in background while running
other application programs. Runs
unattended scheduled backups to
floppy disks, network servers and
any other DOS device. Rejects bad
floppy disks and detects corrupted
files during backup. Detects floppy-
drive capacity and automatically detects changes to PC.

SNMP

Product   **HP OpenView Extensible SNMP
Agent (Rel.1.0)**
Company   Hewlett-Packard Co.
3000 Hanover St.
Palo Alto, CA 94304-1181
800-752-0900; 800 387-3867 (CD);
415-857-1501
Direct sales: 800-637-7740 (HP
Direct)
FAX: 800-333-1917
Tech support: 800-858-8867
Tech support BBS: 415-852-0256
Specs   Mfr. suggested list price: $1,000-
$300,000
Release date: 1992
Application: Network Management
Compatible with: HP 9000 series 300,
400, 700, 800/HP-UX; Sun
SPARCstation/SunOS
Minimum RAM required: 8MB (HP);
12MB (Sun)
Site licensing available: No
Summary   Monitors systems and their applica-
tions and printers. Interacts with
SNMP management station.
Manages devices like routers, bridges
and hubs, as well as computers,
printers, applications, users and
databases.

Product   **NetView (V.2, Rel.4)**

Company   IBM (International Business
Machines)
Old Orchard Rd.
Armonk, NY 10504
800-426-3333; 914-765-1900
Direct sales: 800-426-7695 (IBM PC
Direct)
Tech support: 800-237-5511
Tech support BBS: 919-517-0001;
800-847-7211 (OS2)

Specs   Mfr. suggested list price: $31,060-
$85,680
Release date: 1993
Application: Network Management
Compatible with: IBM/MVS/XA,
MVS/ESA, VM/ESA, VSE/VSAM,
ACF/VTAM
Lease price: Lease $386-$3,750 per
mo.
Customer support: Maint. fee $90-
$205 per mo.

Summary   Handles problem reporting, messages, alerts and management service units. Restores services after
interruption, substitutes resources
for those that fail, reroutes traffic and
reactivates resources, and handles
startups and shutdowns automatically. Includes NetView Graphic
Monitor and Resource Object Data
Manager. Supports SNA, TCP/IP, OSI
and APPN network protocols.

Product   **NetView for Windows (V.1.0)**
Company   IBM (International Business
Machines)
Old Orchard Rd.
Armonk, NY 10504
800-426-3333; 914-765-1900
Direct sales: 800-426-7695 (IBM PC
Direct)
Tech support: 800-237-5511
Tech support BBS: 919-517-0001;
800-847-7211 (OS2)

Specs   Mfr. suggested list price: $1,895
Application: Network Management
Compatible with: Windows 3.X

Additional hardware/software required: Windows 3.X

Summary   Turns Windows workstation into low-
end SNMP management platform for
hubs, bridges, routers and switches.
Object-oriented database with
Object Browser Support enables user
to access records while real-time
graphical presentation of network
performance monitors Token-Ring
and Ethernet LANs. Notifies operator
when performance thresholds are
exceeded.

Product   **NetWare Management System
(V.2.1)**
Company   Novell, Inc.
122 East 1700 South
Provo, UT 84606-6194
800-453-1267; 801-429-7000
FAX: 801-429-5155
Tech support: 800-638-9273

Specs   Mfr. suggested list price: $2,495
Release date: 1993
Application: Network Management
Compatible with: Windows 3.X
Minimum RAM required: 12MB
Disk storage required: 40-80MB
Additional hardware/software re-
quired: Windows 3.X; Novell NetWare
Network compatibility: Novell
Site licensing available: Yes

Summary   Network management platform.
Reduces network traffic by allowing
management data to be processed
locally. Components include agents,
server and console. Tracks workstations, file servers and devices without forwarding all management data
across network to single location.
Includes SmartLink which integrates
NMS snap-in applications.

Product   **VisiNet Enterprise for Windows
(V.2.5)**
Company   VisiSoft, Inc.
2700 Northeast Expwy., Ste. B-700
Atlanta, GA 30345

Specs
800-847-4638; 404-320-0077
FAX: 404-320-0450
Tech support: Use main no.
Mfr. suggested list price: $795-$2,495
Release date: 1993
Application: Network Management
Compatible with: Windows 3.X
Minimum RAM required: 4MB
Disk storage required: 4MB
Additional hardware/software required: Windows 3.X
Network compatibility: LANtastic; LAN Server; Novell; NetBIOS; Banyan; LAN Manager; SNMP; NT Advanced Server
Source language: C; C++
Customer support: 1 yr. phone support
Site licensing available: Yes

Summary
Online, hardware independent, Windows-based LAN network management system. Provides graphical view of all information about network in hierarchical map format. Script language allows user to directly address network OS to set alarms.

Product **Microsoft System Manager (MSM)**
Company Microsoft Corp.
One Microsoft Way
Redmond, WA 98052-6399
800-426-9400; 206-882-8080
Direct sales: 800-MSPRESS
FAX: 206-635-6100
Tech support: 206-454-2030; 206-637-7098 (Windows)
Tech support BBS: 206-936-6735

Electronic Mail and Associated Products

Product **cc:Mail**
Company Lotus Development Corp.
800 El Camino Real, W
Mountain View, CA 94044

800-448-2500; 415-961-8800
FAX: 415-961-0840

Summary
Electronic mail system for PC LANs. Supports WAN connectivity with any combination of server-to-server, LAN-to-LAN, and remote PC-to-LAN messaging, as well as connection to other e-mail systems. Provides notification of new mail, distributed mail server software, single common post office, encrypted compressed messages and user directory files, paper mail terminology and tools, automatic conversion among popular graphic displays, and remote PC access. Includes notification of new mail messages provided by bell tone and either flashing desktop icon or pop-up dialog box.

Product **tPost LAN (V.5.1)**
Company Coker Electronics
1430 Lexington Ave.
San Mateo, CA 94402
415-573-5515

Summary
Electronic mail package for LANs and multi-user systems with built-in gateway to remote LANs and stand-alone field PCs. Includes function key-driven routines, private and public distribution lists, attachments, remote command execution, e-mail-to-fax option, and forms option.

Product **Cross+Point (V.5.24)**
Company Cross International Corp.
854 Walnut Street, Ste. B
Boulder, CO 80302
303-440-7313
FAX: 303-442-2616

Summary
Electronic mail system with groupware, computer conferencing, or thought processing. Includes bulletin board, on-line messaging, and windowing. Includes encryption and pop-up notification and fax/e-mail interface to many PC-fax boards.

Handles internetworking for LAN-to-LAN communications.

Product	**DaVinci eMAIL for DOS & Windows (V.2.5)**
Company	DaVinci Systems Corp.
	P.O. Box 17449
	Raleigh, NC 27619
	800-328-4624; 919-881-4320
	FAX: 919-787-3550
Summary	Memory-resident electronic mail program. Provides pull-down menus, mouse support, and security. Any number of files can be attached to any message. Receivers are notified of incoming messages by pop-up and tone.

Product	**All-In-1 Desktop for MS-DOS (V.1.1)**
Company	Digital Equipment Corp.
	146 Main St.
	Maynard, MA 01754-2571
	508-493-5111
	FAX: 508-493-8780
Summary	Allows MS-DOS-based PC users to access All-In-1 applications on VAX. Includes individual and group calendaring, group conferencing, electronic mail, facility for launching application from within All-In-1, auto-dial function, phone book, facility for logging phone numbers called and length of calls, and decision-support tools.

Product	**Edge Office**
Company	Edge Systems, Inc.
	1245 Corporate Blvd., Fourth Floor
	Aurora, IL 60504-6420
	708-898-0021
	FAX: 708-898-5406
Summary	Consists of integrated modules including Event Notification, File Cabinet, Telephone Book, Telephone Message Notepad, Electronic Mail, Time Manager, Reverse Polish Notation Calculator, ASE editor, and Document Routing.

Product	**Futurus MAIL Plus (V.2.11)**
Company	Futurus Corp.
	211 Perimeter Circle Parkway, Suite 910
	Atlanta, GA 30346
	800-327-8296
	FAX: 404-392-9313
Summary	A peer-to-peer e-mail system including phone messaging and real-time chat modules. Available in both Windows and DOS platforms. Provides instant notification of all module functions. User-configurable options allow for individual needs and tastes. Offers access to faxes, including zoom in, zoom out, flipping and printing. Offers seamless plug-and-play communication with all mainframe e-mail packages.

Product	**The Major BBS (V.5.11)**
Company	Galacticomm, Inc.
	4101 Southwest 47th Ave., Suite 101
	Ft. Lauderdale, FL 33314
	305-583-5990
	FAX: 305-583-7846
Summary	Multi-user bulletin board system. File upload and download, teleconferencing, classified ads, system information, electronic mail, user information display/edit, shopping, and entertainment/games. Supports up to 256 simultaneous users. E-mail offers file attachments carbon copies, return receipts, message forwarding/quoting, and distribution lists.

Product	**PROFS Extended Mail**
Company	IBM
	Old Orchard Road
	Armonk, NY 10504
	800-426-3333; 914-765-1900

Product	**Officepower**
Company	ICL Business Systems
	9801 Muirlands Blvd.

Irvine, CA 92718
714-458-7282
FAX: 714-458-6257

Summary
Multifunctional office management system. Word processing, electronic filing, e-mail, appointment calendars, telephone and address dictionaries, phone message log and routing, full-function math, accounting, and electronic spreadsheets. Optional PC, Mac, Unix integration with GUI.

Product **PostMark E-Mail**
Company Network Associates
80 East 100 North
Provo, UT 84606
801-373-7888

Summary
Combines its MHS-compatible e-mail system with ASCII-standard word processor. Performs standard e-mail functions and group discussions.

Product **Notes**
Company Lotus Development Corp.
55 Cambridge Pkwy.
Cambridge, MA 02142
800-343-5414; 617-577-8500
FAX: 617-225-1299

Summary
Gives you high-powered groupware with strong e-mail. The high price and heavy RAM usage may turn you away, but its unique detailed features lure you on.

Product **Promulgate/PC**
Company Management Systems Designers, Inc.
131 Park St., NE
Vienna, VA 22180
703-281-7440
FAX: 703-281-7636

Summary
Electronic mail gateway that allows 3+Mail and 3+Open Mail users to transparently exchange messages with Unix-based systems. Requires 3Com EtherLink card.

Product **Microsoft Mail**
Company Microsoft Corp.
One Microsoft Way
Redmond, WA 98052
800-227-4679

Summary
Provides users with access to MCI from any LAN. Sends messages, spreadsheets, faxes, and any type of file. Sends and receives messages through remote electronic mail systems (REMS) account to IBM PROFS, DEC VAX-mail, All-In-1, Wang Office, 3Com 3+ Mail, and CompuServe. Requires Consumers Software's Inter-Network.

Product **Wildcat! (V.4.0)**
Company Mustang Software, Inc.
P.O. Box 2264
Bakersfield, CA 93303
800-999-9619; 805-395-0223
FAX: 805-395-0713

Summary
BBS system. Offers e-mail, file transfer, questionnaires, and bulletins. Provides customizable display files and security for 50 levels of users. Messaging capabilities include ability to reply, forward to third parties, send carbon copies, request return receipt, and print. Net/multiline available. Versions available supporting 1—250 lines with or without Pro! series utilities.

Product **Notework**
Company ON Technology Group
1 Cambridge Center, Kendall Square
Cambridge, MA 02142-9773
800-697-9273; 617-374-1400
FAX: 617-374-1433

Summary
Pop-up e-mail program. Includes pop-up telephoning, messaging, and file transfer. Allows user to print, export, and confirm receipt of messages, customize editing commands, attach files to notes, notify others of incoming calls, and send urgent messages.

Product   **X.400 Gateway**
Company   Xsoft (Div. of Xerox Corp.)
            3400 Hillview Ave.
            Palo Alto, CA 94303
            800-428-2995; 415-424-0111
            FAX: 415-813-7162
Summary   Provides communications connec-
            tivity between TCP and OSI elec-
            tronic mail networks. Exchange of
            mail messages between X.400-based
            e-mail services and Unix systems'
            mail applications is transparent.
            Conforms to government's GOSIP
            standard and complies with Defense
            Communications Agency's OSI mi-
            gration strategy.

Product   **QuickTalk**
Company   SilverSoft, Inc.
            1301 Geranium St., NW
            Washington, DC 20012
            202-291-8212
Summary   Calls up electronic mail system and
            enters text directly into word proces-
            sor or spreadsheet. Uploads or
            downloads file while in background.
            Converts up to 40 different strings of
            characters while reading in file or
            text.

Product   **OfficeNet**
Company   Source Data Systems, Inc.
            950 Ridgemount Dr., NE
            Cedar Rapids, IA 52402-7222
            800-553-7305; 319-393-3343
            FAX: 319-393-5173
Summary   Includes word processing, electronic
            mail, scheduling and calendars,
            spreadsheet, file management,
            phone list, notepad, and calculator
            functions.

Product   **CompletE-MAIL/MHS**
Company   Transend Corp.
            884 Portola Rd.
            Portola Valley, CA 94025
            415-851-3402

            FAX: 415-851-1031
Summary   LAN-based e-mail system. Supports
            mail handling service standard.
            Creates, exchanges, and manages
            messages, DOS files, and electronic
            files. Intuitive, icon-based window-
            ing user interface. Incorporates word
            processor or imports data from user's
            word processor.

Product   **LAN Office**
Company   Wang Laboratories, Inc.
            One Industrial Way, Mail Stop 014-
            A1B
            Lowell, MA 01851
            800-225-0654; 508-459-5000
Summary   Includes electronic mail, time man-
            agement, directory services, note
            services, user profile customization,
            and menu modification. Compatible
            with Banyan VINES, Novell Advanced
            NetWare, 3Com 3+ Share, and IBM
            PC LAN Program.

Product   **WordPerfect GroupWise**
Company   WordPerfect Corp.
            1555 N. Technology Way
            Orem, UT 84057
            800-321-4566; 801-225-5000
            FAX: 801-222-4477
Summary   Office automation package for LANs.
            Includes shell menu for integration
            of programs, clipboard, electronic
            mail, notebook with auto-dial fea-
            ture, scheduler, file manager, calcula-
            tor, calendar, macro editor, and
            program editor. Includes Novell's
            wide-area message handling service
            (MHS). Includes WPScheduler,
            WPNotebook, and WPFile Manager.

LAN Fax Gateways and Related Products

Product   **FaxPress**
Company   Castelle

3255-3 Scott Blvd.
Santa Clara, CA 95051
800-289-7555; 408-496-0474
FAX: 408-496-0502

Specs   Price: $3,295-$4,595
Number installed to date: 1,000
Date announced: 1994
Shareable devices: Facsimile
Network compatibility: Ethernet;
IBM Token-Product-Ring

Product   **GammaFax CP-4/AEB/LSI**
Company   GammaLink
1314 Chesapeake Terrace
Sunnyvale, CA 94089
800-FAX-4PCS; 408-744-1400
FAX: 408-744-1900

Specs   Price: $2,995
Date announced: 1993
Group compatibility: CCITT Group 3
Document transmit rate: 14.4Kbps
Standard features: Broadcasting;
Background operation; Auto cover
page; Scheduling

Product   **NetFax FaxServer**
Company   OAZ Communications, Inc.
44920 Osgood Rd.
Fremont, CA 94539-6101
800-NET-FAX3; 510-226-0171
FAX: 510-226-7079

Specs   Price: $1,995
Release Date: 1992
System compatibility: PC-MS/DOS;
OS/2
Network compatibility: Novell

Summary   Networked-based computer fax solution for sending, receiving, viewing
and managing fax messages.
Includes fax board, fax server software and fax client software for DOS
and Windows users.

Product   **PureFax Plus Fax Server**
Company   Pure Data, Inc.
1740 S. I-35
Carrollton, TX 75006
800-662-8210; 214-242-2040

FAX: 214-242-9487
Specs   Price: $995
Date announced: 1993
Network compatibility: Ethernet;
Token Ring
Shareable devices: Facsimile

ISDN Adapters and Equipment

Product   **Pipeline 50 Workgroup Access
Server**
Company   Ascend Communications, Inc.
1275 Harbor Bay Pkwy.
Alameda, CA 94502
800-ASCEND-4; 510-769-6001
FAX: 510-814-2300

Specs   Price: $1,495-$1,695
Date announced: 1994
Description: Ethernet to BRI ISDN
router
Local or remote: Remote
Configuration: Standalone
Number of LAN interfaces: 1
Network compatibility: Ethernet
IEEE standard: IEEE-802.3 10Base2;;
10BaseT
LAN speed: 10Mbps
Protocols supported: IP; IPX; PPP
Number of WAN interfaces: 1
Serial interfaces supported: T1;
ISDN; 56K bps services

Product   **Everyware STD/BRI Bridge CB-400**
Company   Combinet, Inc.
333 W. El Camino Real
Sunnyvale, CA 94087
800-967-6651; 408-522-9020
FAX: 408-522-4600

Specs   Price: $2,190
Date announced: 1991
Description: ISDN BRI to Ethernet
bridge
Local or remote: Remote
Number of LAN interfaces: 1
Network compatibility: Ethernet

Media type: Thin coax; UTP
LAN speed: 10 Mbps
Number of WAN interfaces: 1
Serial interfaces supported: RS-232
Packet filtering rate: 14,400 pps

Product	**PC IMAC**
Company	DigiBoard
	6400 Flying Cloud Drive
	Eden Prairie, MN 55344-3322
	800-344-4273; 612-943-9020
	Direct Sales: 800-437-7241
Specs	Price: $795-895

Date announced: 1993
Description: ISDN Terminal adapters
Compatibility: ISA; EISA; MCA
Line access standard: Basic Rate
Interface (2B+D)
Physical interfaces supported: RJ-45
Central Office switch supported:
AT&T 5ESS; Northern Telecom DMS-100
Command set: Hayes AT
Additional Features: Circuit switched data

Product	**IMAC**
Company	DigiBoard
	6400 Flying Cloud Drive
	Eden Prairie, MN 55344-3322
	800-344-4273; 612-943-9020
	Direct Sales: 800-437-7241
Specs	Price: $1,695

Date announced: 1991
Network compatibility: Ethernet
Configuration: Standalone
Serial interfaces supported: RS-232
Number of LAN interfaces: 1
LAN speed: 10Mbps
IEEE standard: IEEE-802.3 10Base2;
10Base5; 10BaseT
Number of WAN interfaces: 1
Packet filtering rate: 14,400 pps
Packet forwarding rate: 250 pps

Summary Additional features: Inverse multi-plexing; ISDN protocol analysis; IP; host

Product	**LD-LAN E-101**
Company	Extension Technology Corp.
	30 Hollis Street
	Framingham, MA 01701-8616
	800-856-2672; 508-872-7748
Specs	Price: $1,195

Description: ISDN Terminal Adapters
Date Announced: 1992
Compatibility: ISA
Line access standard: Basic Rate
Interface (2B+D)
Physical interfaces supported: RS-232C
Rate adaptation standard: V.120
Central Office switch supported:
AT&T 5ESS; Northern Telecom DMS-100

Product	**LD-LAN E-201**
Company	Extension Technology Corp.
	30 Hollis Street
	Framingham, MA 01701-8616
	800-856-2672; 508-872-7748
Specs	Price: $1,495

Description: ISDN Terminal Adapters
Date Announced: 1992
Compatibility: EISA
Line access standard: Basic Rate
Interface (2B+D)
Physical interfaces supported: RS-232C
Rate adaption standard: V.120
Central Office switch supported:
AT&T 5ESS; Northern Telecom DMS-100

Product	**LANline 5240I**
Company	Gandalf Systems Corp.
	9 North Olney Ave., Cherry Hill
	Industrial Center-9
	Cherry Hill, NY 08003-1688
	800-GANDALF: 609-424-9400
	FAX: 609-751-4376
Specs	Price: $2,695

Date announced: 1994
Description: Bridge to Ethernet
Local or remote: Remote
Configuration: Standalone

Number of LAN interfaces: 1
Network compatibility: Ethernet
LAN speed: 10 Mbps
Number of WAN interfaces: 1
Serial interfaces supported: RS-232;
V.35
Additional functions: Integral ISDN
terminal adapter

Product	**ISDN PC Adapter**
Company	Hayes Microcomputer Products, Inc.
	5835 Peachtree Corners, E
	Norcross, GA 30092-3405
	800-96-HAYES; 404-840-9200
	FAX: 404-441-1213
Specs	Price: $1,199
	Date announced: 1990
	Compatibility: ISA
	Line access standard: Basic Rate
	Interface (2B+D)
	Reference point: S/T Interface
	Physical interfaces supported: RJ-11
	Rate adaption standard: V.120
	Central Office switch supported:
	AT&T 5ESS; Northern Telecom DMS-100; National ISDN-1
	Command set: Hayes AT
	Additional features: Circuit switched data; packet switched data; built-in diagnostics

Product	**RemoteExpress ISDN LAN Adapter**
Company	Intel Corp.
	5200 NE Elam Young Parkway
	Hillsboro, OR 97124-6497
	800-538-3373; 503-629-7354
	FAX: 503-629-7580
Specs	Price: $499
	Date Announced: 1994
	Compatibility: ISA
	Line access standard: Basic Rate
	Interface (2B+D)
	Physical interfaces supported: RS-232C

Network-Operating Systems

Product	**LANtastic (V.6.0)**
Company	Artisoft, Inc.
	2202 N. Forbes Blvd.
	Tucson, AZ 85745
	800-846-9762; 602-670-7100
	FAX: 602-670-7101
Summary	A peer-to-peer LAN that connects up to 500 users. Provides printer, disk, CD-ROM and file sharing, e-mail and local and network disk backup. Supports NetBIOS-compatible adapters, chat and voice mail with sounding board adapters on each PC. Includes resource caching and despooling feature.

Product	**CorStream**
Company	Artisoft, Inc.
	2202 N. Forbes Blvd.
	Tucson, AZ 85745
	800-846-9762; 602-670-7100
	FAX: 602-670-7101
Summary	Server for LANtastic operating system that combines LANtastic NLM and Novell NetWare OS. Provides fault tolerance, file system/media management, mission-critical reliability and applications capability. Built on 32-bit multitasking, multi-thread OS and can seek data across multiple-disk drives. Allows user to install as much memory as needed for optimal throughput.

Product	**VINES (V.5.54)**
Company	Banyan Systems, Inc.
	120 Flanders Rd.
	Westboro, MA 01581-1033
	800-222-6926; 508-898-1000
	FAX: 508-898-1755
Summary	Integrated, distributed network OS for local or global internetworking and management of PCs, minicomputers and mainframes. Creates en-

terprise-wide multi-vendor networks. Offers transparent WAN and LAN bridging. Provides fine-grained security, expanded printer support and high-capacity disk support.

Product **OS/2 LAN Server (V.3.01)**
Company IBM
Old Orchard Rd.
Armonk, NY 10504
800-426-3333; 914-765-1900
Summary Supports OS/2 Requestor portion of IBM's OS/2 Extended Edition (V.1.2) Includes most of Microsoft LAN Manager's capabilities. Supports 16 and 32-bit OSs. Provides double-byte character set, Windows support and OEM enabling. Provides disk mirroring/duplexing and local server security. CD-ROM version available.

Product **InvisibleLAN (V.3.44)**
Company Invisible Software, Inc.
1142 Chess Dr.
Foster City, CA 94404
800-982-2962; 415-570-5967
FAX: 415-570-6017
Summary Peer-to-peer network OS. Designed for use over industry-standard coaxial cable and twisted-pair wiring. Operates with both DOS and Windows. Includes expanded memory managers, menu-driven or command-line installation and initialization, online help, disk-caching utilities, file sharing, printer spooling, e-mail, security and automatic reconnection.

Product **Windows NT**
Company Microsoft Corp.
One Microsoft Way
Redmond, WA 98052-6399
800-426-9400; 206-882-8080
FAX: 206-883-8101
Summary Client/server 32 bit preemptive multitasking OS. Runs 32-bit, MS-DOS, Windows, POSIX and character

based OS/2 1.X applications. Accesses up to 2G of virtual memory per application and terabytes of storage. Includes event viewer for monitoring the system, security and applications event logs and event logger for displaying details. Provides point-and-click access to file manager, printer manager, control panel, user manager, disk administrator, event viewer, performance monitor, backup and command prompt.

Product **NetWare (V.4.2)**
Novell, Inc.
122 East 1700 South
Provo, UT 84606-6194
800-453-1267; 801-379-7000
FAX: 801-429-5155
Summary LAN OS. Various levels for enterprise-wide and workgroup computing. Provides user transparent connectivity, internetworking capabilities, multiple remote connections, LAN to host communications, data protection, resource accounting, security, and programming tools. Available on CD-ROM.

Product **PowerLAN**
Company Performance Technology
800 Lincoln Center, 7800 I-10, W, Ste. 800
San Antonio, TX 78230
800-443-LANS, 210-979-2000
FAX: 210-979-2002
Summary Peer-to-peer network OS that supports up to 255 users. Features printer sharing and network disk sharing, low memory requirements, administrative tools and printing capabilities.

Network Management Suites

Product   **Monitrix—The Network Manager (V.3.0)**

Company   Cheyenne Software, Inc.
3 Expressway Plaza
Rosyln, NY 11577
800-243-9462; 516-484-5110
FAX: 516-484-3446

Summary   Network management VAP or NLM. Tracks file server, network printers, and individual network nodes. Provides alarm capabilities to indicate when disk-drive capacity drops below certain threshold, when printer goes offline, or when a problem is detected with a network node. Performs diagnostic tests by checking transmission paths between two network nods. Offers topology map.

Product   Lanscope (V.2.1d3)

Company   Connect Computer Co., Inc.
9855 West 78th St., Suite 270
Eden Prairie, MN 55344
612-944-0181
FAX: 612-944-9298

Summary   LAN management system. Provides menuing security, usage tracking, software-usage control, network resource management, printer spooling, user productivity, and network management. Modules include menuing system, Audit Trail, Hot Key Workstation Utilities, and Turnstyle Software Metering.

Product   **Frye Utilities for Networks— NetWare Management (V.2.0)**

Company   Frye Computer Systems, Inc.
19 Temple Pl.
Boston, MA 02111-9779
800-234-3793; 617-451-5400
FAX: 617-451-6711

Summary   Allows user to retrieve and edit information needed to troubleshoot, diagnose and manage network. Edits and updates Syscon, Pconsole, Fconsole, Printcon, Printdef, Volinfo and Filer information. Provides detailed explanations of all errors and terms and recommendations for solutions. Provides single-screen to show all the server's user activity in real-time graphic, numeric and text formats.

Product   **Brightwork Utilities for Netware (V.1.0)**

Company   McAfee Associates, Inc.
2710 Walsh Ave., Ste. 200
Santa Clara, CA 95051-0963
800-866-6585; 408-988-3832
FAX: 408-970-9727

Summary   Suite of applications for small and medium-sized LANs. Tracks network software and hardware. Allows user to support and troubleshoot Windows or DOS workstations on LAN. Monitors system performance, security, capacity and configuration. Provides LAN user with access to printers attached to any PC on the network.

Product   **LANalyzer Network Analyzer**

Company   Novell, Inc.
2180 Fortune Dr.
San Jose, CA 95131
800-243-8526; 408-434-2300
FAX: 408-435-1706

Summary   Provides protocol analysis to mid-sized networks. Captures network packet data on NetWare 3.X LANs and performs limited amount of decoding. Troubleshoots IBM mainframes and AS/400 computers, networked applications running on IBM equipment and related front-end devices.

Product   **SaberLAN Workstation (V.5.0)**

Company   Saber Software Corp.
5944 Luther Lane, Ste. 1007

Dallas, TX 75225
800-338-8754; 214-361-8086
FAX: 214-361-1882

Summary Integrated set of Network utilities. Provides tools for designing customized menus, tracking software licenses, managing disk space and catching potential trouble spots. Offers graphical and object-oriented front end to Windows. Includes printer anagement utilities for DOS and Windows.

Product **Norton Administrator for Networks (V.1.0)**
Company Symantec Corp.
10201 Torre Ave.
Cupertino, CA 95014-2132
800-441-7234; 408-253-9600
FAX: 408-446-9750

Summary Allows network managers to control software and hardware inventory, distribute software and manage licensing system security and antivirus protection from central console. Automatically builds database of information each time user logs onto machine, capturing information on system resources and configuration.

TCP/IP and Related Products

Product **LANtastic for TCP/IP (V.2.1)**
Company Artisoft, Inc.
2202 N. Forbes Blvd.
Tucson AZ 85745
800-846-9726; 602-670-7100
FAX: 602-670-7101

Summary Provides terminal emulators that enable users to access applications, share printer and transfer and manipulate files residing on remote hosts as if users were directly connected.

Product **BW-Connect NFS for Windows NT**
Company Beame & Whiteside Software, Inc
706 Hillsborough St.
Raleigh, NC 27603-1655
800-INFO-NFS; 919-831-8989FAX: 919-831-8990

Summary 32-bit multithread kernel implementation of NFS client. Allows Windows NT users to gain access to file and print resources on other systems using NFS protocol.Includes client/server TCP/IP applications such as ftp and Telnet.

Product **SNMPc (V.3.3)**
Company Castle Rock Computing, Inc.
20863 Stevens Creek Blvd., Ste. 530
Cupertino, CA 95014
800-331-7667; 408-366-6540
FAX: 408-252-2379

Summary Incorporates Simple Network Management Protocol (SNMP) to help user oversee TCP/IP networks by monitoring network performance and status and by reporting on network faults. Provides a hierarchical map of the network that graphically displays each node and network segment. Displays part of the map in main window at all times, which can be scaled and moved at any time. Includes real-time graphical or tabular display of counters that trigger alarms when preset limits of network elements are exceeded. Works in Microsoft Windows environment.

Product **Super TCP for Windows**
Company Frontier Technologies Corp.
10201 N. Port Washington Road
Mequon, WI 53092
414-241-4555
FAX: 414-241-7084

Summary TCP/IP connectivity package for Windows. Features Windows DLL, Windows sockets API, NFS client/server, FTP/TFTP client/server, Multi-Session VT320 tn3270, E-Mail, WinSock 1.1 compliancy, News Reader, NetPrint, Talk, Fax client/server, SNMP/MIB and SLIP.

Product	**TCP/Connect II for Windows**
Company	InterCon Systems Corp.
	950 Herndon Parkway, Ste. 420
	Herndon VA 22070
	800-638-2968; 703-709-5500
	FAX: 703-709-5555
Summary	Allows Windows users to communicate with varied computer systems using TCP/IP protocols. Provides terminal emultaion, file transfer, e-mail, electronic news, print services and SNMP agent. Implemented as DLL. Provides VT220 and tn3270 terminal emulation.

Product	**cc:Mail Link to SMTP**
Company	Lotus Development Corp. (cc:Mail Division)
	800 El Camino Real, W
	Mountain View, CA 94040
	800-448-2500; 415-961-8800
	FAX 415-961-0840
Summary	Provides communication link between cc:Mail users of Simple Mail Transfer Protocol-based mail systems. Enables users to prepare and send messages as if they were sending to someone on same e-mail system. Works as TCP/IP node connected to Ethernet network. Includes all TCP/IP and FTP software required on PC side. Users can communicate with users of Unix Mail, Internet, Bitnet, IBM PROFS, DEC VMSmail, DEC VAX All-In-1, DG AOS/VS Mail, and HP DeskMate. Transfers binary and text files and fax items as mail attachments.

Product	**PC/TCP Network Software**
Company	FTP Software, Inc.
	2 High Street

North Andover, MA 01845-2620
800-282-4FTP, 508-685-4000
FAX: 508-794-4488

Summary	Communicates with computers supporting the TCP/IP family of protocols. Contains utilities for file transfer, terminal emulation, mail, NFS file sharing, remote backup, printing, and network testing.

Product	**TCP/IP for OS/2 EE (V.1.1)**
Company	IBM
	Old Orchard Rd.
	Armonk, NY 10504
	800-426-3333; 914-765-1900
Summary	Allows OS/2 EE V.1.2 system attached to an IBM Token-Ring, IEEE 802.3 LAN, or Ethernet V.2 LAN to interoperate with other systems in TCP/IP networks. Incorporates Transmission Control Protocol (TCP), Internet Protocol (IP), Internet Control Messaging Protocol (ICMP), TELNET client/server, Simple Mail Transfer Protocol (SMTP) client/server, Trivial File Transfer Protocol (TFTP) client/server, and remote execution client/server. IBM no. 73F6071, 73F6072, 73F6073, 73F6074, 73F6075.

Product	**LAN Workplace**
Company	Novell, Inc.
	122 East 1700 South
	Provo, UT 84606-6194
	800-453-1267; 801-429-7000
	fax: 801-429-5155
Summary	Provides users with concurrent access to LANs and TCP/IP hosts. Gives access to UNIX systems and other network resources using TCP/IP protocol suite.

Product	**OpenConnect/FTP**
Company	OpenConnect Systems Corp.
	2711 LBJ Freeway, Ste. 800
	Dallas, TX 75234-6400
	214-484-5200
	FAX: 214-484-6400

Summary   Allows bi-directional file transfer be-
            tween IBM systems and TCP/IP hosts
            in interactive and batch mode. FTP
            Server allows file transfer to and from
            TCP/IP hosts and supports log-on
            security validation and binary and
            ASCII file transfers.

Product   **SmarTerm**
Company   Persoft, Inc.
            465 Science Dr.
            Madison, WI 53744-4953
            800-EMULATE; 608-273-6000
            FAX: 608-273-8227
Summary   Emulates DEC VT320, 220, 100, 52,
            and TTY. Includes ASCII, binary file
            transfer, and Kermit, Xmodem, and
            PDIP error-free file transfer. Includes
            background operations, softkeys,
            pop-up windows, and 132-column
            support. Includes LAT protocol.
            Includes TELNET with support for
            multiple sessions and named ser-
            vices for popular PC implementa-
            tions of TCP/IP, including
            Wollongong's WIN/TCP and Excelan's
            LAN Workplace for DOS.

Product   **TCP**
Company   3Com Corp.
            P.O. Box 58145, 5400 Bayfront Plaza
            Santa Clara, CA 95052-8145
            800-638-3266; 408-764-5000
            FAX: 408-764-5001
Summary   Allows PCs to communicate and
            share resources within diversified
            TCP/IP environments. Allows users
            to link to TCP resources while still
            maintaining connections to NetWare
            and other workgroup servers.

Product   **Chameleon**
Company   UniPress Software, Inc.
            2025 Lincoln Hwy. Ste. 209
            Edison, NJ 08817
            800-222-0550; 908-287-2100
            FAX: 908-287-4929

Summary   TCP/IP package for MS Windows.
            Includes terminal emulation, file
            transfer, advanced networking,
            chameleon NFS, electronic mail and
            NetRoute IP router.

Product   **TCP Connection**
Company   Walker Richer and Quinn, Inc.
            1500 Dexter Ave., N
            Seattle, WA 98109-3051
            800-872-2550; 206-217-7500
            FAX: 206-217-0293
Summary   Add-on for WRQ's Reflection pack-
            age. Designed for PC-to-host con-
            nections using TCP/IP networking
            software. Includes TCP/IP stack and
            LAT and Telnet Connections.

LAN Analysis Products

Traffic Monitoring Software

Product   **LT Stat (V.3.0)**
Company   Blue Lance, Inc.
            1700 West Loop South, Ste. 1100
            Houston, TX 77027
            800-TKO-BLUE; 713-680-1187
            FAX 713-622-1370
Summary   LAN utility that manages disk utiliza-
            tion, security, and system configura-
            tion. Generates reports including
            server, user and group configuration,
            trustee assignment, accounting re-
            ports, effective rights, menu file,
            NetWare message and error, log-in
            scripts, directory, volume and user
            utilization, duplicate file, and last
            updated file reports.

Product   **FRESH Utilities (V.2.3)**
Company   Fresh Technology Group
            1478 N. Tech Blvd., Suite 101
            Gilbert, AZ 85234
            800-545-8324; 602-497-4200
            FAX: 602-497-4242

Summary   Assortment of 11 utility programs designed to allow network administrators or users to monitor activity and maximize productivity on a network. Includes online help. Enables network administrators to generate reports on the activity of server, groups, users, and queues. Command-line utilities include FTLight, FTLogout, FTDirsiz, and others.

Product   **LANWatch Network Analyzer (V.3.1)**
Company   FTP Software, Inc.
2 High Street
North Andover, MA 01845-2620
800-282-4FTP; 508-685-4000
FAX: 508-794-4488
Summary   Network analyzer for LANs. Useful for developing and debugging protocols and for installing, troubleshooting, and monitoring networks. Includes an analyzer that increases the amount of data, speed, and ways to manipulate data.

Product   **BindView Network Control System (NCS) (V.3.5)**
Company   The LAN Support Group, Inc.
2425 Fountainview Dr., Ste. 390
Houston, TX 77057
800-749-8439; 713-789-0881
Summary   Management and reporting utility for Novell NetWare LANs. Prints custom-tailored, professional audit and management reports detailing file server configurations. Documents system configuration and user configuration data as safeguard against lost or damaged bindery. Allows customization.

Product   **TXD (TC8310) (V.1.01)**
Company   Thomas-Conrad Corp.
1908R Kramer Lane
Austin, TX 78758
800-332-8683; 512-836-1935
FAX: 512-836-2840

Summary   Analyzes network performance and diagnoses problems on Novell NetWare LANs. Determines internetwork configuration, interrogates all nodes, analyzes critical data from one or all nodes, and reports unusual activity levels with interpretation of what levels represent. Executes point-to-point communication testing.

Product   **NetProbe**
Company   3Com Corp.
3165 Kifer Rd.
Santa Clara, CA 95052-8145
800-638-3266; 408-562-6400
FAX: 408-970-1112
Summary   Network analyzer designed for pinpointing problems in Ethernet and Token-Ring networks. Locates nonresponding workstations, internet route malfunctions, network failures, and overloaded network servers. Requires 3Com's EtherLink, EtherLink Plus, or TokenLink adapter board.

Network Traffic Analyzers

Product   **LANProbe II**
Company   Hewlett-Packard Co.
3000 Hanover Street
Palo Alto, CA 94304-1181
800-752-0900; 415-857-1501
FAX: 800-333-1917
Specs   Price: $2,995-$3,995
Date announced: 1994
Function: Protocol analyzer
Protocols supported: Ethernet, Token Ring
Power provision: through interface

Product   **Pentascanner**
Company   MicroTest, Inc.
4747 North 22nd Street
Phoenix, AZ 85016-4708
800-526-9675; 602-952-6400
FAX: 602-952-6401

Specs
Price: $4,195
Date announced: 1993
Function: Protocol Analyzer
Packaging: Portable/handheld
Protocols supported: 10BaseT,
10Base2, 4 Mbps Token Ring, 16
Mbps Token Ring, ARCnet, Fast
Ethernet, AppleTAlk, ATM.
Interfaces supported: T1, E1, ISDN
Visual monitors provided: Backlit
LCDs
Printer interface provided: No
Disk storage provided: No

Product **Expert Sniffer Portable Analyzer**
Company Network General Corp.
4200 Bohannon Dr.
Menlo Park, CA 94025
800-695-8251; 415-473-2000
FAX: 415-321-0855
Specs
Date announced: 1994
Function: Protocol analyzer
Packaging: Desktop/standalone
Protocols supported: Token-Ring;
Ethernet; FDDI
Interfaces supported: RS-232C
Visual monitors provided: Compaq
DeskPro 486/66, 486/66M display
Power provision: AC and battery
Printer interface provided: Yes
Disk storage provided: Yes

LAN Remote Control Software

Product **Remotely Possible/LAN for Windows (V.4.0)**
Company Avalan Technology
116 Hopping Brooke Park
Holliston, MA 01746
800-441-2281; 508-429-6482
FAX: 508-429-3179
Summary Native Windows LAN remote control
software which allows aster PC on
any network to remotely control
slave PC with mouse. Features multiple levels of password protection and
user ID.

Product **NETremote+ (V.5.2)**
Company McAfee Associates, Inc.
2710 Walsh Ave., Ste 200
Santa Clara, CA 95051-0963
800-866-6585; 408-988-3832
FAX: 408-970-9727
Summary Remote access and user support
software for LAN. Allows network
manager to provide instant support
for users anywhere on LAN or WAN
by seeing a remote user's screen and
controlling a remote user's keyboard.
Includes built-in diagnostics and
async module allowing user to dial
into or out of network.

Product **Remote2 (V.3.0)**
Company DCA
1000 Alderman Drive
Alpharetta, GA 30202
800-348-3221; 404-442-4000
FAX: 404-442-4366
Summary Allows remote operation of PC and
software from any location via terminal or PC. Supports Crosstalk and
Xmodem file transfers. Includes
guard utility that allows host user to
restrict access of guests to drives, directories and individual files on host.

Product **ReachOut/Network (V.4.0)**
Company Ocean Isle Software, Inc.
1201 19th Place, 2nd Fl.
Vero Beach, FL 32960-0631
800-677-6232; 407-770-4777
FAX: 407-770-4779
Summary Remote control application that allows administrator to monitor and
control client. Pinpoint and fixes
problems on user's PC without leaving the desk. Features include remote mouse support, chat window,
pull-down point and shoot menus
and context-sensitive help.

Product **Norton pcAnywhere/LAN (V.4.5)**
Company Symantec Corp.
10201 Torre Ave.
Cupertino, CA 95014-2132
800-441-7234; 408-253-9600
FAX: 408-446-9750
Summary PC-to-PC remote communications
software for network-based PC users.
Permits one workstation to control
another on a LAN and also control
communications with off-site PCs,
laptops, and terminals.

Product **Close-Up/LAN—The Network
Remote**
Company Norton-Lambert Corp.
P.O. Box 4085
Santa Barbara, CA 93140
805-964-6767
FAX: 805-683-5679
Summary Allows user to share screens and keyboards with one, many, or all users
on a network. Enables users on LAN
to share printers, modems, faxes,
and computers. Can be used for
teaching, training, and conferencing.

Product **CO/Session LAN II (V.6.2)**
Company Triton Technologies, Inc.
200 Middlesex Turnpike
Iselin, NJ 08830
800-322-9440; 201-855-9440
FAX: 201-855-9608
Summary Remote control software that allows
remote users to access home office
LANs to run local applications and
exchange files.

LAN Remote Comm Servers

Product **LAN Distance**
Company IBM
Old Orchard Rd.
Armonk, NY 10504
800-426-3333; 914-765-1900

Summary Allows a portable computer or remote PC to access a LAN as if it were
on a network. Consists of the LAN
Distance Remote and the LAN
Distance Connection Server.

Product **LANexpress Remote LAN Access
System (V.1.0)**
Company Microcom, Inc.
500 River Ridge Drive
Norwood, MA 02062-5028
800-822-8224; 617-551-1000
FAX: 617-551-1021
Summary Hardware/software package that lets
mobile users dial into their host
LANs via cellular or land lines and
launch remote nodes and remote
control application on one call from
Windows interface. Includes
LANexpress Remote, LANexpress
Server, 8 built-in DeskPorte Fast or
TravelPort modems, expressWatch,
SNMP-based management software
and Microcom's Carbon Copy for
Windows.

Product **LANRover**
Company Shiva Corp.
63 Third Ave., Northwest Park
Burlington, MA 01803
800-458-3550; 617-270-8300
FAX: 617-270-8599
Summary Remote access to NetWare, TCP/IP,
or NetBEUI protocols. Available with
4 or 8 external Modems.

Product **NetModem/E**
Company Shiva Corp.
63 Third Ave., Northwest Park
Burlington, MA 01803
800-458-3550; 617-270-8300
FAX: 617-270-8599
Summary Remote access to NetWAre protocols
via V.42 bis/V.32 bis modems.

Network Access Servers

Product **Communique**
Company CommVision
510 Logue Ave.
Mountain View, CA 94043
800-832-6526; 415-254-5720
FAX: 415-254-9320
Specs Price: $11,495-$16,495
Network compatibility: Ethernet
LAN speed: 10Mbps
Shareable devices: Integrated
NetWare based remote node, remote
control dial-in/out, gateway, fax, e-
mail, and bulletin board services.

Product **ERS/FT**
Company Cubix Corp.
2800 Lockheed Way
Carson City, NV 89706-0719
800-829-0554; 702-883-7611
FAX: 702-882-2407
Specs Price: $23,000

Product **ChatterBox/Plus**
Company J&L Information Systems, Inc.
9600 Topanga Canyon Blvd.
Chatsworth, CA 91311
818-709-1778
FAX: 818-882-1424
Specs Price: $2,695-$5,095
Shareable devices: Printer; modem;
hard disk
Network compatibility: Ethernet;
Token Ring
LAN speed: 4; 10; 16 Mbps

APPENDIX

B

Publications

Books
Magazine
Online Services

The following is a list of books, magazines, and online services that may prove useful to you as reference sources.

Books

Derfler, Frank J., Jr. *Guide to Connectivity, 3rd Edition.* Emeryville: Ziff-Davis Press, 1995, and *Guide to Linking LANs.* Emeryville, California: Ziff-Davis Press, 1992.

Derfler, Frank J., Jr., and Freed, Les. *Building the Information Highway.* Emeryville: Ziff-Davis Press, 1994; *Get a Grip on Network Cabling.* Emeryville: Ziff-Davis Press, 1993; *Guide to LANtastic.* Emeryville: Ziff-Davis Press, 1993; *Guide to Modem Communications.* Emeryville: Ziff-Davis Press, 1992; *Guide to Windows for Workgroups.* Emeryville: Ziff-Davis Press, 1993; and *How Networks Work.* Emeryville: Ziff-Davis Press, 1993.

Eager, Bill. *Using the World Wide Web.* Que Corporation, 1994.

Mueller, Scott. *Upgrading and Repairing PCs, 4th Edition.* Indianapolis: Que Corporation, 1994.

Norton, Peter. *Peter Norton's Complete Guide to DOS 6.22, Premier Edition.* Sams, 1994.

Novell's Guide to Personal NetWare. San Francisco: Sybex Inc.

Nowshadi, Farshad. *Managing NetWare.* New York: Addison-Wesley Publishing Company, 1994.

Magazines

Byte
McGraw-Hill, Inc.

Communications Week
600 Community Drive, Manhasset, NY 11030
708-647-6834

InfoWorld
155 Bovet Road, Suite 800, San Mateo, CA 94402
415-572-7341

Network World
161 Worcester Road, Framingham, MA 01701
508-875-6400

PC Magazine
One Park Avenue, New York, NY 10016-5802
212-503-5100

PC Week
P.O. Box 1770, Riverton, NJ 08077-7370
609-786-8230

Online Services

America Online
8619 Westwood Center Drive,
Vienna VA 22182
703-448-8700
Fax: 708-917-1201

CompuServe Information Service
CompuServe, Inc. (subsidiary of H&R Block, Inc.)
P.O. Box 20212, 5000 Arlington Centre Blvd.
Columbus, OH 43220
800-848-8199; 614-457-8600
Fax: 614-457-0348

Prodigy
Prodigy Services Co.
445 Hamilton Ave.
White Plains, NY 10601
800-PRODIGY; 914-993-8000
Fax: 914-684-0278

ZiffNet
25 First Street
Cambridge, MA 02141
800-848-8990

INDEX

NUMBERS AND SYMBOLS

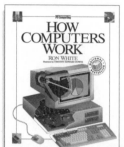
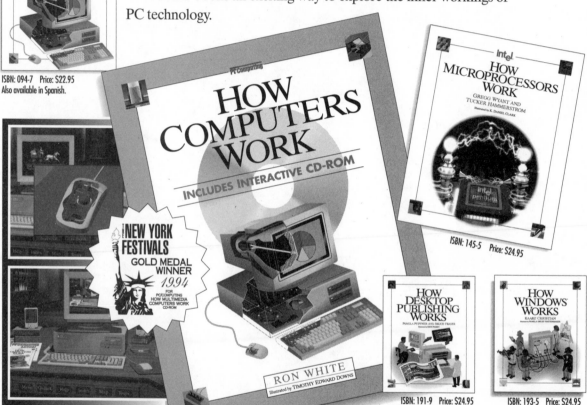

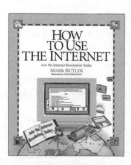

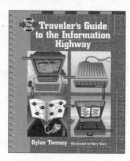

Ziff-Davis Press Survey of Readers

Please help us in our effort to produce the best books on personal computing.
For your assistance, we would be pleased to send you a FREE catalog
featuring the complete line of Ziff-Davis Press books.

1. How did you first learn about this book?

Recommended by a friend . . . . ☐ -1 (5)

Recommended by store personnel . . . .☐ -2

Saw in Ziff-Davis Press catalog . . . .☐ -3

Received advertisement in the mail . . . .☐ -4

Saw the book on bookshelf at store . . . .☐ -5

Read book review in: _____ ☐ -6

Saw an advertisement in: _____ ☐ -7

Other (Please specify): _____ ☐ -8

2. Which THREE of the following factors most influenced your decision to purchase this book? (Please check up to THREE.)

Front or back cover information on book . . .☐ -1 (6)

Logo of magazine affiliated with book . . . . . .☐ -2

Special approach to the content . . . .☐ -3

Completeness of content . . . .☐ -4

Author's reputation. . . . .☐ -5

Publisher's reputation . . . .☐ -6

Book cover design or layout . . . .☐ -7

Index or table of contents of book . . . .☐ -8

Price of book . . . .☐ -9

Special effects, graphics, illustrations . . . .☐ -0

Other (Please specify): _____ ☐ -x

3. How many computer books have you purchased in the last six months? _____ (7-10)

4. On a scale of 1 to 5, where 5 is excellent, 4 is above average, 3 is average, 2 is below average, and 1 is poor, please rate each of the following aspects of this book below. (Please circle your answer.)

Depth/completeness of coverage	5	4	3	2	1	(11)
Organization of material	5	4	3	2	1	(12)
Ease of finding topic	5	4	3	2	1	(13)
Special features/time saving tips	5	4	3	2	1	(14)
Appropriate level of writing	5	4	3	2	1	(15)
Usefulness of table of contents	5	4	3	2	1	(16)
Usefulness of index	5	4	3	2	1	(17)
Usefulness of accompanying disk	5	4	3	2	1	(18)
Usefulness of illustrations/graphics	5	4	3	2	1	(19)
Cover design and attractiveness	5	4	3	2	1	(20)
Overall design and layout of book	5	4	3	2	1	(21)
Overall satisfaction with book	5	4	3	2	1	(22)

5. Which of the following computer publications do you read regularly; that is, 3 out of 4 issues?

Byte . . . .☐ -1 (23)

Computer Shopper . . . .☐ -2

Home Office Computing . . . .☐ -3

Dr. Dobb's Journal . . . .☐ -4

LAN Magazine . . . .☐ -5

MacWEEK . . . .☐ -6

MacUser . . . .☐ -7

PC Computing . . . .☐ -8

PC Magazine . . . .☐ -9

PC WEEK . . . .☐ -0

Windows Sources . . . .☐ -x

Other (Please specify): _____ ☐ -y

Please turn page.

6. What is your level of experience with personal computers? With the subject of this book?

	With PCs	With subject of book
Beginner.............	☐ -1 (24)	☐ -1 (25)
Intermediate..........	☐ -2	☐ -2
Advanced.............	☐ -3	☐ -3

7. Which of the following best describes your job title?

Officer (CEO/President/VP/owner)........	☐ -1 (26)
Director/head..........................	☐ -2
Manager/supervisor.....................	☐ -3
Administration/staff....................	☐ -4
Teacher/educator/trainer...............	☐ -5
Lawyer/doctor/medical professional.......	☐ -6
Engineer/technician....................	☐ -7
Consultant............................	☐ -8
Not employed/student/retired............	☐ -9
Other (Please specify): _____	☐ -0

8. What is your age?

Under 20.............................	☐ -1 (27)
21-29................................	☐ -2
30-39................................	☐ -3
40-49................................	☐ -4
50-59................................	☐ -5
60 or over...........................	☐ -6

9. Are you:

Male.................................	☐ -1 (28)
Female...............................	☐ -2

Thank you for your assistance with this important information! Please write your address below to receive our free catalog.

Name: _____

Address: _____

City/State/Zip: _____

Fold here to mail.   3091-07-21

_____

_____

_____